STUDIES IN ARCHITECTURE

EDITED BY ANTHONY BLUNT AND RUDOLF WITTKOWER

VOLUME XII

THE THEORY OF CLAUDE PERRAULT

WOLFGANG HERRMANN

THE THEORY
OF
CLAUDE PERRAULT

WOLFGANG HERRMANN

A. ZWEMMER LTD
LONDON

IN MEMORIAM

RUDOLF WITTKOWER

Contents

List of Plates

TEXT FIGURE

Abbreviations

Commentaires   Paris, Faculté de médecine, *Commentaires de la faculté de médecine.*

Comptes   *Comptes des Bâtiments du Roi*, Paris, 1881 ff.

Essais   Claude Perrault, *Essais de Physique*, Paris, 1680 & 1688.

Mémoires   Charles Perrault, *Mémoires de ma vie*, (ed. Paul Bonnefon, Paris, 1909).

Ordonnance   Claude Perrault, *Ordonnance des cinq espèces de colonnes selon la méthode des anciens*, Paris, 1683.

Procès-verbaux   *Procès-verbaux de l'Académie Royale d'architecture* (ed. H. Lemonnier), Paris, 1911 ff.

Register   Paris, Académie des Sciences, Archive: Registers.

Vitruvius   *Les dix livres d'architecture de Vitruve*, (trad. Claude Perrault), Paris, 1673.

Photographic Sources

Bibliothèque Nationale, Paris: 5, 16, 20, 21, 22

British Museum, London: 2, 3

J. Colomb-Gérard, Paris: 36

Louvre, Cabinet des Dessins: 17

Nationalmuseum, Stockholm: 14

Service Photographique, Paris: 28

Preface

NO book on Perrault has yet been written. It may seem strange, then, that the present study is mainly confined to a presentation of his views on the theory of architecture. When I chose Perrault as the subject of research, I expected that in the end I would have a clearer understanding of his achievements as an architect and of his standing as a writer on architectural theory. But as my studies advanced I found that, while his work as a writer, both on science and on architecture, was gradually brought into focus, the image of Perrault, the architect, receded more and more and almost dissolved. Eventually I had to admit that his architectural activities were too limited to have justified the inclusion of a separate chapter which, as I see it, would necessarily have led to a negative result. It seems to me more rewarding to concentrate on that sphere in which Perrault had been most active and from which his most original ideas stem.

The main part of the book gives an analysis and interpretation of Perrault's views on architecture and tries to discover what he thereby hoped to achieve. He failed to have these views accepted; more than that, he was invariably misunderstood. Still, in the history of ideas even misconceptions are effective. For this reason, the last chapter, reviewing the aftermath of Perrault's ideas, is carried through to the end of the nineteenth century, since at this comparatively recent period a new interpretation was offered.

I am deeply grateful to Sir Anthony Blunt and John and Eileen Harris for spending much of their time reading the manuscript. Their numerous suggestions, corrections and criticism were of great help.

I also wish to take the opportunity of expressing my thanks to the Secretaries of the Institut de France for permitting me to work in the Archive of the Académie des Sciences and to the Librarian and Staff of the RIBA Library for the constant help I received from them in my research.

CHAPTER I

Perrault's Life and Work

CLAUDE PERRAULT'S fame rests on two works of paramount importance: the translation of Vitruvius and the design for the Colonnade of the Louvre. The quality of the translation is still respected, while his authorship for the design has often been disputed.

He was once called 'the French Vitruvius' by an admirer, and he had this in common with the Latin author, that his knowledge of the theoretical side of architecture was comprehensive, while the occasions for its application were few.[1] Here, however, the comparison ends. Vitruvius was a professional architect, Perrault a medical man who devoted some time to architectural matters. Vitruvius wrote a corpus filled with the traditional knowledge then available to the architect, Perrault a treatise of more restricted scope, containing his particular theory, the subject matter of the present book.

In this preliminary chapter his scientific work and architectural activity will play a part in the narrative, since some knowledge of these pursuits is needed in order to form a picture of the kind of man Claude Perrault was.

He was born on 25 September 1613 the third son of Pierre Perrault, *avocat* at the Parlement de Paris. Fourteen years later, the fifth and last son was born, named Charles, who by the unpretentious task of writing down fairy tales for his children made the family's name famous. He was also the most successful of the five brothers and was able through his

---

1. La Font de Saint-Yenne, *L'Ombre du Grand Colbert*, The Hague, 1749, p. 96. The same expression used by Duperron, *Discours sur la peinture et sur l'architecture*, Paris, 1758, p. 30. Soufflot proposed to place two busts above the doors of Marigny's *salon*: one of Vitruvius, the other of Perrault (Paris, Arch. Nat. o¹ 1541 – 126).

considerable influence in official circles to further the career of his elder brother Claude.[2]

The Perraults belonged to the privileged section of the bourgeois class and were, it seems, fairly comfortably off. The family owned, through the mother, a country house in the Seine valley east of Paris, conforming in this respect to the way of life led by the wealthier members of their class. A pitiful poetical attempt, probably by a friend of the father, and a few hardly more skilful drawings by Claude, which accompany the poem, give some idea of the place where the family spent their leisure and where, in later life, the brothers entertained friends [3] (Pls. 2, 3).

The house stood on a hill above the village of Viry.[4] What we learn about the interior décor suggests for Claude's upbringing a background of some culture and refinement: one room large enough to be used as a *salon de musique*, the walls hung with tapestries or painted with landscapes *en grisaille*, and in a smaller room, as depicted on one of Claude's drawings, paintings and sculptures and a richly decorated, fashionable fireplace.

At the time of these drawings Perrault was a medical student, twenty-four years of age. Two years later, he received his first degree, the *baccalauréat*.[5] Being accepted at the Ecole de Médecine of Paris meant studying more years and spending more money than would have been necessary at a provincial university; but it also meant that in the end his social standing would be much enhanced. When, in 1642, he passed his

2. André Hallays, *Les Perrault*, Paris, 1926. There is much information on Charles Perrault in G. Rouger's introduction and biographical summary to the *Contes de Perrault*, ed. Garnier, Paris, 1967.

For portraits of Claude see N. Schiller, 'L'iconographie de Claude Perrault,' *Comptes rendus du 91e Congrès national des Sociétés savantes, Rennes, 1966, Section des Sciences I*, Paris, 1967, pp. 215 ff.

3. 'Le Voyage de Viry Par le Sr. C. revue, corrigé et augmenté par l'auteur en cette seconde édition à Paris 1637' (London, Brit. Mus. MS Add. 20,087). At end of volume (fol. 14): 'Par Mr Corneillau Concr. au chastelet. Ce poème est le premier mais il est de beaucoup augmenté par le mesme auteur et les figures sont faictes par mon frère le Médecin M. Perrault.' (The original orthography has been retained, here and in all subsequent quotations; only the accentuation has always been modernized.)

On the structure of society in Paris at that period, see Orest Ranum, *Paris in the Age of Absolutism*, New York, 1968.

4. There can be little doubt that the house on the hill, drawn by Perrault more distinctly than those of the village (Pl. 3), is the house of the Perraults. On conjectures about its location see Rouger, op. cit., p. LVI, note 2.

5. J. Colombe, 'Portraits d'ancêtres', *Hippocrate*, XVI, 1949, nos. 4, 5.

doctorate and was from then on known – to distinguish him from his brothers – as *Monsieur Perrault, le médecin*, he became a member of an exclusive group: only about one hundred doctors were licensed in Paris at any one time throughout the seventeenth century, with an annual increment of not more than five to ten.[6]

One detail about his studies should be mentioned as it has some bearing on his being entrusted later-on with the task of translating Vitruvius: medical students had to have a sound knowledge of the Greek language. This was rare in the seventeenth century even among *hommes de lettres*, but was, of course, a prerequisite for the commentator on the Greek terms used by Vitruvius.

His studies completed, Perrault, as *docteur régent*, became a member of the medical faculty at the University of Paris. The obligations imposed by the faculty were manifold. Apart from the mandatory attendance at numerous annual functions, the most onerous, though much esteemed, duty was to teach at the Ecole. In contrast to present practice, medical teaching was then not a vocation; any *docteur régent* could be elected to hold a chair for two years. Thus, in 1651, when Guy Patin was Dean, Perrault was proposed and accepted as professor of physiology.[7] In this capacity, he lectured throughout 1652. This was the year when the Fronde had reached its climax with troops battling at the Porte St Antoine and Condé's men storming the Hôtel de Ville where *notables* from the Parlement and the Corps de Ville had assembled. During these hectic times, Perrault went every day to the Rue de la Bûcherie where, in the new amphitheatre, he explained to the students the functions of the human body. In the following year, he was professor of pathology, opening his course on 11 January when all those present, including the Dean, 'were carried away in admiration for his eloquence and uncommon

6. ibid., p. 4.

For general information on medical life in Paris and on the organization of the Faculty, see Paul Delaunay, *La vie médicale aux XVIe, XVIIe, et XVIIIe siècles*, Paris, 1935; René Fauvelle, *Les étudiants en médecine de Paris sous le Grand Roi*, Paris, 1899; and A. Corlieu, *L'ancienne faculté de médecine de Paris*, Paris, 1877.

7. Paris, Faculté de Médecine, *Commentaires de la faculté de médecine*, t. 13, fols. 446 v and 496 v.

manner.'[8] Ten years later, he was one of seven 'Docteurs régents et Professeurs de l'Eschole' charging a former Dean, who had held office from 1660 to 1662, with unfair distribution of a certain fund, earmarked for the remuneration of professors. Since Perrault had received the normal fee of 90 *livres* per annum in 1652 and 1653, this claim seems to indicate that he lectured once more during this later period.[9] He also fulfilled other obligations. Several times he presided over the presentation of theses, had on one occasion a formal dispute with another doctor about a then much-discussed biological problem, and was present at the faculty meetings whose annual register he often signed.[10] In addition, he had, of course, to attend to his medical practice about which we know little, except that Boileau's sister-in-law was one of his patients and that, through her, Boileau himself became one. Years later, Boileau derided Perrault's skill as a doctor. These offensive remarks, however, were made when Boileau thought his integrity as a poet had been questioned by the Perraults.[11] According to Arnauld, Boileau knew very well that 'Monsieur Perrault le médecin passes among his colleagues for a skilled physician'.[12] It is true that we certainly 'shudder' today when reading Perrault's detailed account of the treatment prescribed by him, in consultation with other doctors, during his eldest brother's dangerous illness:

8. ibid., t. 14, fols. 16, 29. 'Magister Claudius Perault Pathologiae professor prima omnium XI Jan 1653 in theatro . . . Anatomia docuit Scholasticoce, quos omnes, et decanus . . . qui adevant in admiratione rapuit suā eloquentiā et conditione non vulgariā.'

9. A. Pauly, *Bibliographie des sciences médicales*, Paris, 1874. Reprint, London, 1954, p. 576. Pauly remarks that the claim concerned 'la repartition des 800 livres attribuées chaque année aux 4 Facultés de l'Université de Paris.' For further details about this fund, see Corlieu, op. cit., pp. 22 f., 145.
Fees paid to Perrault, *Commentaires*, t. 13, fol. 555 r., t. 14, fol. 56 v.

10. He presided over theses on 29 August, 1652 and 3 September, 1652 (*Commentaires*, t. 13, fols, 535 r., 533 v.), also on 24 January, 1664 and 13 March, 1664 (Paris, Bibl. Nat. Tracts 1182 e). The dispute took place in 1652 (*Commentaires*, t. 14, fol. 34) about: 'An fiunt membranae foetum obvolutura ab uteri aut seminis calore?'
His signature appears for the last time in 1663 (t. 15, fol. 30 v.)

11. Boileau, *Réflexions critiques sur Longin, Oeuvres*, ed. Gidel, Paris, 1873, III, pp. 299 f.
On the reasons behind the animosity between Boileau and Perrault, see Hans Kortum, *Charles Perrault und Nicolas Boileau*, Berlin, 1966, pp. 110, 152.

12. cit. by Albert Laprade, *François D'Orbay*, Paris, 1960, p. 53, n. 4. In another letter Arnauld said: 'J'ai été l'ami particulier du Médecin' (*Lettres de Monsieur Antoine Arnauld*, Nancy, 1727, VII, p. 398).

with unremitting purging and blood-letting they tried – in vain – to save his life,[13] but it would be quite wrong to draw from this treatment any conclusions as to Perrault's medical proficiency. He followed, as most competent practitioners do today, the acknowledged method of the time. All that can be said is that Perrault conformed to the standard expected from a doctor, and that the hankering after originality, for which the Perraults were often blamed, is at least not borne out by what we know about his medical work.

Thus, during the first two decades of his professional career Perrault led a life typical of a member of the medical faculty. When, in 1666 at the age of 53, he joined the newly-formed Académie des Sciences, he gave up his general practice in favour of scientific work.[14] From then on he attended only his relatives, his friends and the poor.[15] Making this change was by no means unusual. Since many branches of natural science, such as Biology, Botany, Physiology, Anatomy and Pathology, still belonged to the physician's domain, they were explored mainly by medical men; with specialization still in its infancy, it was common that they extended their researches, as Perrault did, to embrace the whole range of these subjects.[16]

Charles Perrault tells in his *Mémoires* of the great difficulty he had in persuading his brother to accept his election to the Academy; although

13. Laprade, op. cit., p. 53: 'Ces pages du *Voyage à Bordeaux* font frémir.'

14. Justel informs Oldenburg on 13 October, 1666 of Perrault's election together with Cureau de la Chambre, Duclos and Gayant (*The Correspondence of Henry Oldenburg*, Madison and London, 1966, III, p. 240).

15. Charles Perrault, *Les hommes illustres qui ont paru en France, pendant ce siècle*, Paris, 1696, I, pp. 67 f.

16. Jacques Roger, *Les sciences de la vie dans la pensée française du XVIIIe siècle*, Paris, 1963, pp. 169 f.: 'tous les savants que nous aurons l'occasion de citer sont des docteurs en médecine ... ils se préoccupent beaucoup plus d'anatomie, de physiologie, de chimie ou de sciences naturelles, que de médecine proprement dite.' (This refers to a period around 1670).

R. Ball, 'European Science in the Seventeenth and Earlier Years of the Eighteenth Centuries,' *Cambridge Modern History*, Cambridge, 1908, V, p. 723: '... the men who were building up the several natural sciences were to be found among the teachers of the medical schools.'

E. Geoffrey Saint-Hilaire, *Histoire naturelle générale des règnes organiques*, Paris, 1854, I, p. 64: '... des médecins naturalistes du XVIIe siècle, plusieurs ne sont plus que nominalement médecins; la zoologie, la botanique, l'anatomie, la micrographie, les occupent entièrement.'

feeling greatly honoured, Perrault was convinced that he lacked 'the necessary qualifications for being placed among so many excellent men'. 'This modesty was sincere,' Charles remarks.[17] There are indications for believing that modesty was, indeed, one of Perrault's distinguishing qualities. Apart from this trait being singled out in obituary notices, his habit, then by no means common, of frankly acknowledging the debt he owed to other scientists, confirms this unassuming attitude.[18] This time, however, his misgivings were not as unjustified as Charles made them out to be.

The list of the new members was, indeed, formidable. It included the septuagenarian Cureau de la Chambre, *médecin du Roi*, of great influence at Court and a founder member of the Académie Française; the anatomist Jean Pecquet whose fame in France was almost as great as that of Harvey; the geometer Pierre Carcavy, friend of Pascal and Descartes; Jean Picard, one of the greatest astronomers of his time; Gilles de Roberval, a famous mathematician; and Christian Huygens, a name already known throughout Europe. Most of them, with publications to their credit, came from the circle of scientists who for many years had assembled every week in the house of Habert de Montmort. Perrault's reaction, when told of his election, is evidence that he did not belong to Montmort's Academy. Nor is his name recorded among the more prominent members of the public who attended some of the other private gatherings which preceded

17. *Mémoires de ma vie*, ed. Paul Bonnefon, Paris, 1909, p. 44.

18. Basnage, *Histoire des ouvrages des Sçavans*, Rotterdam, November 1688, pp. 310 f.: 'Mais ce qu'il y avoit en luy de plus estimable, c'est qu'il ne tiroit aucune vanité de ce qui en auroit beaucoup donné à d'autres. . . . On peut s'imaginer combien cela le préservoit de l'air dogmatique si insupportable dans presque tous les sçavans, et combien sa conservation en estoit plus aisée et plus agréable. Quand on a bien du mérite, c'en est le comble que d'être fait comme les autres.'

The *Commentaires* (t. 16, fol. 391) add to the usual notice about the death of a member of the faculty the remark that 'etsi scientarum omnium perfecta haberet congnitio minime superbe erga collegas suas aliosque litteratos vires magna honestate servavit.' The last two lines of the verse under his portrait (Pl. 1) read: 'Et modeste Il n'usa de toute sa lumière, Que pour voir non pour estre vue.'

For acknowledging his debt to other writers or naming those who had come independently to the same result, see his *Essais de Physique*, Paris, 1680, I, preface, pp. 138, 174; III, p. 5; *Ordonnance*, p. XXVII. On the possible reason for his pretentious attitude when telling Leibniz about his architectural activities, see page 30, note 82.

the establishment of the official academy: this, of course, does not exclude the possibility of Perrault's presence at their meetings, but obviously he had not yet made a name as a scientist.[19]

It would, however, be wrong to believe that Perrault entered the Academy only because his influential brother was able to exercise discreet pressure behind the scenes. Of course, without this backing his name would hardly have been included in the list of suitable candidates. Yet, no sponsor could have been successful if Perrault's experience in anatomical work and interest in scientific research had not justified the recommendation. Evidence of this interest can be seen in the fact that some years before the inauguration of the Academy, Huygens had been staying for a few days as guest of the Perraults at their house in Viry. Of course, it need not necessarily have been Claude who established the contact, but since, a few years later, the two were carrying out physical experiments at Viry on several occasions, it is at least a plausible assumption.[20] Moreover, the active part that Perrault was soon to play in the work and the discussions within the Academy shows that his studies must have prepared him well for holding his own when conversing with these eminent men, however diffident he felt about it.

The minutes constantly mention Perrault in connection with work he

19. On the Académie des Sciences, see Harcourt Brown, *Scientific Organizations in Seventeenth-Century France*, Baltimore, 1934; A. J. George, 'The Genesis of the Académie des Sciences,' *Annals of Science*, III, 1938, pp. 372 ff.; R. Taton, *Les origines de l'Académie Royale des Sciences*, (1966); P. Gauja in *Académie des Sciences troisième centenaire*, Paris, 1967, I, p. 1 ff.; E. C. Watson, 'The Early Days of the Académie des Sciences as Portrayed in the Engravings of Sébastien Le Clerc,' *Osiris*, VII, 1939, pp. 556 ff. The statement by Roger, op. cit., p. 171, that the Perraults were 'membres actifs du groupe Thévenot' is made without indicating the source. It may have been based on the equally undocumented assertion by Martha Ornstein, *The Rôle of Scientific Societies in the Seventeenth Century*, Chicago, 1928, p. 144 that 'Colbert knew of these meetings at Thévenot's through Perrault and others,' which, in its turn, may go back to M. Caullery, *Histoire des sciences biologiques*, Paris, 1924, p. 77, stating that 'Colbert, sous l'inspiration de Claude Perrault, l'architecte du Louvre et de l'Observatoire, fit, en 1666, l'Académie des Sciences.'

20. In October 1663, Conrart addresses a letter to Huygens 'chez Monsieur Perrault à Viry'. (*Oeuvres complètes de Christian Huygens*, The Hague, 1888 ff., IV, p. 414). For subsequent contacts between the Perraults and Huygens, see Jacques Barchilon, 'Les frères Perrault à travers la correspondance et les oeuvres de Christian Huygens,' *XVIIe siècle*, 1962, pp. 19 ff.

had performed or contributions he had made to a discussion.[21] Often the suggestions for some particular research or experiment came from him, at other times discussions which had taken place in the assembly were reflected and substantiated in the pages of his *Essais de physique*, a collection of studies on which Perrault worked for many years. These and many commentaries in his *Vitruvius* show how varied were the subjects that interested him. Noticing the equally wide range over which the discussions at the weekly meetings moved, one realizes what his membership meant to him; it must have fulfilled his highest expectations. His curiosity, his inclination for solving intricate problems by conjectures, his inventiveness in technical matters – they had all found an outlet in his new career as an academician. Science was important to him; in fact, it played such a dominant part that in order to see his life in the right perspective, it will be necessary to give at least a short survey of Perrault's scientific activities.

In the first full meeting of the Academy, he outlines a working programme for the anatomical and botanical section. The quality of his paper is remarkable, full of original ideas.[22] He underlines the danger of relying too much on the eye in anatomy instead of directing the search by meaningful conjectures, warning at the same time that we should approach this novel field with as much humility and wisdom 'as we should have strength and honesty in throwing off ancient prejudices'.[23]

---

21. The main source for the work done within the Academy are the Registers, kept in the archives of the present Académie des Sciences. They contain, in many volumes, the minutes of the weekly meetings and various *mémoires* by members on special subjects. The years between 1670 and 1674 are, unfortunately, missing. This period is covered, although in abridged form, by the publications edited by two successive secretaries of the Academy: J.-B. Duhamel, *Regiae Scientiarum Academiae Historia*, Paris, 1698, and Fontenelle, *Histoire de l'Académie Royale des Sciences*, Paris, 1733.

The Academy also has notes in Perrault's handwriting (kept in a *Dossier Perrault*). They contain mostly anatomical observations and excerpts from the writings of contemporary authors: Gassendi (his book on Peiresc), Bartolini, Glisson, Malpighi, Riolan. Among the excerpts from the last-named author are many Greek citations, proof that Perrault, in contrast to his brother Charles, knew Greek well.

22. *Register*, I, fols. 22 ff. and fol. 200 (19 January, 1667).

23. ibid., fol. 24: 'car bienque la connoissance du corps humain dépende principalement de son inspection . . . la Raison fournit aussi des lumières pour s'y conduire qui ne servent pas seulement à s'éclairer sur l'usage des parties que l'on a trouvées, mais mesme sur la nécessité ou la probabilité

In his botanical programme he touches on two theories which were to a considerable degree his own: the circulation of the sap in plants in analogy to the circulation of the blood (then still spurned by the Faculty) and Panspermatism, a new hypothesis about the generation of life which, though never widely accepted, was his most original contribution to biology.[24]

He also proposed the study of 'human bodies and other animals', that is to say, the then hardly-known discipline of comparative anatomy. This was accepted by the Compagnie which, from then on, spent much of its time on dissections. Until the end of his life, Perrault belonged to a team of scientists who dissected, in the rooms the Academy occupied in the Bibliothèque du Roi, animals which mostly came from the Royal menageries (Pl. 4). Whenever, for twenty years, the minutes refer to these regularly-performed dissections, Perrault's name is mentioned. At the beginning of this period he undertook the actual operations, but soon he seems to have specialized in the equally-important task of preparing drawings and writing exact descriptions of the parts found.[25] The first set of these were published anonymously as pamphlets in 1667 and 1669,[26] but it soon must have become obvious to Colbert that this

de celles que l'on espère de découvrir et qu'il peut arriver assez souvent que faute de ce conseil on travaille inutilement pour des organes ... que la Raison faict juger n'estre point nécessaires ... il est nécessaire de joindre toujours les observations avec le Raisonnement ... à condition aussy que l'on apportera autant de prudence et de modestie pour ne pas courir estourdiment après ces nouvelles observations que l'on aura eu de Force et de Sincérité pour se défaire des anciennes préventions.' Similarly in a controversy with a Dr Walter Needham of London: '... il arrive souvent que l'on voit des choses, sans sçavoir qu'on le voit et l'on peut aussi sçavoir que des choses sont, bien qu'on ne les voye pas. ... Si nous n'avons eu que des yeux pour découvrir ce qu'il y a à apprendre dans les dissections, celles qui ont donné lieu à la découverte ... ne nous auroit (sic) fourny qu'une confirmation de la pensée chimérique des anciens.' (Essais, I, pp. 325 ff.; already read to the Assembly on February 13, 1675).

24. Essais, I, pp. 173 ff., III, pp. 302 ff.

25. François Vernon wrote on 12 June, 1669 to Oldenburg from Paris that he 'had opportunity to see a dissection of a horse made by Monsr Pecquet & Gaignan, as operators: Galois, Their Secretary, Copied, and Peraut, a very knowing Dr of Physick designed.' (op, cit., VI, p. 6)

26. Extrait d'une lettre écrite à Monsieur de la Chambre qui contient les observations qui ont esté faites sur un grand Poisson disséqué dans la Bibliothèque du Roi le 24 Juin 1667 – Observations qui ont esté faites sur un Lion disséqué dans la Biblothèque du Roy le 28 Juin 1667 tirées d'une lettre écrite à Monsieur de la Chambre, Paris, 1667.

Description anatomique d'un caméléon, d'un castor, d'un dromedaire d'un ours, et d'une Gazelle, Paris, 1669.

academic work, if properly publicized, was immensely suitable for enhancing the reputation of the Académie des Sciences and, at the same time, for presenting Royal patronage in the most favourable light. It was decided to reproduce drawings and descriptions in a magnificent folio, to be published by the Imprimerie Royale, at which the first edition appeared in 1671.[27]

The preface underlines the co-operative nature of the work; neither on the title-page nor in the text is any member of the team mentioned. There are, however, passages in the preface which sound as if they come from Perrault's pen. In any case, even if others collaborated, he certainly identified himself with their final formulation. 'We only put forward facts', the anatomists claim, 'and these facts are the only forces which we want to use against the authority of the great men who have written before us; while speaking of them with all the respect they deserve, we realize that faults which appear in their works are only there because it is impossible to find anything that has achieved ultimate perfection.' It is better, they continue, to point out these faults than to value them for no other reason than that they have been made by great men and because they have been approved by the common consent of centuries. They hope that their readers will not belong to the great number of people who have 'a blind veneration for the works and the opinion of the ancients.'[28] It is well to remember these sentences when, later on, we come to discuss Perrault's architectural theory.

In the year following the publication, the team of anatomists accumulated so much new material that a second, much enlarged, edition became necessary. It appeared in 1676. 'Dressez par M. Perrault' one reads on the title-page, indicating that the overall responsibility for the

27. *Mémoires pour servir à l'histoire naturelle des animaux*, Paris, 1671. Later, the dissections took place in the *Jardin du Roi*.
28. 'Nous estimons que ceux qui seront capables de ces réflexions n'auront pas la malignité de se prévaloir de l'autorité qu'on donne au grand nombre de ceux qui, n'en estant pas capables, veulent que l'on ait comme eux une vénération aveugle pour les ouvrages et pour les sentimens des Anciens.'

Mémoires was his. His own particular contribution consisted probably in the descriptions and drawings, since Pecquet and Gayant and, replacing them, Duverney are specifically mentioned in the *avertissement* as the members who performed the actual dissections. In the same year, the botanical companion to the anatomical volume was published, edited by Dodart.[29] While he stresses the fact that this undertaking, too, was the result of teamwork, Dodart nevertheless mentions the special contributions made by some members. Evidently, Perrault was also active in this field: he was one of a team of five who examined the results in detail, gave, together with Mariotte, 'much attention and thought' to the matter and, in particular, 'did much work in comparing the descriptions (of rare plants) with the real ones.'[30]

Among the various researches undertaken by the Academy, was one experiment which had great topical interest. Two years earlier, the first blood transfusion between animals had been performed in London. Members now wished to form their own opinion about the operation and its after effects and, consequently, arranged for the experiment to be carried out on two dogs. After this had been performed on several occasions, the subject was debated in March 1667. Perrault's remarks, highly critical about the feasibility of the process (hailed by many as a panacea) make interesting reading even today. They are proof of his understanding of and respect for the living organism and, although he expressed his views in the primitive notions of the time, his foresight of the complex nature of blood is remarkable. It would be strange, he concludes, 'if one could change blood as one changes shirts.'[31]

---

29. *Mémoires pour servir à l'histoire naturelle des plantes*, Paris, 1676.

30. ibid., Preface. The value of his contribution to botanical research is stressed by L. Pantefol in *Troisième centenaire*, II, p. 130.

31. *Register*, I, fols. 211–38; Fontenelle, op. cit., I, pp. 37 f.: 'M. Perrault désapprouva fort cette méthode, fondé principalement sur ce qu'il est bien difficile qu'un animal s'accomode d'un sang qui n'a pas été cuit et préparé ches lui-même.' Perrault published his *mémoire* in 1688 (*Essais*, IV, pp. 403 ff.); he is then still convinced of 'l'impossibilité que la nature trouve à s'accomoder d'un sang étranger' (p. 407), and points to the 'mutuelle conspiration qui est entre les différentes parties, qui conviennent toutes dans un certain caractère particulier à chaque individu' (p. 425).

The controversy was carried into the pages of the *Mercure de France* (13 January, 14 March, 16 and 28 June 1667, and 2 February 1668), until the transfusion was finally forbidden.

When, at the end of 1669, he again outlines a programme for the following year (as he had also done at the beginning of 1668), he suggests as suitable subject for research the muscle movements of the intestine, a process he himself was to investigate for the next five years, by which time his studies were advanced enough for him to communicate his manuscript on the *mouvement péristaltique* to the Compagnie. A few years later, it was published in the first volume of his *Essais de physique*.[32] The second and third volume contained his studies on sound and perception, and the comprehensive treatise on the *Mécanique des animaux*; subjects on which he reported to his colleagues in advance of publication in 1677 and 1679 respectively. Subjects that had been debated in the Academy, with Perrault taking part, were also incorporated in the *Essais*, such as special theories on weight, elasticity and on the solidifying of fluids. In this field, he himself had made experiments during the severe winter of 1669, as he also had taken measurements over many months to determine the effect rain and snow had on the water level of Paris.[33]

There were other experiments which he pursued, independent of his work in the Academy. On one of the many occasions when Huygens stayed at Viry, he assisted him in measuring the speed of sound and with experiments on refraction. Through Huygens's correspondence we learn that Perrault made some experiments with metal lenses for telescopes and also with a special kind of black clay he had found at Viry.[34] To judge from the many occasions on which he wrote or spoke about the properties of chalk, he must have made extensive experiments with this material.[35]

In June 1675, the Academy received, through Colbert, a command

32. I, pp. 129 ff.

33. *Register*, I, 4 February 1668 (Program), VI, 30 November 1669 (Program), VIII, 2 February 1675 (Mouvement péristaltique), 1 December 1675 (sound), X, 1 February 1679 (Mécanique, extending over 15 meetings), IV, 4 August 1668 (Waterlevel), VI, 10 August 1669 (freezing water).

34. *Oeuvres*, XIX, p. 372, X, p. 323, VI, p. 497, VIII, p. 479. The design of a waterclock, attached to a letter to Huygens dated: Viry, 28 October 1669 (*Oeuvres* VI, p. 506) must be by Pierre Perrault, since Claude was at that time in Bordeaux (see below p. 26).

35. *Register*, December 1667: discussion on properties of chalk, with Perrault's *mémoire* attached; *Vitruvius*, p. 37, note 1; *Essais*, IV, pp. 297 ff.

from the King to work forthwith on a *Traité de Mécanique* which was to include 'an exact description of all machines...at present in use in France and Europe'.[36] This meant for Perrault the prospect of seeing his numerous designs reproduced in a publication which, no doubt, would match the splendour and distinction of the volume on the anatomy of animals.

Perrault was much interested in the construction of machines: at a time when mechanics seemed to lead to a deeper understanding of physical phenomena, this interest was natural for a scientist trying to explain the working of animal structure.[37] In addition, the translation of Vitruvius, completed only a few years earlier, had forced him to make himself familiar with constructional problems, since only then could he succeed in offering reasonable interpretations of the obscure terms in which Vitruvius had described machines and instruments then in use. A number of his reconstructions of ancient machinery were shown in engravings; models had been made of some which formed the nucleus of a collection kept in the Bibliothèque du Roi, among them two weight-lifting machines of his own invention.[38]

As a start towards realization of the *Traité de Mécanique*, members decided to compile a catalogue of this collection, beginning with models used in architecture and agriculture. However, apart from this catalogue, the submission of a few theoretical treatises and a resolution about the size of the plates needed for the illustrations, no other steps were taken to comply with the royal command.

Perrault, however, was constantly inventing new machines or improving existing ones. Any constructional problem he encountered, any inefficiency he observed, became a challenge to him for devising different

---

36. Fontenelle, op. cit., p. 199.
For details concerning this project, see the editor's remarks in Huygens, *Oeuvres*, XIX, pp. 181 ff.

37. Charles Perrault in the *Epître* to the *Recueil de plusieurs machines de nouvelle invention. Ouvrage posthume de M. Perrault*, Paris, 1700: '...ceux qui regardent attentivement les Ouvrages de la Nature, en rendent raison par la Méchanique, comme s'ils avoient esté appellez au Conseil du Créateur quand il les forma la première fois.'

38. *Vitruvius*, pls LVII–LXIV.

and better methods. The list of machines and instruments designed by him is impressive, as is the variety of matters dealt with: it ranges from a number of machines connected with warfare to a portable sun-dial watch, from various types of weight-lifting and water-raising machines to a device for improving the sound of an organ. Complying with a request made by Louvois, he designed an instrument for measuring rainfall and evaporation; prompted by an article in the *Journal des Sçavans*, he constructed, and had a model made, of a fixed telescope with a movable mirror of which he sent a detailed description to Huygens who, however, saw difficulties about its application to large telescopes, as he also had thought Perrault's bomb-throwing machine, published in his *Vitruvius*, to be unworkable.[39] Colbert's plan to bridge the Seine at Sèvres caused Perrault to devise a construction allowing a single span of nearly two hundred feet, and, having witnessed in 1674, the exciting event of the transportation and lifting into position of two huge stones for the pediment of the Louvre, he designed a much improved version of the complicated and hazardous contraption used, and published it in the second edition of *Vitruvius*.[40] (Pls. 6–7). When he became doubtful about the prospects of the official *Traité*, he prepared his own publication. At the time of his death, he had completed the descriptions of ten machines designed by him over a period of more than twenty years.[41]

Thus, during the whole of that period, Perrault's scientific work took up most of his time; he attended the meetings of the Academy, took part in the discussions, submitted *mémoires*, performed or, at any rate, was present at the dissections carried out at first in the Bibliothèque and later

---

39. A number of these machines were published in the *Recueil*, the rest in his *Vitruvius* (p. 286: pocket watch; p. 325: Organ; p. 337: bomb-throwing device), the latter, together with another version, also in François Blondel, *L'art de jetter les bombes*, The Hague, 1685, pp. 492 ff., 523 ff. The drawing for the tubeless telescope is attached to Perrault's letter to Huygens, *Oeuvres*, VIII, p. 508.

Huygens's criticism *Oeuvres*, VIII, p. 531, IX, p. 471. See, however, the appreciative remark by A. Wolf, *A History of Science, Technology, and Philosophy in the 16th and 17th Centuries*, London, 1935, p. 66.

40. On the machines for the pediment of the Louvre, see Appendix I.

41. *Journal des Sçavans*, 1689, p. 81: 'Dans le temps même qu'il fut attaqué de sa dernière maladie, il travailloit à un recueil de nouvelles machines de son invention. On a déjà commencé à les graver.'

in the Jardin du Roi, wrote a great number of anatomical descriptions and watched over their publication, made scientific experiments, constructed machines and instruments and made extensive studies in various fields, the result of which appeared in 1680 in the first three volumes of his *Essais*. During the next eight years, he continued his researches, elaborating in particular his animistic theory of perception which makes up, with many other subjects, the fourth volume.[42]

He was active until the end. We are told, as late as March 1688, that 'he never stops working on machines of great ingenuity', that 'some new volumes of the Essais de Physique' are going to be published 'in a few days time', and that he is working with two of his colleagues on a third, enlarged and improved edition of the *Histoire des animaux* which will contain 'many very interesting new descriptions'.[43] Perrault had been engaged on this work for at least four years, bringing text and drawings of the preceding edition up-to-date and preparing new ones of which ten were found among his papers.[44] It must have been in connection with this task of verifying previous observations that he performed, in the autumn of 1688, the dissection of a camel, an operation that proved

42. In 1671, Perrault was appointed a member of a commission, consisting of six doctors and five *bourgeois*, set up to investigate the allegation that yeast made from beer was dangerous to health (*Journal des Sçavans*, 1671, pp. 45 ff.).

43. Huygens, *Oeuvres*, IX, pp. 263 f.: letter of 3 March 1688 from de La Hire to Huygens.

44. According to the *avertissement* to tome III of the *Mémoires de l'Académie Royale des Sciences depuis 1666 jusqu'à 1699* Perrault made additions and corrections in his copy of the second edition of the *Histoire naturelle*. After his death Duverney became 'maître de tous les papiers originaux'. Among these papers was 'une seconde suite de l'Histoire Naturelle des Animaux, écrite et désignée par M. Perrault même: elles contient la Description de seize Animaux.' Duverney prepared, but never published, a new edition without, however, making use of Perrault's additional manuscript. This was found among Duverney's papers and was published in 1733, together with the edition prepared by Duverney, as third part of tome III. Perrault's manuscript and a planned third edition in 1688 is also referred to in a handwritten note in one of six volumes (I, 2, fol. 450) in which all engravings that had been published by the *Imprimerie Royale* were to be collected. (now in the British Museum, Pressmark 1750 c 7). The preparatory work for this third edition was quite advanced at the time of Perrault's death: paper had been bought, plates been trimmed (the new edition was to be smaller than the first two) and the secretary been paid for expenses (*Comptes des Bâtiments du Roi*, Paris, 1881 ff., II, pp. 782, 785, 1009, 1015). The fact that the new edition was given up when Perrault died, proves that he was the driving force |behind the whole undertaking. Cf. J.-A. Hazon, *Notices des hommes les plus célèbres de la Faculté de Médecine en l'Université de Paris*, Paris, 1778, p. 123: '... les Mémoires ... qui ont été imprimés au Louvre en 1676, et dont le second volume resta, après sa mort, à l'Académie pour le revoir.'

fatal to him. Perrault contracted an infection and died of blood poisoning, aged seventy-five, on 9 October 1688.[45]

Almost half a century had passed since the day on which he had taken his first medical degree. All the available evidence suggests that from that time on, he followed a consistent course which, it is true, changed direction when he became a member of the Academy, but which he never abandoned in preference to another occupation. One can be sure that he felt his essential life-work to be well attested when, on the title-pages of his books, he was described as *M. Perrault de l'Académie Royale des Sciences Docteur en Médecine de la Faculté de Paris.*

Perrault was justified in feeling satisfied about his work. During his lifetime he achieved the reputation of being a competent and versatile scientist, and the fact that his work was referred to fairly frequently in the scientific literature of the next century and also in modern books on the history of science proves that it was sufficiently original to leave its mark and to have some influence on later thought. Of course, nothing he wrote as an anatomist, physiologist or physicist comes anywhere near in importance to the outstanding place which the Colonnade of the Louvre holds in the history of art, a monument with which his name has always been closely linked. For that reason, it has been too readily assumed that his scientific work could have occupied only a secondary position in his life: however, even though in this field he was not one of the leading figures of his time, his contributions to science were not negligible. It would lead us too far afield to recount the response Perrault's anatomical and physiological researches and his more general conjectures found, in his own time and among the writers of succeeding centuries. Here, it must suffice to list the names of the more important authors: Leibniz and Huygens, who knew him and recognized his capability; the eminent contemporary philosophers Pierre-Sylvain Regis and Johann Christian Sturm, who devoted whole chapters to a discussion of his ideas; Georg Ernst Stahl, the founder of the vitalistic school of medicine, Albrecht von Haller, Buffon, La Mettrie and Maine de Biran, who knew his books

45. Charles Perrault, *Hommes illustres*, p. 68.

and must have benefited in some way, even though not all acknowledged it. Tracing the name of Perrault, the 'medical man', through the literature of two and a half centuries – of which a more detailed account is given in an appendix[46] – one is left with a picture of a man who, without ever having set up one of the major stepping-stones on which progress of science depends, was nevertheless keenly aware of the tasks that lay ahead and, trying to deal with them and having an original mind, produced work that was good enough to survive him. It is well to be clear about his standing as a scientist; not for its own sake, but in order to understand that Perrault could very well regard the pursuit of science as his true vocation. Without taking this possibility into consideration, the rôle he played in the architectural sphere can easily be overrated.

'Monsieur Perrault . . . a lu Vitruve, il a fréquenté M. le Vau et M. Ratabon, et s'est enfin jeté dans l'architecture,' wrote Boileau in 1676 to the Duc de Vivonne.[47] Boileau, filled with rancour towards Perrault, gave this particular information only in order to ridicule Perrault's pretension of having been the architect responsible for the design of the Colonnade. Nevertheless, the facts may very well be true. We know from the illustrations to the *Voyage à Viry* that the young Perrault had some understanding of architectural composition and perspective or, if that seems too high a claim considering the indifferent quality of his drawings, at least was interested in these subjects. The next design of which we know, a huge obelisk meant to be erected in honour of the King on the left bank of the Seine, dates from almost thirty years later[48] (Pl. 5). Even if he employed another hand for the drawing itself, the invention was his and shows a considerable advance over his early attempts. It is, therefore, quite probable that he had kept up his interest in architecture by reading, as Boileau suggests, architectural treatises, including of course Vitruvius, and by conversing with the first *architecte*

46. Appendix II.
47. *Oeuvres*, ed. Saint-Surin, Paris, 1821, IV, p. 24.
48. Paris, Bibl. Nat., MS Anc. franç., 24,713, fol. 151. The accompanying text is dated 20 October 1666. A variant of this design in the Nationalmuseum Stockholm, Coll. Tessin-Hårleman 2428; ill. in Laprade, op. cit., App. C4.

du Roi and the *surintendant des bâtiments* about architectural topics (no doubt, putting this knowledge to good use when, after the death of his mother in 1657, some rebuilding was done at the house in Viry).[49] It was by no means unusual for an educated person to take an active, though purely intellectual, interest in architecture which then, by its clearly defined system, had a strong rational appeal.[50]

Perrault had made the design for the obelisk a few days after his election to the Académie des Sciences. It is possible that Colbert had previously seen another design by Perrault, a plan for the eastern façade of the Louvre, submitted, so Perrault and his brother claimed in later years, as early as 1664;[51] but, in any case, Colbert was, no doubt, aware – or had been made aware – that this comparatively unknown member of the Academy had qualities that were not often found combined: medical training, a lively interest in the wide range of natural sciences, taste for architecture and, probably, a good knowledge of its theoretical aspect. Here, obviously was the right man to carry out satisfactorily a work that badly needed to be done. Thus, Perrault received the most important commission of his life: to translate Vitruvius into French.[52]

It is not possible to say precisely in which year Perrault started on this work. The first engravings were paid for in January 1668, so that the drawings from which they were copied must have been ready some time in 1667. Of the few notes which provide clues as to the time in which they were written, none can be dated before 1667, some must be

49. Charles Perrault, *Mémoires*, p. 34, declares that the new building was done under his direction (although he admits that his brothers 'avoient grande part au dessein de ce bâtiment') and that it was due to him that 'la rocaille d'une grotte' was then built. This cannot be correct, since an artificial grotto, with water running over rocks and shells, was already the showpiece of the garden when, in 1637, M. Corneillau described it in detail and Perrault made a drawing of its outer appearance (see above, p. 2, note 3).

50. Neither was it unusual in the seventeenth century for a scientist to be attracted to architecture: Louis Savot, who wrote an architectural treatise in 1624, had been a medical man, François Blondel and Nicolaus Goldmann were mathematicians. In England, a close parallel to Perrault's life history is that of Robert Hooke, but specially, of course, that of Sir Christopher Wren (see below pp. 156 f).

51. Charles Perrault, *Mémoires*, p. 53; Claude Perrault in conversation with Leibniz (about 1676). Leibniz's résumé was published in *Journal général de l'Instruction Publique*, XXVI, 1857, pp. 235 f.

52. *Les dix livres d'architecture de Vitruve, corrigez et traduits nouvellement en François avec des Notes et des Figures ... par M. Perrault*, Paris, 1673. I quote, unless otherwise stated, after the second enlarged edition of 1684.

as late as 1672.[53] The probability that Perrault completed the formidable task of translating the text and commenting on it within the comparatively short span of six or seven years is borne out by his own remarks. Apologizing for the imperfection of his translation and pointing out that it was intended for the use of architects, not scholars, he explains that those who had planned it had not been prepared to wait the long time needed for completing the study of all extant manuscripts and of all ancient monuments, nor to allow him enough time for dealing exhaustively with all the physical, historical or mathematical questions referred to by Vitruvius.[54] It was only in preparing the second edition that he had sufficient leisure to make up for the 'haste' with which he previously had to work, 'not having been able in the first edition to give all the time required for throwing light on the many different matters which this work contains'.[55]

It is evident from these remarks that Colbert did not simply give official support to a work which Perrault had already in hand, but that the initiative came from him. His decision to entrust Perrault with the task proved to be the right one. Perrault gladly met the challenge which Vitruvius's comments on so many different subjects presented to him. If others ridiculed Vitruvius for 'telling, regardless of relevance, all he knew or even did not know', Perrault, though himself reporting these remarks, probably welcomed Vitruvius's weak side.[56] It gave him the opportunity of dealing with many subjects that interested him, of adding to his explanatory notes the results of modern research, often his own.

---

53. *Comptes*, I, p. 281.

References to the collection of machine models in the *Bibliothèque du Roi* must have been written after 1667, to the Tutelles in Bordeaux (pp. 92 n. 30, 108 n. 13, 217 n. 8, 298 n. 3) probably after his journey of 1669. The machine by Francini ('qui . . . l'a fait construire il y a environ deux ans' p. 319 n. 8) was published in 1669 which gives a date of 1671 for this note. In the same year the great salon of the Observatoire was vaulted (p. 152 n. 10) and the measurement of the earth's circumference (p. 25 n. 9) calculated. The crossing of the Rhine (p. 245 n. 2) took place on 12 June 1672, the siege of Ostende (p. 347 n. 4) in the same year. A reference to a catapult in the Arsenal in Brussels (p. 332 n. 1), Perrault probably inserted after his visit to Holland in 1671 (Huygens, *Oeuvres*, VII, p. 57).

54. First edition, Preface.

55. Second edition, *Avertissement*.

56. ibid., p. 32 n. 2.

They range, to name only a few of the more extended ones, from the organic structure of trees and the properties of timber to those of chalk and drinking water, from wall paintings and colour pigments to the construction of walls and chimneys, and, above all, to the subject that interested him so much, the construction of machines and instruments.

Perrault comments on these, and many other subjects, with expert knowledge. His bent for exploring technical problems makes him also discuss at length purely practical questions, such as novel ways for constructing masonry, timber roofs and drainage, or the most efficient way of laying foundations. He deals with equal proficiency with the essential part of Vitruvius's treatise, the four books that are exclusively devoted to architecture. With full knowledge of the considerable literature on the Vitruvian text he weighs up the various interpretations, often suggesting new ones, and never misses an opportunity of developing his own particular views on architecture.

He carried out his commission as translator and commentator simultaneously with his academic work. Reading through the minutes of the Academy, one finds that many subjects on which he commented, other than purely architectural ones, were at one time or other discussed in the meetings. On many of these occasions, Perrault himself had thrown much light on the subject; but, obviously, the quality and depth of many notes owe much to the frequent opportunities he had of discussing these problems with his fellow academicians. The Académie d'Architecture, which could have performed a similar rôle for the architectural comments, was established too late to have been of much assistance, although there may also have been other reasons for its less marked influence, a problem to which we shall return presently.

A few remarks in his scientific papers reveal the ease with which Perrault's mind could glide from one sphere of interest to the other. In his arguments against blood transfusion he uses as analogy to the unique quality of an animal's blood the fact that 'the perfect construction of a palace can only be achieved with material that had been cut and adapted to the particular structure', and points out that the blood of one dog cannot nourish the flesh of another dog, just as 'the stone which is cut for a vault not only cannot be used for the construction of a wall, but not even for another vault than the one for which it had been cut.'[57] When in the preface to the *Histoire des animaux* it is said that the measurements of the animals described are given in relation to the human body because 'it was necessary to agree one measure and one module, in the same way as it is done in architecture,' we can be sure that this remark was inserted by Perrault, as it was due, no doubt, to him that buildings of a style he had adopted in his illustrations to Vitruvius appear again, in spite of the incongruity, on two occasions in the background of illustrations depicting wild animals (Pls. 8–9). Naturally, he liked to display his knowledge acquired in the course of his architectural studies. Of the three *mémoires* on the properties of chalk, submitted to the Academy in December 1667, his is the only one that refers to the remarks made on the subject by Vitruvius and Cesare Cesariano, to those of 'Barbaro, Philibert de Lorme, Palladio and all the others who have written about architecture'.[58]

When his *Vitruvius* was completed, it was brought out in a splendid folio edition and dedicated to the King (Pl. 10). In November 1673, Perrault presented a copy to the members of the architectural academy who had eagerly awaited it ever since, in February of that year, they had rejected as unsatisfactory the only translation then available.[59] To judge from the great number of meetings which they devoted to the reading of Perrault's edition and their scrutiny of text and commentaries, they recognized its quality. Perrault's achievement was, indeed, outstanding; he had produced the first authoritative and well-annotated French translation which, written in the international language of the educated, became a standard work known in all parts of Europe. Perrault's

57. *Essais*, IV, pp. 425 f. This comparison, he concludes, 'peut faire concevoir que le secours que l'on pourroit donner à la Nature par l'infusion d'un sang étranger, quelque pur et bien conditionné qu'il puisse être, seroit pareil au soulagement que recevroit un Architecte empêché à équarrir les pierres dont il veut construire un mur à plomb, si on lui en apportoit de parfaitement bien taillées pour un mur en talus.'

58. *Register*, I, 17 December 1667. Copy of his *mémoire* is entered in the *Register*.

59. *Procès-verbaux de l'Académie Royale d'architecture* (ed. H. Lemonnier), Paris, 1911, I, p. 21 (28 February 1673), and p. 50 (20 November 1673).

contemporaries praised it almost unanimously, and even in modern times it is given an honourable place amidst the many translations that have been published over the centuries. Of course, advances in archaeological and philological research made it obsolete, but it is a tribute to its accomplishment that almost 150 years passed before a new French translation was undertaken and that even thereafter Perrault's text and notes were taken over, wholly or in great part, into editions of Vitruvius published as late as the middle of the nineteenth century.[60]

Perrault's edition was also valuable because of the many illustrations with which he tried to make text and interpretation more intelligible. A great number of them, woodcuts inserted throughout the book, are simple explanatory diagrams; others are more illustrative, relating mainly to the Orders, but they too are no more than a visual record of what had been stated in the text. A few, however, are imaginative and stand out from the others (Pls. 11–14). In one or two instances they derive from Palladio's or Serlio's designs, but on the whole they are the result of independent work.[61] The restraint with which any superfluous ornament is avoided, the emphasis laid on the constructive part of the building – its columns, pilasters and entablatures – the exquisite delicacy with which niches, reliefs or simple festoons are arranged to give rhythmic articulation to the bare walls – all this creates the beautiful quality of classical simplicity that is akin to buildings seen in Claude's or Poussin's paintings. Of course, Perrault's own taste influences his conception of the buildings described by Vitruvius; but it must be noted that his designs, unlike those of the two painters, are conscious reconstructions, adhering, as far as possible, to the information given in the text. The extreme simplicity is only partly due to his taste. It is as much the result of scholarly honesty, and springs from the same attitude that guided him in his reconstruction of the Jewish Temple which he was asked to devise a decade later.[62]

60. See Appendix III for some contemporary and modern comments on his translation.

61. Perrault's reconstruction of the 'Egyptian' house (pl. LIV) follows closely Palladio's (I quattro libri, Venice, 1570, book II, p. 42); those of the atrium (pls LI and LII) may have been influenced by Palladio's design II, p. 10 and Serlio's Tutte l'opere d'architettura, Venice, 1619, book III, fol. 123.

With admirable persistence he resisted the temptation to adorn the Temple, in the conventional way, with the full gamut of classical decoration, but, relying only on the few details and measurements he found in the text, presented it in its awesome primitiveness (Pl. 15).

In April 1667, Colbert set up a *petit conseil* to advise him on the proposed eastern façade of the Louvre. This council consisted of three men: Le Vau, the *premier architecte du Roi*, Le Brun, the *premier peintre du Roi*, and Claude Perrault.[63] The appointment of Perrault seems strange – at least as long as this *conseil* is considered as a partnership of professional architects. The inclusion of Le Brun in itself shows that this was not Colbert's intention. It is true that at about the same time Perrault, as a member of the Académie des Sciences, was engaged in the planning of the Observatoire, intended to be the future home of all sections of the Academy [64] (Pl. 16), but even allowing for this evidence of Perrault's having acquired knowledge that, for an amateur, was remarkable, he was certainly not an architect. His election to this three-man council must have been due to some other qualification by which, it was expected, he would be able to contribute to their deliberations. For a building as outstanding and representative as the Louvre façade, a design had to be obtained that was satisfactory in every respect. Not only had it to fulfil a complex building programme, and to represent convincingly the power and glory of the Crown, it had also to be 'correct', that is to say, it had to conform to the stringent demands imposed by classical dogma. For Colbert, the obvious choice for filling this place must have been the man who, through his important work on Vitruvius, was on his way to becoming an outstanding expert on architectural theory. Thus, Perrault joined the other two in his capacity as, one might say, the *premier théoricien du Roi*. That this was, indeed, essentially the task he performed as a member of the *conseil* – and within the framework of

62. Maimonides, *De Cultu Divino* (ed. Ludovicus ... de Veil), Paris, 1678. (see my article 'Unknown Designs for the "Temple of Jerusalem" by Claude Perrault' in *Essays in the History of Architecture presented to Rudolf Wittkower*, I, pp. 143 ff.).

63. Piganiol de la Force, *Description de Paris*, Paris, 1742, p. 629.

64. The *Observatoire* and Perrault's authorship has recently been dealt with in detail by M. Petzet, 'Claude Perrault als Architekt des Pariser Observatoriums,' *Zeitschrift für Kunstgeschichte*, XXX, 1967, pp. 1 ff.

classical architecture it was by no means an unimportant one – is confirmed by Charles Perrault. As the secretary of the council he kept a register which, he tells us in his *Mémoires*, 'is full of very interesting things that would be most useful to those who are fond of architecture. Because my brother was constantly contradicted by Monsieur Le Vau and Monsieur Le Brun, he had to make dissertations all the time, or rather give lectures on architecture, which he brought back in writing to the next meeting. I possess the originals which I am glad to keep.'[65]

It can be assumed that Perrault, too, produced a plan, but whether his was finally chosen in preference to those submitted by Le Vau and Le Brun (as both Charles and Claude asserted) remains doubtful. In any case, if there was a plan by him, it probably was among the designs, kept by Charles in two volumes, which were destroyed a hundred years ago when, during the Commune, the Bibliothèque du Louvre was burnt down. Of the many plans still extant none has been identified with certainty as Perrault's work.[66]

When, in the following year, it was decided to erect at the Porte St Antoine a triumphal arch, the matter may have been considered by the *petit conseil* and a basic design established. This would explain the striking similarity between Le Brun's and Perrault's designs. Perrault's variant, however, was accepted, being, indeed, superior to Le Brun's. The dimensions of this arch were enormous, and would have dwarfed the Arch of Constantine in Rome (Pl. 17); however, the arch was never completed, work having stopped soon after it had risen a few feet above the foundation; eventually, in 1716, it was demolished.[67]

These then are the three buildings which are traditionally ascribed to Perrault: the Colonnade, the Observatoire and the Arc de Triomphe

65. op. cit., p. 87.

66. On Perrault's contribution to the planning of 1667 see the following recent publications: A. Laprade, op. cit., pp. 52 ff., 143 ff.; Tony Sauvel, 'Les auteurs de la colonnade du Louvre,' *Bulletin Monumental*, CXXII, 1964, pp. 323 ff.; A. Braham and M. Whiteley, 'Louis le Vau's Projects for the Louvre and the Colonnade,' *Gazette des Beaux-Arts*, LXIV, 1964, pp. 285, 347 ff.; M. Petzet, *Akten des 21ten Internationalen Kongresses für Kunstgeschichte in Bonn 1964*, Berlin, 1967, III, pp. 159 ff.

67. Pierre Clément, *Lettres, instructions et mémoires de Colbert*, Paris, 1868, V, pp. 277, 522. J.-F. Blondel, *Architecture françoise*, Paris, 1752, II, pp. 136 ff.

(Pl. 18). The degree of his involvement varies with each building and is difficult to assess. His contributions to these projects are made within a period of not much more than three years – from the beginning of 1667 to about 1670. These were the most eventful, and most stimulating years of his life, full of activity. Besides his own extensive researches and the work carried out for the Academy, which must have taken up a good part of his time, he was engaged in the exacting task of translating Vitruvius, was involved in the discussions taking place in the *petit conseil*, and was preparing designs for the three buildings mentioned. All these pursuits are crowded into these few years.[68]

Thereafter, his interest in architectural design and the part this activity played in his life seems to have undergone a change. During the years just dealt with, Perrault had been connected with the planning of monuments outstanding in size and quality: this made it necessary for him to give a certain degree of sustained attention to the project and its progress, and to deal occasionally even with technical matters. But now, from 1670 on, this is changed. His designs became sporadic, his concern for architecture more like that of a gifted amateur. We hear of a design he made for a French Order when an official competition had been arranged, while on another occasion he sent in, as many others did, the *grand dessein* for turning the Louvre and the Tuileries into one huge, integrated complex, a plan to which belong two still-extant designs for the main staircase.[69] Then again, he designs bronze doors for the *grands appartements*

68. In addition he submitted, in June 1669, together with a number of other architects, a plan for the rebuilding of Versailles, which Colbert much criticized, as he did those of the others with the exception of Le Vau's plan (Charles Perrault, *Mémoires*, p. 112, Clément, op. cit., V, pp. 284 ff.). A few years earlier, he was probably responsible for some decorative details of the Grotte de Thétis at Versailles, though not for the planning of the grotto itself (Liliane Lange, 'La grotte de Thétis et le premier Versailles de Louis XIV,' *Art de France*, I, 1961, pp. 133 ff.).

69. The competition was announced in the *Gazette de France*, No. 133 (14 November 1671). Perrault's design is mentioned by A.-Ch. Daviler, *Cours d'architecture*, Paris, 1691, II, p. 298 and J.-F. Blondel, op. cit., IV, 4, 62 note p. cf. L. Hautecoeur, *Histoire de l'architecture classique en France*, Paris, 1948, II, pp. 352 ff.; H. Lemonnier, *L'art français au temps de Louis XIV*, Paris, 1911, pp. 197 ff.

For the *grand plan* see J.-F. Blondel, op. cit., IV, pp. 9 f. and pls I, II; L. Hautecoeur, *Le Louvre et les Tuileries de Louis XIV*, Paris, 1927, pp. 189 f. A copy of the plan was sent in 1679 to Huygens's brother-in-law who refers to it in an interesting letter (*Oeuvres*, VIII, p. 154).

The designs for the staircase of the Louvre project are in the Nationalmuseum Stockholm, Collection Tessin-Hårleman; they were published by R. Josephson, 'Quelques dessins de Claude Perrault pour le Louvre', *Gazette des Beaux Arts*, LXIX, 1927, II, pp. 171 ff.

at Versailles and submits the sketch to Colbert.[70] Some years later, on
Colbert's advice, he seeks the opinion of members of the Académie
d'Architecture on a plan for raising the height of the corner pavilions of
the Colonnade by superstructures.[71] At about the same time, believing
that the church of Ste Geneviève, near which he lived, needed rebuilding,
he designs, probably assisted by his brother, the façade and interior of a
splendid new church, the drawings of which are still preserved.[72] From
this time also date the engravings, already mentioned, of his reconstruction of the Temple of Jerusalem; he received this commission because
the accuracy with which his illustrations interpreted Vitruvius's text
made him seem the right person for doing the same for the Temple from
the Latin translation of Maimonides's edition of the Mishnah. Even if
more designs had been preserved or recorded, it seems unlikely that they
would alter the picture of his architectural activity during this period.
Not being connected with any particular building project, he makes
designs whenever an occasion presents itself. The latest of these are the
engravings for the Temple, published in 1678. After that date, this
particular pursuit comes to an end. The last decade of his life he devoted
exclusively to scientific and theoretical studies.[73]

A curious remark once made by Colbert points to the same conclusion
regarding Perrault's relation to architecture. In September 1669, Perrault,
in the company of his brother Jean and a few friends, had started on a
journey through France which, after two months, was cut short in
Bordeaux through the tragic death of Jean.[74] Perrault kept a diary on this
journey the day-to-day entries of which give a vivid picture of his personality: a keen observer, obviously enjoying the constant changes that

70. Mentioned in a letter by Perrault dated 27 January, 1674, Paris, Bibl. Nat., MS Mélanges
Colbert 167, fols. 245 a & b.
71. *Procès-verbaux*, I, pp. 137, 252, 260 (March 1677, December 1678, January 1679). T. Sauvel, op.
cit., p. 344, refers to the practical reasons that led to the idea of raising the height of the pavilions.
72. M. Petzet, 'Un projet des Perrault pour l'église Sainte-Geneviève à Paris', *Bulletin monumental*,
CXV, 1957, pp. 81 ff.
73. L. Hautecoeur, *L'architecture classique*, II, p. 461: 'Claude Perrault n'apparaît plus comme
architecte après 1680.'
74. 'Voyage à Bordeaux,' publ. by P. Bonnefon as an appendix to the *Mémoires*, pp. 139 ff.

go with travelling, meeting the unexpected with a great sense of humour, intent on visiting everything that was of importance – châteaux as well as more modest buildings, ancient churches and new ones – noticing constructional details and marking down any deviation from the classical canon. The pages are filled with competent little sketches, making even clearer his entries which become very detailed when they describe what were probably the first Roman ruins he had ever seen, the so-called Piliers de Tutelle, a Gallo-Roman Temple, and the Amphitheatre, both in Bordeaux[75] (Pls. 20–22). But he is just as fascinated by a huge naval arsenal, not yet completed but already employing two thousand men, where he watches the making of ropes and the casting of guns and describes what must have been one of the earliest dry-docks operated by sluices. There is nothing that fails to interest him, whether it is the production of salt by evaporation, a particular herb or the anatomy of a fish he is eating for the first time. His descriptions are factual and remain so when he describes his brother's last illness. Although all the Perrault brothers were known to have been close to each other, he never shows his emotion, except once, when he admits that the deterioration in his brother's condition 'me mit en une étrange peine'. When he attends the funeral service, the strange rites – unknown to the Parisian – rouse his interest and, having returned to his quarters, he describes them with the same attention to detail with which he had noted the measurements and decorations of the Piliers de Tutelle.

While Perrault was in Bordeaux, Colbert had received bad news from the local engineer in charge of the fortifications: a bastion of the main fortress on the left bank of the Garonne had collapsed. Colbert, greatly alarmed at the threatening prospect of large sums of money having been spent in vain, remembered that Perrault was in Bordeaux and that through him he could have a first-hand, independent report. Therefore, he wrote to the Chevalier du Cherville, the *commissaire* in charge of all fortifications, urging him to contact Perrault, to show him

75. The sketches are certainly better in quality than those of an 'amateur médiocrement doué'. (Laprade, op. cit., p. 331).

everything and to discuss with him what could be done. It is when he introduces Perrault to him that he makes the remark to which we referred.
'You have,' Colbert wrote, 'at the moment in Bordeaux Monsieur
Perrault who knows as much about architecture and good constructions
as his brother, my clerk.'[76] As much as Charles, not more! Obviously,
Colbert did not think of Perrault as an architect. He was for him an amateur like Charles, though he evidently trusted his judgment. As it
happened, Perrault had already left when the letter arrived, but he had
visited the fortress before his brother fell ill, had inspected the damage
and had discussed the matter with the engineer. After his return, he
submitted his report to Colbert, pointing out that the senseless ornamentation applied to the bastion had been detrimental to its solidity and
that 'he had found the piles too short and not driven home properly'.
Colbert's remark and Perrault's report indicate that, while he was not
considered to be an architect, his architectural knowledge was uncommon
for an amateur.

The same ambiguity is noticeable in relation to the Académie d'Architecture. Ever since its minutes were published at the beginning of this
century, the question has been asked, without any clear-cut answer being
given, whether Perrault 'belonged to the Academy'. He attended the
meetings only on rare occasions. Félibien, who acted as secretary, does
not list him among the six architects appointed at the outset, but, on the
other hand, names him, together with Blondel, who attended regularly,
as members who 'were also present'.[77] Against this, it can be held that the
members themselves considered a meeting to be *complète* without
Perrault's being present.[78] This puzzling question can be clarified to some
extent by a document relating to an occasion when members had been
asked for their considered opinion on a matter of some importance. By
1675, the building of the Collège des Quatre Nations was so far advanced that a decision had to be made about the location of Mazarin's

76. Clément, op. cit., V, pp. 23 ff. The various letters are also reproduced in a note to the 'Voyage
à Bordeaux,' pp. 188 f.
77. Lemonnier in *Procès-verbaux*, I, p. XVIII, II, p. XI; Laprade, op. cit., pp. 58, 298.
78. *Procès-verbaux*, II, pp. 71, 119.

tomb inside the chapel. The Academy was approached, whereupon members visited the chapel on 15 July 1675. After Monsieur Foucault, one of Mazarin's executors, had on this visit outlined all the considerations which he wished to be taken into account and after he had submitted these in two *mémoires* to the Academy, it was decided to set out in a formal report the result of their visit. This, however, was not done until 3 March of the following year when the document containing the opinions of every member was read out to Monsieur Foucault; it was also pointed out to him that Hardouin-Mansart's *mémoire* was included, although at the time of their visit he had not yet been admitted to the Compagnie.[79] This report was not entered in the register of the Academy, but was handed to Foucault who copied it into the '3me registre des délibérations concernant . . . le Collège Mazarin.'[80] There we find the *mémoires* of all members, and included among them are – Charles and 'Perrault, le médecin'. Clearly, this means that when the Academy was approached as an official, representative body, both Perraults were considered to be full members. It was not a matter of being received at these occasions as *ex officio* members, since other officials of Colbert's staff, as for instance the *intendant des bâtiments* Coquart de la Motte, were not asked to attend and, in any case, Claude Perrault held no official appointment. The fastidiousness with which the Compagnie dealt with Mansart's somewhat uncertain claim to be included in the list shows that similar doubts did not exist regarding Perrault.

He was a member, but came rarely to the meetings. It is true that the absence of his name from the minutes of most meetings is no conclusive proof of his non-attendance; there was no necessity for him to sign because no attendance money was due to him – nor, for that matter, to Blondel, both receiving their remuneration through the Académie des Sciences. Since, however, he affixed his signature in 1680 and 1681 when, because of his work on the five Orders, he attended meetings regularly,

79. ibid., I, p. 104 (15 and 29 July 1675), p. 105 (5 August 1675), p. 112 (9 March 1676).
80. 'Troisième Registre contenant la suitte des délibérations concernant l'exécution de la fondacion du collège et académie appellez Mazarin', Paris, Bibl. de l'Institut, MS 368, fols. 154–179 (Perrault's *mémoire* on fols 169v–171v).

it is, I think, fair to conclude that he, although a full member of the Academy, of his own free will rarely exercised his right of attendance.

The two academies to which he belonged, that of Science and the Academy of Architecture, meant different things to him. The one was *his* academy, the focal point of his professional life, the other an interesting assembly to which he went whenever it suited him. Architecture appealed to him all his life, but his connection with the planning and execution of actual buildings was limited to a period lasting only a few years, whereas his scientific work never flagged, nor was ever interrupted. It would be quite wrong to assume that he ever became 'an architect in the widest sense of the term.'[81] The most convincing proof that this had never been his wish are his own words. In a reply he once gave (and later reported to Leibniz) he had said that 'he was not an architect by profession, neither did he wish to give up everything for the sake of architecture.'[82]

If his involvement in the practical side of architecture was short-lived and is difficult to assess, there existed, however, one aspect for which his interest, once aroused, did not abate: the theory of architecture. His contribution in this sphere is the subject of the following chapters.

81. Petzet, *Louvrekolonnade*, p. 163. Also P. Bonnefon, 'Charles Perrault', *Revue d'histoire littéraire de la France*, XI, 1904, p. 366: 'L'un (des frères) de médecin devient architecte,' and H. Rigault, *Histoire de la querelle des anciens et des modernes*, Paris, 1856, p. 130: '. . . Claude, génie créateur dans l'art qu'il adopta définitivement, l'architecture . . .'
82. Leibniz, op. cit., (see note 51), p. 235.
The whole tenor of what Perrault told Leibniz on this occasion, with the boastful claim of having been asked to become the 'premier architecte du Roi', contradicts the modest attitude for which at other times he was praised (see above p. 6). I think that these are reactions typical for a man who in his own profession feels competent enough to be unassuming, but when embarking on a sphere where his knowledge is less thorough and well grounded, tries to compensate by becoming over-assertive.

CHAPTER II

Proportions and Beauty

'BEAUTY,' declared Perrault in 1674, 'has hardly any other foundation than *fantaisie*,' and since for that reason, so he argues,
everybody has different ideas of how to achieve aesthetic perfection, rules are necessary for shaping and rectifying these ideas. Every
sphere of human activity is in need of rules. They are, indeed, so indispensable that, when nature has failed to provide them 'as it did in the
case of language, fancy and custom . . . it is up to human agencies to
furnish them, and, in order to do so, a definite authority, taking the
place of reason, should be generally agreed to.'[1]

These sentences from the preface to Perrault's edition of Vitruvius are
like a blueprint of everything he intended to achieve when venturing
into the field of architectural theory. In that context, the authority
called for is, of course, Vitruvius, but Perrault himself must have had
doubts about Vitruvius's eligibility for the rôle of supreme arbiter,
because ten years later he introduced his book on the rules of proportions as a 'kind of supplement to what has not been treated in sufficient
detail by Vitruvius'.[2]

In one of the first meetings of the Academy of Architecture Vitruvius
had been declared 'the first and wisest of all architects and . . . the leading

1. *Vitruvius*, 1st ed., Preface: 'Car la beauté n'ayant guère d'autre fondement que la fantaisie,
qui fait que les choses plaisent selon qu'elles sont conformes à l'idée que chacun a de leur perfection,
on a besoin de règles qui forment et qui rectifient cette Idée: et il est certain que ces règles sont
tellement nécessaires en toutes choses, que si la Nature les refuse à quelques-unes, ainsi qu'elle a
fait au langage, aux charactères de l'écriture, aux habits et à tout ce qui dépend du hazard, de la
volonté et de l'accoutumance; il faut que l'institution des hommes en fournisse, et que pour cela
on convienne d'une certaine autorité qui tienne lieu de raison positive.'
Similarly in *Ordonnance* (see following note), p. XIV: '. . . des règles certaines et arrestées . . .
doivent toujours estre recherchées en toutes les choses qui en sont capables.'
2. *Ordonnance des cinq espèces de colonnes selon la méthode des anciens*, Paris, 1683, Epître.

authority among them.'[3] Nevertheless, Perrault's reflection on Vitruvius's competence cannot have made a great stir among the architectural profession which, at that time, was used to and accepted a certain degree of criticism directed against the 'father of architecture'. What architects must have found provoking was Perrault's suggestion of linking beauty with chance, fancy and custom. Passing from the preface to Perrault's commentaries on Vitruvius's text, they were told that beauty, the arbitrary foundation of architecture, 'depends on authority and custom,' that proportions please although their beauty 'is nothing real', that, in fact, they 'could be changed without shocking either common sense or reason.'[4] These comments were published in 1673. However, within the small circle of men who were interested in classical dogma and were, in addition, in frequent contact with Colbert's influential secretary, Charles Perrault, the unorthodox views of his brother Claude were known and discussed before this date. These specialists were indeed so much disturbed by his views that as soon as the Académie d'Architecture had been formed, Perrault's challenge was taken up. Members discussed what 'had been called in question', as the secretary noted in the minutes, no doubt, referring to Perrault – namely the very nature of proportion 'whether a positive rule for it existed or whether it was arbitrary and was only introduced by habit and custom.' At the next meeting the majority of members were of the opinion that 'a positive beauty existed in architecture', but, 'the contrary opinion having been upheld' – probably by Perrault himself, who may have attended the meeting – they deferred a decision, which they thought to be of great importance, to a time when 'Monseigneur Colbert would honour the Company with his presence'.[5] This opportunity offered itself rarely, Colbert's time being taken up by matters of greater importance; nevertheless, he attended their meeting in

3. *Procès-verbaux*, I, p. 6 (4 February 1672).
4. *Vitruvius*, p. 12, note 13: 'Le fondement que j'appelle arbitraire, est la Beauté qui dépend de l'Autorité et de l'Accoutumance.'
   ibid., p. 105, note 7: '. . . la beauté de ces proportions, bien qu'elle n'eust rien de positif.'
   ibid., p. 106, note 12: '. . . la proportion qui fut premièrement donnée à la colonne Dorique et à l'Ionique a esté changée ensuite, et pourroit encore l'estre sans choquer ny le bon sens ny la raison.'
5. *Procès-verbaux*, I, p. 5 (21 and 28 January 1672).

July of the following year.[6] Yet, strangely enough, the whole issue seems to have been forgotten, until, quite unexpectedly after an interval of almost nine years, it was debated once more. In the meantime, Colbert's son, the Marquis d'Ormoy, had taken over the function of *surintendant* from his father. He attended a number of meetings in 1680 and 1681, but the discussion had to wait until 18 August, 1681 when the attendance was 'en grand nombre', Perrault also being present.[7]

The question put before the assembly was 'to find out if what is pleasing in architecture and could be called good taste is something real and positive, or whether it pleases us only because of custom and prejudice or for being in company of things that have a natural beauty.'[8] The phrasing of the problem is almost identical with the one Perrault intended to use in his *Ordonnance*, published two years later. This seemingly odd coincidence is resolved through an entry in the minutes of the Académie des Sciences towards the end of 1681 which lists various manuscripts ready for publication, among them 'un volume intitulé Ordonnance des cinq espèces de colonnes suivant la méthode des anciens' by 'Monsieur Perrault'.[9] Undoubtedly, the members of the Académie d'Architecture had seen this manuscript or another copy of it. The irksome problems with which Perrault had confronted them as far back as 1672 had thus turned up again. In the intervening years they probably suppressed the irresolution and irritation they had then experienced – suppressed them so successfully that even when they examined Vitruvius in Perrault's translation, a study that occupied more than forty meetings, they never

6. ibid., I, p. 40 (17 July 1673).

7. ibid., I, p. 321.

8. loc. cit.,: '. . . de sçavoir si ce qui plaist en architecture et que l'on peut appeler le bon goust a quelque chose de réel et de positif dans la nature, ou s'il ne nous plaist que par accoutumance et par prévention, ou pour estre accompagné de choses qui ont une beauté naturelle.'

9. *Register*, X, 5 December 1681: 'Le Roi ... estant entré dans l'Académie, Monseigneur Colbert fit voir à sa Majesté les ouvrages imprimez de l'Académie et une partie de ceux qu'on doit imprimer.' (Pl. 19. The engraving dates from 1671 (Frontispiece for the *Mémoires des animaux*). It depicts an imaginary event, since no other royal visit than the one of 1681 has been recorded by Fontenelle). It is interesting to note, and has some bearing on Perrault's relation with the Académie d'Architecture, that the *Ordonnance*, a purely architectural treatise, was sponsored by the Académie des Sciences.

reverted to this problem, although they must have read Perrault's relevant notes.[10] No doubt they thought the less said the better and hoped that in this way they had disposed of these eccentric views for good: but they had underestimated Perrault's inquisitive mind and ambitious disposition and now found that, after all, they had to go over this intractable ground once more. They knew that this time they had to speak their minds.

Respect for Colbert's son and courteous consideration for Perrault's presence made them temper their opposing view by giving it no more than 'high probability,' but it was a rejection just the same. Thus, leading architects under the chairmanship of François Blondel had given their verdict on the central maxim of Perrault's theory. Yet the man who had not been deterred from reiterating one of his biological theories, although it was, as he almost proudly claimed, one of those most widely rejected, was unlikely to be discouraged by the disapproval of professional architects: and, within eighteen months, the *Ordonnance* was in the press. When it appeared in the spring of 1683, it presented to a wider public, in systematic form, a new architectural theory which until then could only have been gleaned from a few notes dispersed over the bulky volume of his edition of Vitruvius. This theory is set out in twenty-seven pages making up the preface to his new book, to which must be added a few pages of the concluding chapter where one aspect of his theory – and it is an important one – is dealt with. The bulk of the book is taken up by a detailed exposition of Perrault's version of the Orders, in which general theoretical problems are hardly ever touched upon. In this chapter, then, we shall concentrate on an analysis of Perrault's theory as developed mainly in the preface, taking also into account some commentaries in his *Vitruvius* that contain the first formulation of his challenging statements; from its second edition we shall consider two or three enlarged notes in which he made, one year after the publication of the *Ordonnance*,

10. They read *Vitruvius* in Perrault's translation in their weekly meetings from 18 June 1674 to 17 June 1675 and from 3 March 1676 to 26 August 1676; during these two periods they only occasionally attended to other matters.

a reasoned reply to his critics, thereby elaborating on some aspects of his theory.

Through his extensive work on *Vitruvius*, Perrault had become familiar with the whole range of modern architectural literature – the numerous translations and commentaries as well as the original treatises written by various architects within the preceding 150 years. Knowledge of the measurements of ancient Roman monuments went, of course, with the study of this literature. He realised that the architects of these monuments had often departed from the rules laid down by Vitruvius and was disturbed by the fact that modern writers frequently disagreed both with Vitruvius and ancient monuments, and also differed among themselves. He finds that 'neither two buildings nor two authors agree and follow the same rules', speaks of the need to 'clear up this perplexing confusion', and, in spite of foreseen opposition, expects that his proposal to 'contain these proportions within definite rules', if accepted, will achieve this aim.[11] At the conclusion of the preface he expresses the hope that through his book he 'will have been the cause that the rules of the architectural Orders will be given the precision, perfection and ease with which to remember them that they lack at present'. Should it be said that his book contains nothing new, he fully agrees, since his intention was nothing more daring than 'to extend the change a little further than has been done so far'.[12]

Of course, these modest statements, particularly the last, were intended to mitigate the onslaught of the professional critics of which Perrault had

11. *Ordonnance*, pp. II f.: '. . . il ne se trouve point, ny dans les restes des Edifices des Anciens, ny parmy le grand nombre des Architectes qui ont traitté des proportions des Ordres, que deux Edifices ny deux Auteurs se soient accordez et ayent suivy les mesmes règles.'

ibid., Epître: 'Il falloit encore débrouiller l'embarras et la confusion où les Auteurs Modernes ont laissé la plus grande partie de ce qui appartient aux cinq espèces de Colonnes.'

'. . . je prévoye (quelque difficulté) à faire recevoir les moyens que je propose pour renfermer ces proportions dans des règles certaines . . .'

12. ibid., p. XXVI: '. . . si quelqu'un . . . vouloit prétendre que mon Livre ne contient rien de nouveau . . . j'en demeureray d'accord en déclarant que mon dessein n'est que d'étendre un peu plus loin, qu'on n'avoit fait, ce changement; pour voir si . . . je pourray estre cause que l'on donne aux Règles des Ordres d'Architecture la précision, la perfection, et la facilité de les retenir qui leur manquent.'

already had a foretaste. Nevertheless, what he claims is true; the proposed
changes are not of great consequence. Furthermore, others before him had
noted the 'confusing variety among authors who in their treatises of the
Orders and their measures have dealt with them in very different ways'.
This had been said by Fréart de Chambray, while Philibert de l'Orme had
already observed, when inspecting ancient buildings in Rome, that none of
their measures were alike, a state of affairs that caused Desgodets to undertake his minute examination of Roman antiquities.[13] As to Perrault's claim
to have brought proportional rules to greater perfection than had ever been
done before, this too cannot have caused excitement among men familiar
with architectural literature, where identical or similar claims were the
order of the day; it could not possibly have stirred up the opposition
which Perrault encountered. They were antagonized not by the claim
itself, but by the arguments sustaining the claim which, to men
committed to classical architecture must, indeed, have seemed subversive.

A fundamental tenet of classical doctrine was the belief in beauty that
was absolute, an integral part of nature, an ideal to be searched for, yet
destined never to be fulfilled. 'True beauty,' Nicole had written a few
years earlier, 'is neither changeable nor fleeting.'[14] This beauty is revealed
through proportions whose rules are, in Bossuet's words, 'eternal and
invariable.'[15] Few architects may have shared Philibert de l'Orme's,
optimistic belief in eventually finding 'divine proportions', or may have
followed Villalpandus and other theological writers who, to cite
Perrault's ironical remark, declared that 'God had by special inspiration
taught all proportions to the architects of the Temple of Solomon'.[16]

13. Fréart de Chambray, *Parallèle de l'architecture antique et de la moderne*, Paris, 1650, p. 5.
Philibert de l'Orme, *Architecture*, Rouen, 1648 (1st ed. 1568), fol. 211 r.
Antoine Desgodets, *Les édifices antiques de Rome*, Paris, 1682. About the conflicting evidence of
Vitruvian rules and ancient monuments see Erik Forssman, *Säule und Ornament*, Stockholm, 1956,
pp. 63 ff.
14. Pierre Nicole, *Traité de la vraye et de la fausse beauté*, Paris, 1698 (1st ed., in Latin 1659), I,
p. 5.
15. J.-B. Bossuet, *De la connaissance de Dieu et de soi-même*, (before 1681), *Oeuvres*, 1840, IX,
p. 652.
16. On de l'Orme's divine proportions see A. Blunt, *Philibert de l'Orme*, London, 1958, pp. 124 f.
Perrault's remark about Villalpandus: *Ordonnance*, p. XVIII.

Yet, the majority took it for granted that true proportions existed, as it were, in the abstract and accepted them as first principles underlying the working of nature. They believed that man, the product of nature, had an inborn responsiveness to these 'natural' and, in this sense, eternal proportions, which he constantly tried to approach in his works of art.

Perrault, no doubt, realized that this basic belief was blocking the way to the general approval he hoped to obtain for his own rules, just as it had been the cause 'that neither Hermogenes, nor Callimachus, nor Philon, nor Ctesiphon, nor Metagenes, nor Vitruvius, nor Palladio, nor Scamozzi, despite their talents, had been able to muster sufficient consent for having their precepts made into the rules of architectural proportions.'[17] Here was a problem 'the solution of which is of the utmost importance for the work I have undertaken.'[18]

He was never at a loss when it came to tackling fundamental problems. In fact, his ability to recognize them and to be undaunted by their seemingly insoluble nature is his most characteristic quality. When, as a physiologist, he encountered the formidable difficulty of explaining mechanically the responses of the nervous system to the perceptions of the senses, he cleared the major obstacle away by boldly rejecting the commonly held view that impulses travel back and forth between the sense organs and the brain, and instead assumed an all-pervading soul which perceives independently from the brain at all parts of the body. Similarly, when dealing with the process of generating life and finding it impossible to accept that life could be created by mechanical means, he brushed this obstacle aside with the hypothesis that at the beginning of the world all seeds were created by God and scattered throughout the world. Conjectures of this sort were called *paradoxes*, a word which in the seventeenth century conveyed something slightly different from its present meaning. Then it signified opinions that were uncommon and unorthodox, suspect only because of the high value which classical man set on universal consent. Perrault is aware that 'there are only a few people

17. ibid., pp. XX f.
18. ibid., p. V.: 'Je ne m'arresterois pas tant sur cette question, quoyque ce soit un problème, dont la résolution est de la dernière importance pour l'Ouvrage que j'ay entrepris ...'

who are not shocked and repulsed by the slightest paradox', yet he admits unashamedly, in his *Essais* as well as in the *Ordonnance*, to having proposed paradoxes, and seems to set great store by them, since he cites, as an example of their meaning, the Copernican pronouncement that 'the earth turns and the sun does not move'.[19]

When faced now with an intricate problem of architectural theory, he reacts in the same way as he did with scientific material. He disposes of the problem by approaching the situation from a novel standpoint, in short, by stating a paradox. In the case of beauty and proportions, all that was needed was to exaggerate the views which he had made known a decade earlier in his *Vitruvius*. Expressing them with greater vigour, intensifying their impact through the context in which they stand, he makes clear that he intends to deny the validity of principles on which classical architecture rested: 'true and natural' proportions do not exist;[20] those which are practised in architecture contribute nothing at all to beauty;[21] accuracy of proportions is immaterial;[22] they could be different without imparing the things that really make a building beautiful.[23]

These views are, indeed, unorthodox and, repeated in various places of the preface, provocative in their effect. Of course, it was not enough to make sweeping statements: Perrault had to prove his case.

In order to do so he had to attack three arguments that gave support to the common belief that architectural proportions express, or attempt to express, absolute, unalterable laws. His repudiations of these arguments

19. *Essais*, II, p. 260, III, p. 350.
20. *Ordonnance*, pp. III f.: '. . . sans qu'ils ayent esté choquez par l'excez des proportions éloignées de celle qu'on voudroit faire passer pour la véritable et la naturelle . . .'
    ibid., p. XIV: '. . . il n'y a point, à proprement parler, dans l'Architecture de proportions véritables en elles-mesmes.'
21. ibid., p. XI: The work can be made beautiful 'sans que la proportion ait rien contribué à cette beauté . . .'
22. ibid., p. I: '. . . la beauté d'un Edifice . . . ne consiste pas tant dans l'exactitude d'une certaine proportion . . .'
    ibid., p. XXIII: '. . . la beauté des Edifices ne consiste point dans l'exactitude de ces véritables proportions . . .'
23. ibid., p. XII: '. . . les Proportions . . . auroient pu en effet estre autrement sans nuire aux autres beautéz . . .'
    ibid., p. XIII: '. . . toutes ces choses pourroient avoir d'autres proportions, sans choquer . . . le sens le plus exquis . . .'

are set out in three different sections of the preface, but the purpose is the same on each occasion: to expose the fallacy that proportions are subject to influence outside man's control.

THE MUSICAL ANALOGY

The concept of ideal beauty presupposes the all-pervading force of the laws of nature, of a harmony inherent in God's creation. Architectural proportions were imagined to be subject to this cosmic order which had been revealed to man, in some miraculous way, in the harmonic musical consonances. Thus the analogy between architectural proportions and musical harmonies seemed natural to men brought up in the classical tradition. It became one of the main arguments for those who advocated 'true and natural' proportions, and for that reason was the first argument Perrault had to attack.[24]

The idea that architectural proportions are comparable to musical harmonies had a long tradition, reaching back to neo-Platonic and neo-Pythagorean thought prevalent during the Renaissance. By the seventeenth century, the conception had lost much of its philosophical quality, but it was still known and expounded. A few years before Perrault had finished work on the manuscript of the Ordonnance, a musician, Ouvrard, had advocated 'the application of the doctrine of musical proportions to architecture'.[25] According to him, the ancient people living at the time of the Temple of Solomon possessed the knowledge of harmonic architecture, the Greeks cultivated it, the Romans looked for it, while the Moderns talk about it without practising it. A close examination of ancient and modern buildings would prove that those not built according to harmonic rules shock the eye.[26] That this was the commonly held view

24. A full discussion of this subject by R. Wittkower, *Architectural Principles in the Age of Humanism*, London, 1962, specially part 4 and, for the later development, pp. 142 ff.

25. René Ouvrard, *Architecture harmonique ou application de la doctrine des Proportions de la Musique à l'Architecture*, Paris, 1679.

26. ibid., pp. 2, 12.

Huygens, who had known Ouvrard, calls his book 'un petit traité assez extravagant, où il vouloit qu'en matière d'architecture on observast les proportions qui font les consonances, comme si l'oeil pouvoit reconnoître quand on s'écarte de ces proportions, de mesme que l'oreille le fait au chant.' (Letter to Leibniz, July 1692, *Oeuvres*, X, p. 298).

is shown by the prominence given to Ouvrard's book in Blondel's
Cours d'Architecture, published shortly after the *Ordonnance*.[27] These views
had already been clearly expressed, in Perrault's presence, at the meeting
of the Academy in 1681 which, we have seen, decided in favour of
'natural' beauty. According to the minutes members also agreed that
visual concord 'cannot be less natural than the number, the orderly
arrangement and the proportions of sounds which produce the harmonic
concord that pleases us in music.' Just as in music we do not need to have
direct cognition of the consonances to find them agreeable, in fact we
cannot help being agreeably affected even without this knowledge, so in
architecture it would be unreasonable to assume that total conscious
knowledge of proportions is a prerequisite for judging them beautiful.[28]

Perrault had already stated in 1673 that 'architectural proportions do
not possess a beauty that has a foundation as positive as is the foundation
of natural things, unlike the beauty of musical harmonies which please
because of a definite and unalterable proportion which is independent
of *fantaisie*.'[29] This was said in a note to Vitruvius's remark that, owing to
the refinement of taste, the height of the Doric and Ionic columns had,
in the course of time, been changed from the initial 6 and 8 modules to
7 and $8\frac{1}{2}$ modules. Perrault accepted this observation as proof of his contention that architectural proportions and musical harmonies belong to
different categories: otherwise, he argued ten years later, architects
would have been sensitive to the slightest lack of precision like musicians
who never differ about the correctness of a consonance.[30] In actual fact,
however, architects not only disagree about the rules that could bring
proportions to perfection, they also, 'while trying and groping in the
course of two thousand years' for this perfection, have reached a point

27. François Blondel, *Cours d'Architecture*, Paris, Part I 1675, Parts II–V, 1683, pp. 756–60.
28. *Procès-verbaux*, I, p. 321.
29. *Vitruvius*, p. 106, note 12: '. . . les proportions des membres d'Architecture n'ont point une
beauté qui ait un fondement tellement positif, qu'il soit de la condition des choses naturelles, et
pareil à celuy de la beauté des accords de la Musique, qui plaisent à cause d'une proportion certaine
et immuable, qui ne dépend point de la fantaisie.'
30. *Ordonnance*, p. III.

where some make the projection of the Doric capital, to take one example, seven times greater than the projection suggested by others 'without anyone having been shocked by the excessive proportions which are far removed from those supposed to be true and natural'.[31] The last sentence directly contradicts Ouvrard's contention that buildings deviating from harmonic porportions shock the eye.

Perrault could have disproved another assumption made by Ouvrard who, trying to explain the different degrees of receptiveness of the two senses, had asserted that 'the eye is not as subtle as the ear and accepts faults'.[32] Perrault's physiological studies of the ear and of sound showed him, on the contrary, that the eye is far better equipped to register differences than the ear.[33] The same studies made him realize how wrong it was to assume that acoustic and visual proportions are transmitted to the mind in identical ways. The reason why the mind is pleasantly affected by harmonic consonances without having any knowledge of their ratio is precisely because 'the ear is incapable of transmitting this knowledge to the mind', whereas in the visual field the situation is the opposite. 'The eye ... can make the mind feel the effect of proportion only through the knowledge which it transmits of this proportion.'[34] Thus, basic physiological differences between the two sense organs gave weight to Perrault's outright rejection of the notion that 'nature has fixed and established with exact precision' architectural proportions, as it had done with musical harmonies.[35]

31. ibid., pp. III f.: 'Ainsi il y a tantost deux mille ans que les Architectes essayant et tastant depuis deux et demy jusqu'à dix-sept, ont esté jusqu'à faire cette saillie sept fois plus grande les uns que les autres, sans qu'ils ayent esté choquez par l'excèz des proportions éloignées de celle qu'on voudroit faire passer pour la véritable et la naturelle . . .'

32. op. cit., p. 9. This passage is cited by Blondel, op. cit., p. 782.

33. *Essais*, II, pp. 255 ff.

34. *Ordonnance*, p. IV: '. . . l'oreille n'est pas capable de donner (à l'esprit) la connoissance de cette proportion: mais l'oeil qui est capable de faire connoistre la proportion qu'il fait aimer, ne peut faire sentir à l'esprit aucun effet de cette proportion que par la connoissance qu'il luy donne de cette proportion.'

On 'musical analogy' see P. H. Scholfield, *The Theory of Proportion in Architecture*, Cambridge, 1958, pp. 72 ff.

35. *Ordonnance*, p. III.

IMITATION OF NATURE

The second argument in support of absolute beauty rested on one of the main principles of classical architecture, that of imitation. It was thought that architecture had, at the beginning, imitated certain natural forms – the proportions and symmetrical arrangement of the human body, the shape of trees, the primitive hut, as well as the constructive elements developed by a primitive craft such as carpentry – and had thus followed nature's eternal laws. Perrault does not dispute that 'imitation ... is a thing of great authority in architecture',[36] but he rejects the claim that this principle of imitation proves that proportions have their origin in nature. Taking the concept of imitation in its most literal sense, he argues that, if architectural beauty were really 'regulated', as he terms it, by imitating nature, then the more exact the copy the greater would be the beauty, and, furthermore, no deviation from the proportions of the models could take place without shocking good taste. Yet this is obviously not so, since, for instance, the ratio between capital and shaft of the column is different from the ratio between head and trunk of the human body, nor can it be said that any tree, the building material of the primitive hut, shows anything like the entasis of columns, nor do the members of the cornice represent faithfully the arrangement of the pieces of carpentry on which they were modelled. No, concludes Perrault, 'imitation of nature ... (is) not the foundation of that beauty which people believe they detect in the proportion and the orderly arrangement of the parts of the column.'[37]

THE AUTHORITY OF THE ANCIENTS

There still remained one authority – the Ancients – to the prestige of whom those who had put their faith in the absolute validity of proportions could appeal. The unquestioning trust in their supremacy was the

36. *Vitruvius*, p. 243, note 10.
37. *Ordonnance*, p. X: 'L'imitation de la Nature, ny la raison, ny le bon sens ne sont donc point le fondement de ces beautez, qu'on croit voir dans la proportion, dans la disposition, et dans l'arrangement des parties d'une colonne.'

most substantial obstacle to change that Perrault encountered. It is true that the days were over when Serlio could urge architects 'always to follow the teaching of Vitruvius as an infallible rule and guide'.[38] Even Fréart, for whom Greece was still 'the divine country,' warned the reader against blind respect, and Blondel, a hardly less fervent admirer of the Ancients, turned against servile veneration.[39] Yet the notion was still strongly held that the Ancients, in some mysterious way, had penetrated the secrets of proportion and that therefore we could follow them even if we did not understand their reasons. 'It is inconceivable,' exclaims Perrault in desperation, 'how deep is the religious reverence of architects for works of antiquity, admiring them in everything, but principally for the mystery of proportions.'[40] Here Perrault was perhaps thinking of a remark which Desgodets had made in the introduction to his great and, as we shall see, for Perrault in other respects, indispensable work. He had spoken of 'the mysteries in architectural proportions', which even the great masters of the profession could not always penetrate, but for which, he confidently believed, good reasons existed. We may fail at times to understand these reasons, but 'we can at least be quite sure that these great examples, which the Ancients have left us, cannot be imitated accurately enough.'[41]

38. *Tutte l'opere d'architettura*, Venice, 1619, book III, fol. 69 v.

39. Fréart, op. cit., pp. 3, 2.
Blondel, op. cit., pp. 169, 250.
For a similar tendency in the literary field see René Bray, *La formation de la doctrine classique en France*, Paris, 1957 (reprint of ed. of 1926), pp. 162 ff.

40. *Ordonnance*, p. XVII: 'Car il n'est pas concevable jusqu'où va la révérence et la religion que les Architectes ont pour ces ouvrages que l'on appelle l'Antique, dans lesquels ils admirent tout, mais principalement le mystère des proportions . . .'
A similar opinion already expressed by Corneille, *La Suivante*, Paris, 1637, Epître: 'Nous pardonnons beaucoup de choses aux Anciens . . . nous faisons des mystères de leur imperfections . . .'
In a dialogue which Perrault intended to prefix to the 'Traité de la musique' (*Essais*, II, pp. 335 ff.), preserved in Paris, Bibl. Nat., MS anc. franç. 25,350 and reproduced by H. Gillot, *La querelle des anciens et des modernes*, Paris, 1914, pp. 576 ff., he speaks of Rapin's book as containing 'la confession de foi de ceux qui révèrent avec tant de religion les mystères de l'Antiquité'. (Gillot, p. 583.).

41. op. cit., Preface.
Blondel, op. cit., p. 748, expresses hope that 'on découvriroit des secrets que l'on n'a point encore enseignez dans l'Architecture'. Henry Wotton, *The Elements of Architecture*, London, 1624, p. 55, also speaks of 'the Mysteries of Proportion'.

Why, retorts Perrault, should one look for mysterious reasons when common sense would suggest that these minute variations, far from being the cause of beauty, are inexplicable only because they have 'no other foundation than chance'.[42] The excessively high opinion which some have for the ancient world and art is, he says in another context, probably the real cause for making these so-called mysteries impenetrable, 'because this opinion results in a search for something which perhaps is not there.'[43] He must have felt even more justified for this critical view when he found that Fréart, whose *Parallèle* was one of the most influential architectural books of the time, accepted the Doric Order as practised by the Greeks without base, not for any valid reason, but because 'their intention . . . would, no doubt, have been very judicious', or when he noticed that Blondel, after having toyed with the idea of ascribing to custom the pleasure we derive from the unnatural, because unfunctional, character of the Corinthian capital, ended up his deliberations with the remark that, after all, 'there may be some hidden and not less natural reason' for it.[44] These were the writers who believed in the exceptional position of Greek architecture because of its closeness to nature, or because the best climate in the world helped their architects to 'see things naturally which we here have to discover after long and painful study'. The Greeks alone, they thought, had produced an architecture, perfect, incomparable and unique; their rules should be inviolable; their buildings, the source of art, should serve as the guiding compass --- the touchstone on which to test the value of our own buildings.[45]

42. *Ordonnance*, p. XIX: '. . . il n'y a pas beaucoup d'inconvénient à croire que les choses dont ils ne pourront trouver de raison, sont effectivement sans raison qui fasse à la beauté de la chose, et qu'elles n'ont point d'autre fondement que le hazard . . .'

43. *Vitruvius*, p. 163, 'Explication de la Planche XLI,' setting out the musical system of the Ancients: 'Quelques-uns croient que ce qui nous rend ces mystères impénétrables, n'est que la trop grande opinion que nous avons des merveilles que l'on dit qu'ils renferment, parce que cette opinion fait que nous y cherchons ce qui peut-estre n'y est point.'

44. Fréart, op. cit., p. 10.
Blondel, op. cit., p. 767.

45. ibid., p. 2; Fréart, op. cit., pp. 3 ff, 6, 9. Commenting on Palladio's and Scamozzi's deviation from antique models, Fréart declares that his 'maxime soy toujours de me conformer précisément au goût des antiques et aux proportions qu'ils ont gardées'. (ibid., p. 76).

For Perrault all this is just 'blind adoration'. To accept everything the Ancients have done without questioning its reasonableness is in his view a sign of infatuation he had not thought possible,[46] or, could it be that this 'blind respect for the ancient monuments' is only a pretence while the real reason is the usual desire of the profession to cloak their affairs in 'mysteries of which they alone are the interpreters?'[47] It is a sign of Perrault's confidence in the soundness of his own case that, whenever he encounters a diametrically-opposed view, he believes it to be so untenable that he invariably suspects the motives of his opponents. Thus, when confronted with those who believe in the superiority of ancient music, he at once doubts their 'good faith' and suspects that they have 'some interest in despising modern works', and, again, when dealing with sceptical philosophers, he alleges that behind their negative stand are 'other motives than the respect they feign to have for the impenetrable profoundness of God's eternal wisdom'.[48]

For a scientist, such as Perrault, the willing acceptance of the ancients as an authority must, indeed, have seemed incomprehensible or, at least, much out of date. From the beginning of the century, the new scientific spirit, critical and empirical, had opposed the dogmatic tradition of the Schools. In biology the authority of Aristotle, in anatomy that of Galen, were seriously challenged. An increasingly independent attitude made

46. *Vitruvius*, p. 206, note 3: '. . . je n'aurois jamais pensé que l'entestement que l'on a pour les anciens pust aller si loin: car je croiois qu'on avoit de la vénération pour les ouvrages de ces grands hommes . . . parce que c'étoient des choses toujours fondées sur la raison . . .' Further on of Blondel: '. . . il a une trop grande vénération pour les anciens Architectes . . .'

In a letter to Huygens (25 August 1684, *Oeuvres*, VIII, p. 531): 'Au reste je suis bien aisé que vous ne soyez pas du sentiment de Monsieur Blondel à l'esgard de l'adoration aveugle qu'il veut que l'on ait pour les Anciens . . .'

47. *Ordonnance*, p. XX: '. . . beaucoup d'autres qui sçavent bien ce qu'ils font quand ils couvrent de ce respect aveugle pour les ouvrages Antiques le désir qu'ils ont que les choses de leur profession paroissent avoir des mystères dont ils sont les seuls interprètes.' Similarly, p. 108.

48. MS anc. franç. 25,350 (Gillot, op. cit., p. 585): '. . . ce n'est pas de bonne foy que les connoisseurs témoignent avoir tant d'estime pour l'antiquité, mais mesme qu'ils ont quelque interest à mépriser les ouvrages modernes.'

Essais, III, p. 3: '. . . il faut croire que ceux d'entre les Philosophes qui soutiennent avec tant d'affectation que nous ne voyons goute dans les ouvrages de Dieu, et que c'est inutilement que l'esprit humain s'amuse à les méditer, doivent avoir d'autres motifs que le respect qu'ils feignent pour la profondeur impénétrable de la Sagesse éternelle.'

new discoveries possible which in turn demonstrated that progress beyond the point achieved by the Ancients was feasible. After the middle of the century, no serious scientist or philosopher could doubt that modern science was superior to that of the Ancients.[49] They were convinced that deference to the opinions of classical authors was detrimental to progress. The writings of Descartes, Gassendi and Malebranche had undermined the authority of Aristotle. Why, asks Malebranche, is it a sign of irreverence to assume that Aristotle, Plato or Epicurus made mistakes? They 'were men like us and of the same species as we'.[50] The Cartesian Rohault reviles the Schools for their 'blind submissiveness' to everything taught by the Ancients which prevents the best scholars from 'making their contributions to the advancement of physics.'[51] The same theme is taken up by Stenon, a leading anatomist of the age, in a lecture on the anatomy of the brain, read by him in the early sixties before an audience of scientists who assembled regularly in the house of Thévenot. This remarkable paper, valid in many respects still today, becomes even more meaningful in our context through the possibility of Perrault's having attended the lecture. A quotation at some length may, therefore, not be out of place.[52] Speaking about the difficulties of successful brain dissection, Stenon emphasizes the necessity of constantly adjusting and changing the manner of dissection according to circumstances. At this point he adds remarks that must have roused Perrault's enthusiasm. The contention that no hard

49. The development of scientific thought in the seventeenth century is thoroughly dealt with in the first part of the important and well documented work of Jacques Roger, *Les sciences de la vie dans la pensée française du XVIIIe siècle*, Paris, 1963. For the evaluation of Perrault's biological studies I am much indebted to this author.

50. N. Malebranche, *De la recherche de la vérité*, Paris, 1674 (*Oeuvres complètes*, ed. G. Rodis-Lewis, Paris, 1962 ff, I, p. 283). See also the general remarks by D. Roustan on p. 467 of a planned edition of Malebranche's works, of which, however, only the first volume appeared in 1938.

51. Jacques Rohault, *Traité de Physique*, Paris, 1671, Preface. A colleague of Perrault, Nicolas Liénard, at one time Dean of the Faculty, prides himself 'de ne m'en estre pas aveuglement tenu au travail et aux expériences des anciens, à celles d'Aristote, d'Hippocrate et de Galien.' (*Dissertation sur la cause de la purgation*, Paris, 1659, p. 21.)

52. *Discours de M. Stenon sur l'Anatomie du Cerveau à Messieurs de l'Assemblée qui se fait chez Monsieur Thévenot*, Paris, 1669 (reprint Copenhagen, 1950).
The lecture must have been given well before date of publication, since Thévenot left Paris and retired to Issy in autumn of 1664 (Albert J. George, op. cit., p. 375).

and fast rules for dissection exist 'will appear very strange to those who . . .
are of the opinion that the anatomical directions given by the Ancients
must be observed in their entirety without changing or adding anything.
I would admit that the Ancients could have given us inviolable rules of
dissection . . . if they had had perfect knowledge about it; but since they
have been in this respect as little enlightened as we are . . . they were
just as incapable of prescribing the true manner of dissection, about which
there will be nothing fixed and constant until more discoveries have been
made. . . . The main reason that has kept many anatomists in their errors
and stopped them from advancing further than the Ancients in their
dissections has been their belief that everything has already been observed . . .; since they took the ancient rules of dissection for inviolable
rules, they did nothing else all their lives but demonstrate the same parts
by the same method; whereas anatomy must not be subjected to any
rules, but must change every time dissection begins.'[53] One would like to
think that Perrault remembered these words when translating Vitruvius
and preparing his book of the Orders.

Of course, these and similar passages by other writers also prove that
'blind submission to the authority of the Ancients' (to use Malebranche's
phrase) still existed.[54] However, by this time, the third quarter of the
century, the orthodox attitude was on the whole only to be found
among the older generation. This was specially the case within the
universities which at one time had been a powerful force, but were by
now much on the defensive and, in view of the great strides forward
made in scientific progress, were bound to lose the battle. Progressive
scientists already took a dispassionate, detached view when judging the
merits of ancient achievement. The sincerity of Perrault's declaration in
the *Ordonnance* that 'he has all the veneration and admiration for the
works of ancient architecture they deserve'[55] is borne out by his attitude

53. ibid., pp. 46 ff.
54. op. cit., edition of 1674, p. 208. In another place, he speaks of 'l'entêtement de certaines gens
pour l'autorité des Anciens' (*Oeuvres*, I, p. 284).
55. *Ordonnance*, p. XX.

as a scientist.[56] He even admits that in physics most new hypotheses are not more than 'explanations of ancient opinions which the moderns have taken somewhat further than their first authors have done'.[57]

Turning now to the arts, he met a very different situation. The two parties – on the one hand, those who believed that the works of the Ancients were of exceptional beauty and should serve as models and, on the other hand, those who judged that modern artistic achievements could surpass those of the ancients – were adversaries of equal strength. In fact, many leading artists had joined the ranks of the 'Ancients'. The prospect was not an easy victory, but a hard, drawn out and of necessity inconclusive fight. Perrault, however, was unaware of this difference and only noticed that the 'Ancients' used the same arguments he knew from scientific literature, arguments that could easily be refuted, and which he rightly thought to be untenable. He, like most 'Moderns', failed to realize that the conception of progress was valid for the scientific, but not for the artistic sphere. 'Because Perrault,' remarked Condillac a hundred years later, 'was more impressed by the errors of the Ancients in physics than sensitive to their poetic beauties, he considered the cult rendered by Despréaux to Homer and Pindar to be the same as the respect the scholastics had for the errors of Aristotle.'[58] The 'excessive respect of architects for antiquity' was for Perrault, indeed, identical with the 'submissive spirit' of the scholastics who were more concerned 'with finding the true sense of Aristotle's text than with discovering factual truth', a remark Perrault took over almost verbatim from Malebranche.[59]

56. *Essais*, I, Preface, p. XI.
57. ibid., p. IX.
58. *Eloges des Académiciens de l'Académie Royale des Sciences*, Paris, 1773, p. 87.
59. *Ordonnance*, pp. XVIII f.: '. . . ce respect excessif des Architectes pour l'Antique qui leu rest commun avec la pluspart de ceux qui font profession des sciences humaines . . .' 'C'est ce qui faisoit qu'autrefois les sçavans n'avoient pour but dans leurs études que la recherche des opinions des Anciens, se faisant beaucoup plus d'honneur d'avoir trouvé le vray sens du texte d'Aristote que d'avoir découvert la vérité de la chose, dont il s'agit dans ce texte. Cet esprit de sousmission . . . s'est tellement nourri . . . par la docilité aux gens de lettres, que l'on a beaucoup de peine à s'en défaire . . .'
Malebranche, op. cit., *Oeuvres* I, p. 290: '. . . il y a eu un fort grand nombre de sçavans qui se sont plus mis en peine de sçavoir le sentiment d'Aristote sur ce sujet, que la vérité de la chose en soi . . .'

Having witnessed the success which scientists had achieved in reducing the reactionary forces, he was confident that he could be equally successful when carrying the contest among architects. Of course, his whole attitude is a reflection of the *Querelle des Anciens et des Modernes*. We can be sure that Perrault belonged to the modern faction, and have it confirmed by Boileau's statement that 'the *médecin* had the same taste about the Ancients as his brother.'[60] Perrault did not touch on the main, hotly-contested question, whether ancient or modern artists were superior; this is not mentioned at all in the *Ordonnance* and only in passing in his *Vitruvius*.[61] However, he used another argument that also goes to the root of the confrontation. Progress, the Moderns believed, would inevitably be impeded if novel ideas were distrusted and rejected for no other reason than that they were novel and did not conform to tradition. When Perrault, in a note to Vitruvius's classification of temples, introduced a new type consisting of a colonnade of coupled columns, 'as executed with great splendour . . . on the façade of the Louvre,' he was well aware that some architects disapproved of that arrangement as not being authorised by the Ancients, although the Ancients themselves had not blamed an architect as inventive as Hermogenes for having made a similar change.[62] Blondel voiced this disapproval and argued at great length against the practice of coupled columns, referring specifically to this note.[63] Perrault, seeing that the attack was directed against this feature, because he had claimed responsibility for it replied forcefully. It is nothing but prejudice, one reads in the enlarged note of the second edition, to believe that any departure from ancient usages leads to licence, caprice and disorder. If 'shutting the door to beautiful inventions' had always been the law, 'then architecture would never have reached the

60. *Oeuvres*, ed. Gidel, III, p. 303.
Also Charpentier in a letter to Longepierre (cit. by Kortum, op. cit., p. 202): 'Monsieur Perrault a perdu son frère qui étoit un grand défenseur des modernes contre les anciens.'
61. Only in his 'Traité de la musique' and its preface (see above, p. 43, note 40) does he use all the arguments brought forward by the Moderns.
62. *Vitruvius*, p. 79, note 16.
63. op. cit., pp. 232 ff.

point to which the inventions of the Ancients, new in their time, have brought it.'[64]

Among writers on architectural theory it was only André Félibien, the future secretary of the Academy, who developed, in general terms, the same notion as Perrault, preceding him by several years. 'If the Ancients,' Félibien wrote in 1666, 'enjoyed the liberty of choosing and adjusting things as they wished . . . why should we today depend so slavishly on their views that we do nothing by ourselves when . . . reason, far from condemning our ideas, approves our new inventions?'[65] It is true that De l'Orme and even Blondel used the same argument; but these are two isolated instances where the claim is made in support of a sixth, the so-called French Order when, naturally, national pride overruled dogmatic principles.[66] On the whole, writers on the arts appeal comparatively seldom to ancient precedents as a warrant for making changes, and considerably less frequently than philosophical and scientific writers.

Here the evidence is overwhelming. After the middle of the century, all progressive minds are in agreement that the introduction of *nouveautés* is the prerequisite for any advance. It is mental laziness, the arguments run, to follow the beaten track in the search for truth; nobody should be blamed for leaving the routes taken by Aristotle and Galen, since they themselves left those taken by their predecessors; not blame, but praise is due to those who try to discover something new in the sciences; to reject an opinion solely for its novelty is a bad maxim, an attitude alien to antiquity; today, in contrast, it still happens that by suggesting a new idea one has to endure the hatred of those who reject indiscriminately all new opinions as false. To contradict the Ancients,

64. *Vitruvius*, p. 79, note 16: 'Si cette Loy avoit eu lieu, l'Architecture ne seroit jamais parvenue au point où l'ont mises les inventions des Anciens, qui ont esté nouvelles en leur temps.'

65. *Entretiens sur les vies et sur les ouvrages des plus excellens peintres anciens et modernes*, Paris, 1685 (1st ed. 1666), pp. 321 f. In the same year, Corneille wrote in his preliminary remarks to *Agésilas*: 'Les premiers qui ont travaillé pour le théâtre ont travaillé sans exemple, et ceux qui les ont suivis y ont fait voir quelques nouveautés de temps en temps. Nous n'avons pas moins de privilège . . . (Les) règles (des anciens) sont bonnes, mais leur méthode n'est pas de notre siècle; et qui s'attacheroit à ne marcher que sur leurs pas, feroit sans doute peu de progrès . . .'

66. De l'Orme, op. cit., fol. 218 v.

Blondel, op. cit., p. 250.

writers complain, is almost considered a crime, to add something new an outrage; yet, in philosophy and the sciences perfection can only be achieved by new ideas, not by upholding traditional views, however venerable they are, nor by resisting new discoveries founded on reason; in the sciences only reason counts, not authority; in religion only authority, not reason, and while in matters of faith innovations are dangerous, in physics they are superior to any false conjectures of Antiquity, for it has no authority. This fundamental dividing line between matters of science and matters of faith is an ever recurring theme, which finds support in St Augustine's dictum: *quod scimus, debemus rationi; quod credimus, auctoritati*. Pascal expressed the same idea in his unpublished preface to the *Traité du vide*, which Perrault, because of the connection between his brother Nicolas and Pascal, may have known in manuscript. Pascal explicitly names geometry, arithmetic, music, physics, medicine and architecture as disciplines where authority is useless, while it has supreme power in religion. We should restrict the respect we have for the Ancients and remember that 'if they had remained in that reserved attitude of not daring to add anything to the knowledge that had been handed on to them . . . they would have deprived themselves and posterity of the fruit of their inventions.' By being bold, they opened up new ways. 'Their example should be the means, not the end of our studies; we should thus try to surpass them by imitating them.'[67]

Scientific literature of the seventeenth century abounds with remarks of this kind, signs of justified pride in scientific achievement and of

67. This paragraph is based in the main on passages found in the writings of the following authors:

Cureau de la Chambre, *Nouvelles conjectures sur la digestion*, Paris, 1636, Preface.

N. Liénard, *Dissertation sur la cause de la purgation*, Paris, 1659, pp. 20 f.

J.-B. Denis, *Recueil des mémoires et conférences sur les arts et les sciences*, Amsterdam, 1682, pp. 64 ff. (5th *mémoire* of 22 March 1672).

J. Rohault, op. cit., Preface.

Claude Fleury, *Dialogues sur l'éloquence judiciaire* (1664), Paris, Bibl. Nat., MS anc. franç. 9521.

Antoine Arnauld, 'Examen d'un écrit qui a pour titre: Traité de l'essence du Corps,' publ. in *Oeuvres*, 1780, XXXVIII, pp. 94, 96. Pascal, 'Préface sur le Traité du Vide,' *Oeuvres de Blaise Pascal*, ed. Brunschvicg, Paris, 1908, II, pp. 129 ff.

happy optimism for its future development. They were taken from the writings of various authors – philosophers, physicists, medical men – and, no doubt, their number could be increased by gleaning the contemporary literature of the remaining disciplines. Those paraphrased are, I hope, sufficient to show that an attitude rejecting ancient authority and welcoming change existed. Perrault grew up in this belief and shared it. '*Nouveauté*,' he declares in the preface to his *Essais*, 'is almost all that can be claimed in Physics, the main purpose of which is to search for things not yet seen.'[68] Of course, he knows that, following a new hypothesis, he may go astray on this so far unknown route. 'But,' he concludes, 'I do not believe that I can be blamed if this should happen, since on the beaten tracks it is impossible not to go astray because they do not lead at all where one wants to go'.[69]

The arguments which he had found convincing in the scientific field did not lose their validity for him when applied to architecture. He uses them in the *Ordonnance*, pointing out that we must 'make the distinction that exists between the respect due to sacred things and the respect which profane things deserve; these we are allowed to examine critically and to censure moderately . . . not being concerned here with mysteries of the kind that religion offers us and which we are not surprised to find incomprehensible'.[70] Every writer on the Orders has corrected and added to the supposedly inviolable laws of the Ancients. The fact that some of these *nouveautés* have been accepted shows 'not only that in these matters

68. *Essais*, I, Preface.

69. ibid., III, pp. 305 f.: 'Tout le danger que je cours en prenant une nouvelle hypothèse, est de m'égarer dans une route qui n'a point encore esté suivie; mais je ne croy pas qu'on me doive blasmer si cela m'arrive; puisque dans les autres toutes battues qu'elles sont on ne laisse pas de s'égarer, parce qu'elles ne conduisent point où l'on vouloit aller.'
Corneille ends the passage, already partly quoted (p. 50, note 65), as follows: 'On court, à la vérité, quelque risque de s'égarer, et même on s'égare assez souvent, quand on s'écarte du chemin battu; mais one ne s'égare pas toutes les fois, quand on s'en écarte; quelquesuns en arrivent plus tôt où ils prétendent, et chacun peut hasarder à ses perils.'

70. *Ordonnance*, p. XIX: '. . . la distinction qu'il y a entre le respect deû aux choses saintes, et celuy que méritent celles qui ne le sont pas; lesquelles il nous est permis d'examiner, de critiquer, et de censurer avec modestie, quand il s'agit de connoistre la vérité; et dont nous ne considérons point les mystères, comme estant de la nature de ceux que la Religion nous propose, et que nous ne nous étonnons point de trouver incompréhensibles.'

change itself is not a reckless undertaking, but even that a change to the better is not as difficult as the passionate admirers of Antiquity wish us to believe.'[71] Reasoning in this way and attacking those who, in the scholastic tradition, 'want to argue by authority,' Perrault pleaded his case: uncritical adoration of the Ancients bars the way to changes which, if architecture is to advance, are indispensable.[72]

These were the three arguments, critically examined by Perrault, on which the common belief in absolute proportions rested. He had proved, to his own satisfaction, no doubt, that proportions, unlike musical harmonies, were not a natural manifestation and invariable in character, that imitation of nature did not vouchsafe this quality either, and that faith in the superior knowledge of the Ancients, which enabled them to penetrate mysteries sealed to us, was a fallacy. Proportions, then, could not be the cause of that beauty which is absolute and eternal. Nevertheless, the fact remained that they were often pleasing to the eye. How is it possible that something, while not the cause, can still produce the effect? With this puzzling question the centre of his theory has been reached; the answer he gives contains his most original ideas.

THE DUALISTIC NATURE OF BEAUTY

He tried to solve this seeming contradiction by methods which he had already used in his scientific work. Developing the animistic theory of sense perception, he came upon the difficulty of making his system embrace every possible action, that is, to include voluntary and reflex actions as well as functions governed by the involuntary nervous system – to use modern terminology. Since for him, as for Descartes, whom in this instance he closely followed, 'thought is inseparable from all actions of the soul,' his problem was to explain how it is possible that

71. ibid., p. XXV: 'car bien que quelques-uns de ces changemens n'ayent pas esté approuvez; il y en a néanmoins un assez grand nombre de reçus et de suivis mêsme en des choses très considérables, pour faire voir que le changement de soy en ce genre de choses, non seulement n'est point une entreprise téméraire; mais mêsme que le changement en mieux n'est point si difficile que les admirateurs passionez de l'Antiquité veulent faire croire.'

72. ibid., p. XIX: 'Comme l'Architecture . . . a souvent esté traitté par des gens de lettres, elle s'est aussi gouvernée par cet esprit plus que les autres Arts; on y a voulu argumenter par autorité . . .'

'there are some actions of which we are not conscious', although 'there is not a moment at which the animal does not think'. He resolved the difficulty by assuming that thought takes place on two levels. 'There is an explicit and distinct thought for the things to which we apply ourselves with care, and an inattentive and confused thought for the things that long practice has made so easy that explicit and exact thought is unnecessary . . . Now we think nearly always in these two different ways simultaneously.'[73] This notion of unconscious or subconscious thinking is, as will easily be recognized nowadays, a fruitful concept that leads Perrault in many cases to an insight into the working of the mind which modern psychological research confirms. But – and this is important in the present context – the notion is, in the first place, a device for making his animistic theory unassailable, whilst its yield of scientific discoveries becomes, as it were, only a by-product. Concerned foremost with the establishment of a plausible system, he carries his notion of the dual layers of thought to extreme lengths, undisturbed when its logic leads him to make strange assertions. In fact, he must have found the concept of dichotomy, when confronted with complex terms, so rewarding that he makes use of it again and again. The assumption of two kinds of reasoning, of judgment, of understanding, and even of volition may be said to proceed directly from the conception of two kinds of thought; but to hear him speak of two kinds of taste, one internal, the other external, two kinds of pleasurable sensation caused by taste and smell, one common to all beings, the other more individual, and two kinds of effusion of the animal spirit, one precipitous, the other less forceful, makes it evident that this approach is typical for his way of thinking.[74]

73. *Essais*, II, pp. 283 f.
74. ibid., II, p. 305 (two kinds of reasoning), IV, p. 31 (two kinds of knowledge), IV, p. 137 (two kinds of taste), II, p. 294 (two kinds of volition), IV, p. 100 (two kinds of discharge of spirits), II, p. 312 (two kinds of judgment).
Others too used this method. Malebranche, op. cit., I, p. 63, speaks of two kinds of truths, those that are *nécessaires*, the others that are *contingentes*; Méré, *Oeuvres*, ed. Boudhours, Paris, 1930 I, p. 96, refers to two kinds of *justesse*, one depending on taste and the *je ne sais quoi*, the other on rules; Leibniz, *Meditationes de Cognitione, Veritate et Ideis*, Philosophische Schriften, Berlin, 1880, IV, p. 422, makes a differentiation that comes nearest to Perrault's, namely of two kinds of knowledge, one *obscura*, the other *clara*.

Dichotomy, having served him well in his scientific work, was now to provide the answer to the perplexing architectural problem of how to account for the fact that proportions, without being the cause of beauty, were obviously closely linked to it. 'One must suppose,' he declares, 'that there are two kinds of beauties in architecture, those that are founded on convincing reasons and those that depend on prejudice,' or, as he also formulates it, 'I oppose to a beauty which I call positive and convincing another which I call arbitrary.' Under positive beauties he lists 'richness of material, the size and magnificence of the building, precision and neatness of execution, and symmetry', while he calls arbitrary those beauties that 'depend on one's own volition to give things that could be different without being deformed a certain proportion, form and shape'. Those belonging to the first group are recognized and appreciated by everyone, since by their very nature they are well defined, to such an extent that any fault would immediately show. However, as far as the second group is concerned, the question still remains of how it is possible that things exist in architecture which 'although they have in themselves no beauty that must without fail please' are yet pleasing to the eye.[75]

LINKED IDEAS

Perrault finds the cause for this strange phenomenon in 'a connection which the mind makes of two things of a different nature: because through this connection it happens that the esteem, which the mind is

75. *Ordonnance*, pp. VI f.: 'Or quoy qu'on aime souvent les proportions conformes aux règles de l'Architecture, sans sçavoir pourquoy on les aime, il est pourtant vray de dire, qu'il doit y avoir quelque raison de cet amour ... Pour bien juger de cela il faut supposer qu'il y a de deux sortes de beautez dans l'Architecture, sçavoir celles qui sont fondées sur des raisons convaincantes, et celles qui ne dépendent que de la prévention, j'appelle des beautez fondées sur des raisons convaincantes, celles par lesquelles les ouvrages doivent plaire à tout le monde ... telles que sont la richesse de la matière, la grandeur et la magnificence de l'Edifice, la justesse et la propreté de l'exécution et la symmétrie ...'

'Or j'oppose à ces sortes de beautez que j'appelle Positives et convaincantes, celles que j'appelle Arbitraires, parce qu'elles dépendent de la volonté qu'on a eu de donner une certaine proportion, une forme et une figure certaine aux choses qui pourroient en avoir une autre sans estre difformes ...'

ibid., p. VIII: 'Il en est ainsi dans l'Architecture, où il y a des choses que ... l'on ne sçauroit souffrir qu'elles soient autrement quoy qu'elles n'ayent en elles-mesmes aucune beauté qui doive infailliblement plaire ...'

predisposed to have for things of which it knows the value, suggests an
esteem for other things of which the value is unknown to it, and thus the
mind begins by slow degrees to esteem them equally.'[76]

This liaison relates to a faculty of the mind for which Locke, a decade
later, coined the term 'association of ideas'. Although the phenomenon
was already known to Plato and more especially to Aristotle, it had to
wait until the seventeenth century to be studied more systematically.
Descartes, discussing the working of memory, mentions the 'liaison des
traces', and Hobbes too, in the same context, has something to say on the
'train of thoughts'.[77] Malebranche devotes a whole chapter to the 'liaison
des idées'. His *Recherche de la vérité* was published in 1674, one year after
Perrault's translation of Vitruvius. Although the systematic way in which
Perrault treats the subject in the *Ordonnance* is still lacking in the *Vitruvius*,
where he touches on the problem in two notes only, he is already then
fully aware that this effect of 'being fond of things by *compagnie* and
custom is to be met with in almost all things that please, even though,
not having thought about it, we do not believe this to be so.'[78] These
words make Perrault the first writer to apply the association of ideas to
the aesthetic field. Those who preceded him – Descartes, Hobbes,
Malebranche – and those who, after him, made their outstanding
contributions – Locke and Berkeley – were interested in the subject
mainly in order to arrive at an understanding of the working of the
human mind, and almost a hundred years passed before Perrault's
observation of the important rôle which the association of ideas plays in

76. ibid., p. VII: '. . . par une liaison que l'esprit fait de deux choses de différente nature: car par
cette liaison il arrive que l'estime dont l'esprit est prévenue pour les unes dont il connoist la valeur,
insinue une estime pour les autres dont la valeur luy est inconnue, et l'engage insensiblement à les
estimer également.'

77. On the history of linked ideas see: H. C. Warren, *A History of the Association Psychology*,
London, 1921; E. Claparède, *L'association des idées*, Paris, 1903; Gordon McKenzie, *Critical
Responsiveness*, Univ. of California, 1949.
The first to have dealt with this aspect of Perrault's theory was L. Tatarkiewicz, 'L'esthétique
associationniste au XVIIe siècle,' *Revue d'esthétique*, 1960, pp. 287 ff.

78. *Vitruvius*, p. 105, note 7: 'Cette raison d'aimer les choses par compagnie et par accoustumance
se rencontre presque dans toutes les choses qui plaisent, bien qu'on ne le croye pas, faute d'y avoir
fait réflexion.' On p. 12, note 13, he also mentions 'aimer par compagnie'.

aesthetics was taken up.[79] Furthermore, Perrault approached this subject with a clearly conceived purpose in mind: to show how erroneous was the belief in the absolute beauty of proportions even though appearance seemed to suggest the contrary. For that reason, his interest centred on one particular aspect of the intricate working of the human mind: the fact that frequently when an association takes place, the quality or attribute of one idea is transferred to the other. He was not the first to notice this transference, but perhaps the first for whom it meant not just an interesting occurrence, but a principal feature of his whole theory. He illustrates the process of this transference by the way 'the esteem we have for the merit and fine grace of courtiers makes us like their dress and manner of speech, although these things in themselves have nothing likeable in a positive sense, since shortly afterwards they shock us without their having undergone any change.'[80] Among Pascal's *Pensées* we find a similar example taken from the same milieu. In fact, Perrault would have done well to use it in this form. Pascal observed that the awe inspired by the military retinue, with which kings are ordinarily surrounded, is transferred to the person of the king, so that 'the world, which does not know that the effect is caused by this habit, believes that it is produced by a natural force.[81] This example would have supported and illustrated Perrault's argument excellently; for, whereas in his example the admiration felt for the ridiculous speech and dress evaporates as soon as they are encountered away from court, Pascal's simile would have demonstrated how difficult it is to discard the belief that the 'respect and terror' emanating from the King's face were due to a natural force, while, in fact, they were

79. See below pp. 152 ff.
80. *Ordonnance*, p. VIII: 'Car l'estime que l'on a pour le mérite et la bonne grâce des personnes de la Cour, fait aimer leurs habits et leur manière de parler, quoy que ces choses d'elles-mesmes n'ayent rien de positivement aimable, puisque l'on en est choqué quelque temps après sans qu'elles ayent souffert aucun changement en elles-mesmes.'
81. Pascal, *Pensées, Oeuvres*, XIII, p. 230 (no. 308): 'La coutume de voir les rois accompagnés de gardes, de tambours, d'officiers, et de toutes les choses qui ploient la machine vers le respect et la terreur fait que leur visage, quand il est quelquefois seul et sans ses accompagnements imprime dans leurs sujets le respect et la terreur parce qu'on ne sépare point dans la pensée leurs personnes d'avec leurs suites qu'on y voit d'ordinaire jointes. Et le monde qui ne sait pas que cet effet vient de cette coutume, croit qu'il vient d'une force naturelle.'

due to an accompanying factor. By analogy, therefore, it is equally difficult to discard the belief that the beauty of proportions was based on some 'natural' force, whereas, in fact, it was due to being seen always in company with positive qualities of beauty. The transference takes place, so Perrault's argument runs, because proportions have always, right from the beginning of architecture, been joined to and seen together with the absolute qualities, such as magnificence, size and symmetry. The power that welded the two groups together and thus caused the effect of one to be taken for the effect of the other, was custom.

FORCE OF CUSTOM

Perrault was greatly interested in the transformation brought about by frequent repetition of actions and impressions, of which he encountered the extraordinary effect in all his researches, whether physiological, psychological or aesthetic. Since he gave to custom a crucial position within his architectural theory, it is important to understand fully the rôle he allotted to it and, since he suggested that it is – even if only indirectly – the cause of beauty, to be clear about the meaning he gave to custom. Almost simultaneously with the *Ordonnance*, Perrault examined its influence on the bodily functions, and here, too, custom becomes a prominent feature of his system. I believe that essentially Perrault's conception of the part played by custom was the same in both fields. For that reason it should be rewarding to see what Perrault, the scientist, has to say on the subject.

As mentioned before, Perrault's conjecture that the soul – or, as we would term it, the mind – is the prime mover of all functions, forced him to assume the existence of two kinds of thinking, one clear and precise, and the other confused and loose. At the beginning of life, so he stipulates, every bodily function is a conscious process, even heartbeat and the digestive process, but, as the child grows up, the continuous exercise of these internal functions makes them work so smoothly that clear and distinct attention becomes unnecessary 'The force inherent in habit that increases the ease with which all actions are conducted . . .

goes so far as to have them exercised even against distinct thought and against our will,' as is witnessed by the impossibility of stopping the heartbeat through conscious thought or preventing one from shutting one's eyes before an impact, although the operative muscle is a voluntary one.[82] It is again through constantly repeated experience that we are able to see objects of the outside world the right way up and not in the reversed position as represented on the retina (an instance of the function of custom confirmed by modern research), or that people with a squint do not see objects double, having been 'accustomed to take the two objects which they actually see for only one'.[83] In fact, 'by means of habit a state of compelling certainty and clear evidence is reached which even our imagination cannot overcome.'[84]

The great power wielded by habit over the human mind had been observed and commented upon by philosophers of all times,[85] but for Perrault its action assumed paramount importance; without it, the radical animistic conception of animal life, which he propagated as his special theory, would have been untenable. Again and again in his articles on sense perception he points to the strange phenomenon, brought about by the repetitive process of custom, of obliterating from consciousness the original conduct of a function, thereby changing its character so completely that what in fact is a voluntary act directed by the soul, is thought to be an independent automatic reaction. 'The power,' he sums up, 'which custom has of making a number of actions insensible has been explained sufficiently often enough in these *Essais* to make those who read them familiar with it; all things that I attribute to custom seem at first incredible only . . . because we are not used to it and, not having given the matter sufficient thought, we hold on to our prejudiced opinions.'[86] In fact, however, long habit causes the soul 'not

82. *Essais*, II, pp. 293 f.
83. ibid., p. 298.
84. ibid., p. 297.
85. On the history of 'custom' see Gerhard Funke, *Gewohnheit*, (Archiv für Begriffsgeschichte Bd. 3), Bonn, 1958.
86. *Essais*, IV, p. 74.

only to lose completely the memory (of directing certain functions), but even the power of perceiving that it has directed them and that, in actual fact, it still directs them.'[87]

This is the aspect of custom which is foremost in Perrault's thought when discussing the subject in the *Ordonnance*. What is important to him is to demonstrate the power that custom is able to exercise over the human mind; in physiology, this power succeeds in changing a voluntary act into a seemingly involuntary one, making it often impossible for the mind to reverse the process; in aesthetics, it produces the transference of attributes, changing arbitrary beauties into seemingly positive ones, again with such strong persuasion that, as Perrault emphasizes, it causes 'a prejudice against which it is very difficult to guard oneself'.[88] Just as the visual experience of the outside world contradicts in many cases the evidence of our senses, so it is in architecture, where various arrangements 'which reason and common sense ought to make appear deformed and offensive... become tolerable... and finally agreeable through custom, which even has the power of bringing it about that people supposed to have architectural taste cannot bear them when they are different.'[89] Other writers had observed the capacity of custom to make forms acceptable even when they do not conform to reason: Fréart, for instance, realizes that the custom of giving a base to the Doric Order 'has prejudiced imagination... to such an extent that at the present time it prevails over reason.'[90] However, the difference in approach between Fréart and Perrault is instructive. Fréart considers the change brought

87. ibid., p. 145.
88. *Ordonnance*, p. XII: 'Il est donc vray qu'il y a des beautez positives dans l'Architecture, et qu'il y en a qui ne sont qu'arbitraires, quoy qu'elles paroissent positives à cause de la prévention, dont il est bien difficile de se défendre.'
89. ibid., p. VIII: 'Il en est ainsi dans l'Architecture, où il y a des choses que la seule accoutumance rend tellement agréables que l'on ne sçauroit souffrir qu'elles soient autrement quoy qu'elles n'ayent en elles-mesmes aucune beauté qui doive infailliblement plaire ... et il y en a mesme que la raison et le bon sens devroient faire paroistre difformes et choquantes, que l'accoutumance a rendu supportables ... et elles sont enfin devenues agréables par l'accoutumance qui a mesme eu le pouvoir de faire que ceux que l'on dit avoir le goust de l'Architecture ne les puissent souffrir quand elles sont autrement.'
90. op. cit., p. 10. Also pp. 2, 97.

about by custom as an abuse the quicker rectified the better: for Perrault, on the contrary, custom is a unique and positive force wielding changes the undoing of which is almost as difficult as the reversion of a biological change caused by custom. Of course, Perrault is well aware that custom is operative on many levels, but in his main argument he is concerned with its fundamental influence, its impelling power that reaches into great depth and effects the transference of attributes with a finality that almost bars us from recognizing that proportions, originally and in themselves, have no positive beauty at all.

The assertion that beauty depends to a great extent on what people are accustomed to, appears to be tantamount to relativity. Perrault is, however, far from subscribing to relativism: it is true that in one place he compares the pleasure we obtain from architectural proportions with that derived from fashions which 'when they change, are not liked any-more, although they remain the same,'[91] but close attention to his main argument makes it evident that the aspect of custom which interests him is the rôle it has played in the development of classical proportions. He sees this as a unique historical fact, which we have to relive when, individually, we are being trained in classical taste. There is no indication anywhere in the *Ordonnance*, or in his notes on Vitruvius, that custom should set the standard or that, installed for ever as a directing agent, it would justify any kind of taste. There is nothing in Perrault even remotely akin to the sceptical attitude of a Montaigne, or of a Pascal in whose opinion 'a different custom will produce different natural princi-ples,' and who made the famous challenging statement that 'three degrees nearer the pole turns the whole jurisprudence upside down, one meridian decides truth.'[92] It was not Perrault, but his opponent Blondel

91. *Ordonnance*, p. VI: '. . . la difficulté est seulement de sçavoir . . . si le plus souvent (l'amour pour les proportions) n'est fondée que sur l'accoutumance; et si ce qui fait qu'un Bastiment plaist à cause de ses proportions, n'est pas la mesme chose que ce qui fait qu'un habit à la mode plaist à cause de ses proportions, lesquelles cependant n'ont rien de positivement beau . . . puisque l'ac-coutumance et les autres raisons non positives qui les font aimer, venant à changer, on ne les aime plus, quoy qu'elles demeurent les mesmes.'
92. *Pensées, Oeuvres*, XIII, nos. 92, 294.

who at the inaugural session of the Academy spoke of 'the perpetual movement' of the arts which never rest for long in one place. 'They have,' he told his colleagues, 'flourished at one time among the Egyptians, the Assyrians and the Medes and then passed to the Persians, Greeks and Romans.'[93] Again it is Blondel, not Perrault, who undertook to vindicate the beauty of a particular Gothic building, the façade of the Cathedral of Milan.[94] Of course, this is not to say that Blondel rather than Perrault tended towards a relativistic point of view. It would be absurd to look for this tendency in François Blondel, who certainly believed in the absolute value of beauty. His remarks – and similar ones by other writers on architectural theory – only underline the split in personality, so typical of an architect brought up in the classical doctrine. Viewing the 'art of building' as one of the fundamental activities of mankind, he is able to unfold a historical canvas on which all nations, from primitive to modern times, are given equal status, but, almost with the same breath when contemplating 'Architecture', he can uphold the grand principle of classical doctrine, the belief in man's inborn responsiveness to the eternal laws of beauty – a conviction that is not shaken by the disturbing thought that it may appear odd that only the Greeks responded to it. Perrault may have entertained similar ideas about the development of the arts, but if so, he did not express them. His sole concern in the *Ordonnance* and the relevant notes in *Vitruvius* is the one style of architecture that for him, as for his contemporaries, had any real value – the classical one. Proportions are important for this style of architecture, but, so goes Perrault's argument, custom has formed them, not any natural laws. Custom had fulfilled this function in the past, and as to the possibility of its influence in the future, this had no bearing on the point Perrault wished to make.

The only time Perrault uses a relativistic argument is in *Essais*, II, p. 394, where, when dealing with ancient music, he sees in the 'diversité du goust qui règne dans certains siècles et dans certaines nations' the reason why 'l'antiquité a aimé jusqu'à l'excès des choses que l'on a haïes depuis jusqu'à l'horreur'.

93. *Cours*, 'Discours.'
94. ibid., pp. 774 ff.

There is one further point on which Perrault could be misunderstood: because he speaks of two classes of beauty, it could be thought that he, as Blondel expressed it, despised the arbitrary qualities or, as has been said, 'relegated the arbitrary beauties to second place.'[95] This is not so. On the contrary, Perrault explicitly states that 'it is evident that knowledge of the arbitrary beauties is the most proper way of forming what is called taste, and that this knowledge alone distinguishes true architects from those who are not.'[96] He does not therefore, contradict himself, as one might be inclined to think after having heard him say that proportions are not the cause of beauty, when he begins the preface to the *Ordonnance* with the categorical statement that 'proportions . . . make the beauty of buildings', or when he refers to them as 'one of the principal foundations of beauty'.[97] All he maintains is that custom plays a great part in lending proportions the semblance, but not the reality, of positive qualities. This, however, is for him no reason to think of them as less effective and inferior qualities, nor to consider the influence exercised by custom as unfortunate or undesirable. Instead, he just accepts it as an indisputable fact.

GRÂCE

Another, in my view erroneous, interpretation of Perrault's aim arises from his definition of arbitrary beauties. He uses the term in *Vitruvius*, but is not specific about it. He calls proportion an arbitrary quality as opposed to the positive and convincing one of rich material and exact execution; but when he tries to define the whole class, he is content with a general reference to 'that beauty which depends on authority and custom'. By this he means the capacity of men of discriminating taste

95. ibid., p. 763; Gillot, op. cit., pp. 501 f.
96. *Ordonnance*, p. XII: '. . . il est constant que la connoissance des beautez arbitraires est la plus propre à former ce qu'on l'appelle le goust, et que c'est elle seule qui distingue les vrais Architectes de ceux qui ne le sont pas.'
97. ibid., p. I; *Vitruvius*, p. 16, note 1.

to promote a habitual preference for certain forms in those who, as
disciples, had submitted to their superior judgment.[98] In the shortened
edition of his *Vitruvius* the system has become involved, arbitrary
beauties being subdivided into two classes, one called *sagesse*, the other
régularité. The object of the first is the 'reasonable use of the positive
beauties', of the second the 'observance of proportional rules'. One
ground for considering proportional rules a source of beauty has a
rational foundation – such as the rule that the part which carries has to
be stronger than the part carried – the other reason is derived from the
habitual esteem for those who invented these proportions, and from the
custom of seeing them observed in ancient monuments.[99]

When he comes to write the *Ordonnance*, his main interest centres
around proportions. In accordance with his chief argument, they belong
to the class of arbitrary qualities, but, of course, there must be other
arbitrary elements as well, which he is now at pains to define, trying to
be more specific about them. He sees them in the way things are shaped
and formed, how contours and profiles are delineated in an agreeable
manner, in the skilful presentation of the character of the different
Orders, and – as he says on the first page of the preface – in the *grâce de la
forme*. Exact proportions, he stresses again and again, do not ensure the
beauty of a building. For that they have to be joined, not only to the
positive beauties, but to the other qualities just mentioned, which, with
the exception of proportions, are all imponderable qualities and are, as

98. *Vitruvius*, p. 12, note 13: 'Car bienque la beauté (arbitraire) soit aussi en quelque façon établie
sur un fondement positif, qui est la convenance . . . que chaque partie a pour l'usage auquel elles
est destinée; néanmoins parce qu'il est vray que chacun ne se croit pas capable de découvrir . . . tout
ce qui appartient à cette raisonnable convenance, on s'en rapporte d'abord au jugement et à
l'approbation de ceux qu'on estime estre éclairez . . .'
   In another note (p. 105, note 7), he contrasts positive beauty with proportions, without, however,
classifying the latter as arbitrary, only pointing out that, in his opinion, they have been 'établies
par un consentement des Architectes qui . . . ont imité les ouvrages les uns des autres, et qui ont
suivy les proportions que les premiers avoient choisies, non point comme ayant une beauté
positive . . .', but only because they appear in company with 'autres beautez positives et convaincantes'.
   99. *Abrégé des dix livres d'architecture de Vitruve*, Paris, 1674, pp. 103 ff.

Perrault no doubt realized, difficult to define, except in general terms.[100]

It may seem that to emphasize the rôle which *grâce* and the other imponderable qualities play in the creation of beauty, and to depreciate the application of exact rules, reveals a point of view in open contradiction to that generally held at Perrault's time. However, as has been shown in recent years in a number of studies on the artistic and literary attitude prevalent during the *Grand Siècle*, there existed a strong trend to ascribe the creation of beauty to qualities, such as *grâce* and the *je ne sais quoi*, and not to pedantic application of rules.[101]

No doubt, the painters, poets, and architects of the seventeenth century set great store by the efficacy of rules, by order and unity, but they were at the same time acutely aware that the artist's independent judgment played a decisive rôle in creative work. The notion of the *Grand Siècle* as the age in which the state and the arts were authoritatively governed, the one by the will of the king, the other by the imposition of strict rules, is, possibly in both spheres but certainly in that of the arts, a simplification that disregards evidence and points to a spirit of the times which in its complexity did not differ from that of other ages. Rules can guide the artist on his way, but are no guarantee for final achievement: something else is needed, 'un mystère de l'art,' as Boileau calls it who, in the same context, advises those who want to emulate the ancient poets to adhere at times to the rule 'not to observe the rules'. Boileau, thought to be the Beckmesser of the *Grand Siècle*, knew, as all the great writers and poets of

---

100. *Ordonnance*, p. VII (see p. 55, note 75).

ibid., p. XXIII: '. . . peut-estre quand ces véritables proportions se trouveroient observées, il n'auroit pas davantage d'agrément, s'il estoit destitué des autres parties, dans lesquelles consiste la véritable beauté, telles que sont entr'autres choses, la manière de décrire agréablement les Contours et les Profils et l'adresse de disposer avec raison toutes les parties qui font les caractères des différens Ordres.'

ibid., p. I: '. . . la beauté d'un Edifice a encore cela de commun avec celle du corps humain, qu'elle ne consiste pas tant dans l'exactitude d'une certaine proportion . . . que dans la grâce de la forme qui n'est rien autre chose que son agréable modification, sur laquelle une beauté parfaite et excellente peut estre fondée, sans que cette sorte de proportion s'y rencontre exactement observée.'

101. S. H. Monk, 'A Grace beyond the Reach of Art,' *Journal of the History of Ideas*, V, 1944, pp. 131 ff.

E. B. O. Borgerhoff, *The Freedom of French Classicism*, Princeton, 1950. Jules Brody, *Boileau and Longinus*, Geneva, 1958.

his time knew, that beauty depended to a great extent on indefinable qualities, on 'a *je ne sais quoi* which charms and without which beauty would have neither grace nor beauty,' and even Bossuet warned his readers against 'too scrupulous regularity'. Doubt about the value of rules made the Chevalier de Méré declare boldly that they 'are disliked by everyone' and ascribe this extraordinary fact to 'a sense of liberty of which we cannot rid ourselves'. *Grâce, délicatesse*, the *je ne sais quoi* are the qualities Méré – and many other men of letters – valued most; they caused Lafontaine to speak of 'grace, more beautiful than beauty'.[102]

The conviction that an excess of regularity is detrimental to the creation of a great work of art was also shared by writers on arts other than poetry and literature. Mersenne's hopeful expectation that the ideal musician of the future would arise through a full investigation of harmonic rules was countered by a correspondent with the warning of not applying rules too exactly 'since grace is created often rather by deviating from rules than by their strict observance.'[103] The same point, with reference to painting and sculpture, was made by Bouhours, author of the first systematic treatise on the *je ne sais quoi*.[104] The appreciation of irrational forces for the creative act can be traced back to the preceding century, to Vasari and Lomazzo, through whom the notion was passed on to Franciscus Junius, an influential writer on art theory. He devoted a whole chapter of his treatise to the subject of grace, which, he says, 'cannot be taught by any rules of art'.[105]

---

102. Boileau, *Discours sur l'Ode, Oeuvres*, III, p. 5; *Dissertation sur la Joconde, Oeuvres*, III, p. 158 (cf. Brody, p. 79).

On Meré see Borgerhoff's exposition pp. 83 ff., where the relevant passages are cited in full.

Bossuet's remark quoted by Henri Peyre, *Le classicisme français*, New York, 1942, p. 150, note 27.

Lafontaine, *Adonis* (written 1658; publ. 1669), *Oeuvres*, ed. Regnier, VI, p. 233: 'Ni ce charme secret dont l'oeil est enchanté, Ni la grâce, plus belle encore que la beauté.'

103. Marin Mersenne, *Correspondance*, Paris, 1932 ff., I, p. 318.

104. P. Bouhours, *Entretiens d'Ariste et d'Eugène*, Paris, 1671 (see Borgerhoff's chapter on Bouhours, op. cit., pp. 186 ff.).

105. Franciscus Junius, *The Antient Art of Painting*, Oxford, 1638, Chapter VI. The quoted remark on p. 323.

For the emergence of the new quality of grace during the 16th century and the important rôle it played in the writings of Vasari and Lomazzo see A. Blunt, *Artistic Theory in Italy 1450–1600*, Oxford, 1956, in particular pp. 93 ff. and pp. 145 ff.

These treatises and essays were, of course, known to the members of the newly formed Académie de Peinture. Here we meet again André Félibien, historiographer for the Academy and for the royal buildings and also secretary to both Academies, those of painting and of architecture. Through the duplication of his charges he was singularly well-suited to transmit ideas from the theory of painting to that of architecture. When, in 1666, he published the first volume of his encyclopedic work, *Entretiens sur les vies et les ouvrages des plus excellens peintres*, he, too, voiced mistrust in the infallibility of rules, warning his readers that 'sometimes it becomes necessary to act against the common rules of art' and that they should not imagine that in painting, any more than in many other arts 'rules have the kind of certainty to be met with in geometry.'[106] An introductory chapter deals with architectural questions and contains 'a conversation on proportion and *grâce*.' Having discussed various aspects of architectural beauty, derived from solidity, function, *bienséance*, order, disposition and proportions, Félibien ends the architectural discourse by pointing out how complex the art of building is, and how admirable the great royal buildings are, not only for their technical and, as it were, rational beauty, but also for 'that *grâce* which is difficult to achieve, which only a few know how to bestow on their works, but which is admired wherever it is met with. As you know well,' he tells the friend with whom he has the discussion, 'there are charms which do not consist simply in beautiful proportions. In works of art as well as in those of nature, we observe beauty of a kind which has neither the *grâce* nor the *je ne sais quoi* that renders some . . . works more agreeable than those that, yet, are more perfect.' What then, is the difference between beauty and *grâce* enquires his friend, and Félibien explains that beauty arises from well proportioned 'corporal and material' parts of a building, whereas *grâce* has its roots in the soul of the artist. Thus, it is possible to have beauty without *grâce* and works which, though conceived in the most beautiful proportions, yet lack the last degree of perfection, a subtle difference which Félibien, like almost every other

106. Paris, 1685 (1st edition 1666), Preface.

French writer on this subject, exemplifies by a comparison with feminine beauty.[107]

It is against this background of aesthetic theory that Perrault's reference to *grâce de la forme* and the other imponderable qualities must be judged. Far from indicating a break on his part with orthodox classical dogma, these passages are, in fact, in line with views voiced by many authors writing during his lifetime on literary and artistic theory. Through his brother Charles he knew the men who frequented literary circles and, through his association with the Académie d'Architecture he was in contact with its secretary. Félibien, no doubt, influenced him by emphasizing the superior rôle which arbitrary qualities were supposed to play in the creative process, but possibly also by placing proportions in a somewhat isolated position, allotting to them a distinct, 'corporal beauty.' In any case, these were current notions, at least among persons of a progressive frame of mind. They may not have been conventional notions, but they certainly were not unusual. To conclude from this part of Perrault's theory that he championed, in defiance of orthodox opinion, the artist's freedom is quite unjustified. If he, with these rather weak passages, could be thought to pursue this aim, then the whole intellectual élite of the age, using much bolder language, could rightly make the same claim.

Perrault really aimed at something that would rather curtail than promote artistic freedom. His explicit aim, as mentioned before, is to 'contain proportions within definite rules'. At the same time, he is aware of one vital fact: if it were true that absolute proportions exist and are the manifestation of natural order, then any attempt in fixing the rules of these proportions is bound to fail; no man, no human institution could possibly have the authority to encroach upon the realm of natural laws. Only in spheres that are free from the rigid application of these laws could man hope to arrange things to his own convenience. Starting from this premise, Perrault had to prove that custom, not unalterable laws, determine proportions. These he assigned to the class of arbitrary values –

107. ibid., pp. 30 ff.

not because he wished to surrender them to artistic licence, but because he wanted to establish the fact that changes can be made, and that it is up to man to accept these, provided they are reasonable and convenient. When he speaks of changes, he has in mind those he is going to propose in the treatise itself; he is not pleading for the right of the architect to make changes at will.

Should it seem doubtful whether this interpretation of Perrault's intention is correct, I hope that examination of his attitude towards a specific problem, which was considered to be of vital importance to the classical architect, will dispel these doubts. It is the problem of changing proportional rules for visual reasons, or, as it may be called for short, the problem of 'optical adjustment'.

CHAPTER III

Optical Adjustment

AFTER Vitruvius has dealt in two books with the Orders and the various types of temples, and has given the proportional rules that have to be observed, he admonishes the architect to take special care in the selection of exact proportions.[1] Less obvious than this advice are the remarks that follow. Once the correct proportions have been decided upon, it is then up to the architect's acumen, which is variously translated as wisdom, skill and, by Perrault, as *esprit*, to make adjustments by 'adding or subtracting from the symmetry (i.e. proportional relations) of the design, so that it may seem to be rightly planned and the elevation may lack nothing.' 'Objects,' he explains, 'appear different close at hand or high above us, because the impression which the eye transmits to our judgment is often misleading. Numerous optical illusions, among them the apparently broken oar when dipped under water, clearly demonstrate that in certain instances reality is wrongly represented so that vision judges things to be different from what they really are'. For that reason, he does not doubt 'that we ought to add or subtract, as needed by the natures of our sites.' In another place, he recommends a rate of diminution gradually decreasing from short to tall columns because of the different height and, consequently, different distances from the eye, so that, unless we make adjustments to counteract the amount of optical deception, the work will look clumsy and un-attractive.[2] The greater the distance that vision has to travel, the more likely is its failure to present objects accurately. Therefore, 'we must always add a supplement to the proportion . . . so that works, which are

1. Vitruvius, *De Architectura*, VI, ii, 1–4.
The passages that follow are given either in M. H. Morgan's or F. Granger's translation.
2. ibid., III, iii, 12, 13.

either in higher positions or themselves more grandiose, may have proportionate dimensions.'³ The eye also fails when viewing 'features which are above the capitals of the columns, that is to say: architraves, friezes, cornices, tympana, pediments, acroteria;' they would appear to recline, unless a correcting adjustment of a forward inclination by the twelfth part of their height is made, an adjustment which would have the result that 'the parts will seem vertical and to measure'.⁴

That the human eye cannot always be trusted in giving a true representation of the outside world, had, of course, been observed long before Vitruvius wrote these passages, but he was the only writer who applied these corrective measures to architecture: at least, his treatise is the only one to survive into modern times. While this alone invested him with great authority, and makes it understandable that his rules of the Orders became a canon from which architects were reluctant to deviate, it seems extraordinary, and certainly needs explanation, that his passages on 'optical adjustment' were repeated again and again, from one treatise to the next, with hardly a voice dissenting. Perrault is puzzled by the 'unanimous opinion of all architects' and by the fact that nobody took the trouble to examine a maxim 'established almost 2000 years ago'.⁵ Matters exist, he reflects, (and may thereby also have in mind a few scientific problems that he had taken on) 'which are so much entrenched in everybody's opinion that the sheer intention of examining them seems to make one ridiculous, although when viewed from close quarters they turn out not to be without difficulties.'⁶ He suspects the cause for this reluctance to investigate the problem to be the belief, held among architects, 'that, because of the authority of Vitruvius, who seems to have

3. ibid., III, v, 9.
4. ibid., III, v, 13.
5. *Ordonnance*, p. 108: 'Cependant que deviendra l'opinion unanime de tous les Architectes, fondée sur l'autorité de Vitruve, qui enseigne ce changement de proportion . . .? Faut-il croire que depuis près de deux mille ans que cette maxime est établie, personne ne se soit donné le loisir de l'examiner . . .? Il faut bien qu'il y ait quelque chose de cela.'
6. ibid., p. 96: 'Il y a des choses tellement établies dans l'opinion de tout le monde, qu'il semble que ce soit se rendre ridicule que de les vouloir seulement examiner, quoy qu'elles se trouvent n'estre pas sans difficulté quand on les regarde de près.'

decided it, a discussion was useless.'[7] We shall see that there might have been more weighty reasons for the constant repetition of Vitruvius's remarks.

Perrault had good reason for connecting this uncritical attitude with the authority of Vitruvius. His task of translating *De Architectura* necessitated a study of architectural literature, then already formidable. From his notes a long list of the works consulted could be drawn up, which includes, naturally, all editions of *Vitruvius*, with and without commentaries, in Latin, French and German, and also the major architectural treatises, from that of Alberti and the great masters of the Cinquecento to those of his own century; an impressive list that includes names like the Englishman Wotton and the German Dürer.

Perrault found that editors who commented on the relevant passages did not question the correctness of Vitruvius's arguments; they were content with elaborating on them.[8] Turning from commentaries on *Vitruvius* to architectural treatises Perrault would notice that their authors, too, reiterated Vitruvius's remarks on optical adjustment.[9] Fréart, to quote one writer, explains that the uncommon proportion of the architrave at the Theatre of Marcellus was due to the architect's being 'only concerned with repairing by optical means what the eye, because of the great distance, must have found wrong in the gracefulness of the general proportions,' and that in the same way 'the mass and prodigious

7. ibid., p. 108: '. . . ceux qui ont esté capables de resoudre les questions les plus subtiles, ont pu avoir négligé celle-cy, dont la discussion leur a paru inutile, à cause de l'autorité de Vitruve qui semble l'avoir décidée.'

8. Cesare Cesariano, *Di Lucio Vitruvio Pollione de Architectura* . . . Como, 1521, fol. LVIII v.
Daniele Barbaro, *I dieci libri dell'Architettura di M. Vitruvio*, Venice, 1556, pp. 102, 171.
G. Philander, *In decem libros M. Vitruvii . . . annotationes*, Rome, 1544, p. 183.
Walter Rivius, *Vitruvius Teutsch*, Nürnberg, 1548, fol. CXCVIII r. Also Sagredo, *Raison d'architecture antique extraicte de Vitruve*, Paris, 1539 (1st edition a few years earlier), fols. 19r, 42, with an illustration showing the need to incline acroterias. This widely read dialogue – 'the earliest architectural book to be published in French' (W. B. Dinsmoor, 'The Literary Remains of Sebastiano Serlio,' *The Art Bulletin*, XXIV, 1942, pp. 69 f.) – ran into several editions, the last of which appeared in 1608.

9. Leone Battista Alberti, *De re aedificatoria*, ed. J. Leoni, *The Architecture of Leon Battista Alberti*, London, 1755, p. 142. Andrea Palladio, *I quattro libri dell'architettura*, Venice, 1570, p. 15.
J. Bullant, *Reigle génerale d'architecture des cinq manières de colonnes*, Paris, 1568, fol. Giii, v.
Philibert de l'Orme, op. cit., fols. 155 r., 172 r., 174 v., 186 v., 192 r., 237 v.

height' of the Colosseum 'required the sophisticated means of optics to make it appear regular'.[10] Thus, Perrault seemed to be right when he spoke of the 'unanimous opinion of all architects' favouring optical adjustment, a conclusion he found confirmed when reading in Vignola's book on the Orders that 'according to the opinion of everybody and of Vitruvius himself it is often necessary to add or subtract . . . in places where vision is deceived.'[11]

The arguments for adjustment were based on the assumption that the visual angle determines the apparent size of the object, so that objects seen at equal angles give the impression of being of equal size. Accepting this theory as correct, Serlio, in 1545, devised a simple geometrical scheme by which the architect could counteract the effect of 'the intervening air wearing out our vision' (as Serlio expressed it) and thus ensure that all parts of a tall building appear to be of equal size, unaffected by visual distortions[12] (Pl. 23). Perrault would have come across the device in a number of publications with illustrations that vary only slightly from the one introduced by Serlio. After it had been reproduced again in the edition of Serlio's works in 1619, it turned up a few years later in handbooks on perspective, that of Hondius in 1625 and of Dubreuil in 1651 (Pl. 24), and, in the second half of the century, in basically similar form in Abraham Bosse's treatise on the Orders. François Blondel dealt in detail with both schemes, that of Serlio and that of Bosse, and judged them on the whole favourably.[13] A different set of illustrations demonstrated the need

10. op. cit., pp. 38, 106, 66.

11. Giacomo Barozzi Vignola, *Regola delli cinque ordine d'Architettura*, Venice, 1596 (1st ed. 1562), preface.

12. op. cit., fol. 9 r. Serlio's explanation of his device on fol. 8 v.

13. H. Hondius, *Brève instruction des règles de la géometrie*, The Hague, 1625, fig. 24.

J. Dubreuil, *La perspective pratique*, Paris, 1651, I, p. 125.

Abraham Bosse, *Traité des manières de dessiner les ordres de l'architecture antique en toutes leurs parties*, Paris, 1664, fol. XLII.

Blondel, op. cit., pp. 711, 713.

Dürer was the first to draw up a scheme for counteracting foreshortening. An illustration in his *Elementa Geometrica*, Lutetia, 1532, p. 116, shows how the apparent size of highly-placed lettering can be corrected (Pl. 25). He remarks that this device can be generally applied. Salomon de Caus. *La perspective avec la raison des ombres et miroirs*, London, 1612, Pl. 37, reproduces a similar drawing, specifically referring to Dürer.

for adjusting highly-placed objects. It appeared for the first time in
Cesariano's commentaries, from which it was taken over by Rivius and,
in simplified form, by Martin and Rusconi (Pls. 26–27). Its purpose was
to provide a visual interpretation of Vitruvius's remarks, not, as was the
case with the other set of illustrations, a practical help for the architect.[14]

All writers on architectural theory who preceded Perrault thus accepted
as an obvious fact the falsifying influence of human vision – with two
exceptions. The dissenting voices were those of an architect, Scamozzi,
and of an art critic, Roger de Piles. Scamozzi, while approving of
Vitruvius's recommendations for adjustments in some instances, rejects
his demand for inclining parts of the entablature forward; Perrault, aware
of this criticism, notes that Scamozzi calls 'all this nothing but *une
chicane de perspective*'.[15] Roger de Piles's objection is of a different kind.
He does not maintain that making changes is wrong; he rejects the
reason advanced for making them. We shall return to his observations.

Perrault goes considerably further in disputing the need for optical
adjustments than either Scamozzi's critical remark or Roger de Piles's
realization that changes are made necessary by a cause different from the
one commonly advanced. Perrault's arguments are set out, in clear and
convincing terms, in a few notes to his *Vitruvius* and, at greater length in
the seventh chapter of the *Ordonnance*. They are based in part on the
results of Descartes's inquiry into optics and the process of vision, in
part on more recent studies by Cartesians, but in important details on his
own researches.[16]

The partisans of optical adjustment presupposed that the eye can be

14. Cesariano, op. cit., fol. LX r.
Rivius, op. cit., fol. CXXVII v.
Martin, *Vitruvius*, fol. 42 r.
G. A. Rusconi, *I dieci libri d'architettura*, Venice, 1660 (1st ed. 1590), p. 65.
15. V. Scamozzi, *L'idea della architettura universale*, Venice, 1615, II, p. 20: 'Questa invero è una
sottilità di prospettiva e piú tosto discorsiva, che da metter in atto ... oltre, che sarebbo anco
cosa ingratada vedere ...' Perrault's remark in *Vitruvius*, p. 102, n. 79.
16. Descartes, *Dioptrique* (publ. 1637), *Oeuvres*, ed. Adam, VI, pp. 130 ff., *Traité de l'homme* (1st
ed. 1664), *Oeuvres*, XI, pp. 151 ff.
J. Rohault, *Traité de Physique*, Paris, 1671, I pp. 344 ff.
Malebranche op. cit. Book I, especially chapters VII–X.

deceived. This, Perrault counters, is not so: if deception occurs, it is not due to the eye, which never fails, but to our judgment, which interprets the optical sensation wrongly.[17] This is, of course, an obvious and by no means novel observation, which in itself does not affect the issue. However, Perrault goes further than that and maintains not only that the eye never fails, but that even the visual judgment 'is as a rule very certain and almost infallible'.[18] It functions without our being aware of its action, or of its extraordinary degree of certainty; it is a faculty that everybody possesses, but uses unconsciously. This judgment is assisted in its correct assessment about size and distance by a number of what today are called clues: the visual angle, a clue that played a prominent part in the arguments for optical adjustment, is only one of them; reduction in brightness of colours and shades, and the comparison between things known with those unknown are further aids, the latter assuring that 'knowledge of distance makes known the size, and the size that is known gives knowledge of the distance.'[19]

Yet, although everybody unconsciously makes use of the certainty of visual judgment, it is not an inborn, but an acquired faculty, acquired through the process of continuously repeated experience, in short, by being subjected to the force of custom. As mentioned in the previous chapter, Perrault was intrigued by the extraordinary influence which custom exercises over all human functions, and spent a great deal of time and ingenuity on the investigation of this phenomenon.[20] When he now proceeds to explain that, mainly owing to repetitive experiences, vision corrects itself, he could speak to the architectural profession authoritatively; a situation that, one can safely assume, gave him a good deal of satisfaction.

17. *Vitruvius*, p. 205, C.
18. ibid., p. 204, C: '. . . la veue n'est pas si sujette à se tromper autant que Vitruve le prétend, non pas seulement, parce qu'en effet la veue de mesme que les autres sens extérieurs ne se trompe jamais, mais mesme parce que le jugement de le veue . . . est pour l'ordinaire très-seur et presque infaillible . . .'
19. *Ordonnance*, pp. 102 ff., where he sets out the 'clues' in greater detail than in *Vitruvius*, p. 204, E.
20. *Essais*, II, pp. 290 ff. His long treatise on 'Des sens extérieurs' in *Essais*, IV, pp .19–163, deals largely with the influence of habit on sense perception.

It seems highly probable, Perrault declares, that vision is poorly
developed at birth; we gradually learn to see effectively, an observation
which modern research confirms.[21] 'By the time we are grown up, long
habit and experience have so often corrected the early errors that we
relapse only on rare occasions.'[22] Gradually, vision becomes more perfect:
nobody is afraid that, because of the converging lines of a long gallery,
he would touch the ceiling by the time the end of the passage is reached,
or not be able to pass a door which from far away he can cover with the
tip of a finger, nor does anyone mistake the shape of a circular window,
when seen from the side, for an oval. On the contrary, experience and
the habit of 'adding at once to the image, as it is in the eye, the circumstances which are known,' make visual judgment so reliable that, even
when 'distance and situation tend to make objects appear different from
what they are', it is not confused and will not accept the image on the
retina as a true representation of things. Everybody can easily judge
'whether a face appearing high up on a window is round or long, nor
will a thin body in this situation appear to be squat, nor an exceedingly
tall one ever be taken for a dwarf.' The precision with which vision
functions is incredibly high, as is daily confirmed by the way 'a coachman
judges from 50 feet away that he shall be able to pass his coach between
two other carriages, although there is no more than 2 inches clearance
by which he can pass.' The hunter aiming at a bird, and the gardener
trying to pick a fruit from a tall tree are both able to judge visually the
correct size of the bird or the fruit, as can the carpenter that of a beam
high above him or the fountain-maker the thickness and height of a jet
of water. Admittedly, these are examples of highly specialized visual
judgments, but they are formed only by experience, in the same way as
ordinary visual judgment is formed. We employ it without being
conscious of doing so, just as 'in all other actions where experience and
custom produce in us a habitual faculty to such a degree that we do a
hundred things necessary to accomplish these actions without thinking

21. *Ordonnance*, p. 103.
22. *Vitruvius*, p. 204, C.

that we do them'. As little as the player on the lute thinks of the cords and stops he has to touch, and yet plays correctly, 'do we think of the rules of perspective; without examining expressly the reasons and different effects of distance and of the weakened tint of objects, common sense only rarely fails to take note of these circumstances.' The occasions when we may be deceived in trusting the image on the eye are indeed rare, and only occur in situations in which we have had little or no experience. These exceptions only confirm that ordinarily we are not deceived.[23]

Perrault's assumption of how vision functions have, naturally, in the course of time been modified and superseded by theories based on more sophisticated physiological and psychological research, yet the main point that matters here, namely that, under normal circumstances, vision is capable of interpreting the retinal sensation correctly is still accepted as basically true. He is, therefore, justified in his conclusion that changing architectural proportions in order to correct visual shortcomings is a bad practice. In his opinion, it should be done on rare occasions only.[24] Because of the high degree of precision of which he had shown visual judgment to be capable, a change of proportions is normally bound to be perceived by the observer. 'For that reason, this change is not only useless; it must be considered to be positively bad.'[25] The increased height of an entablature, increased because it crowns a tall column, will be perceived at once as an adulteration of a proportion that was based on the reasonable relation between load and support, and will only result in the eye's being offended. As for Vitruvius's advice to incline highly placed parts, such as statues, in order to make them appear to be in a

23. The foregoing paragraph is condensed from Perrault's note on the subject in *Vitruvius*, pp. 204 ff.

24. ibid., p. 81, note 24: '. . . je dis librement ma pensée sur l'abus que je prétens que les Architectes font ordinairement du changement des Proportions suivant les différens aspects; mon opinion estant que l'on ne le doit pratiquer que rarement . . .'

25. *Ordonnance*, pp. 105 f.: 'Cette exactitude du jugement de la vue . . . estant donc aussi précise qu'elle est, il n'y a pas beaucoup de difficulté à concevoir que l'éloignement des objets n'estant pas capable de tromper . . . ces proportions ne peuvent estre changées qu'on ne s'en apperçoive, et que par cette raison ce changement n'est pas seulement inutile, mais qu'il doit estre même reputé vicieux.'

Similarly, in *Vitruvius*, p. 175, note 10.

perpendicular position, nothing like the desired effect will be achieved, 'because if they lean forward, they will unfailingly appear to lean forward.'[26] It can, therefore, be said that 'it is senseless to distort and mar proportions in order to prevent them from looking distorted, and to make a thing defective by intending to correct it.'[27] In fact, while architects extol the change of proportions, they do not practise it, and in the rare cases when they have done so, as, for instance, on the pediment of St Gervais with its figures of 'enormous size', the effect is bad and shocks everybody.[28] (Pl. 28).

In short, Vitruvius's assertions were untenable. Nevertheless, they seemed to find support in the practice of the ancients; at least, some of the discrepancies between the 'correct' proportions and those observed on ancient monuments were generally thought to be explicable in this way. Barbaro reproaches those who, with great arrogance, draw rash conclusions from the obvious disparity between the Vitruvian proportions and those actually applied, thereby ignoring completely Vitruvius's often repeated advice 'not to use always the same proportional rules', but to add or subtract according to the nature of the place.[29] A century later, Fréart ascribes, as already mentioned, the unusual proportions of some Roman monuments to the architect's intention of compensating for the effects of perspective.[30] Blondel, too, when advising architects to deviate in certain cases from the usual proportions, points to the example given by the architects of the 'three columns on the Campo Vaccino', of those 'half-buried at the foot of the Capitol', and of the entablature – 'of an exorbitant and colossal size' for the 'Temple of the Sun on the Quirinal'.[31]

---

26. *Ordonnance*, p. 106.
27. ibid., p. 108: 'Enfin pour conclure en un mot, je croy que lors qu'on y aura bien pensé, on trouvera qu'il n'y a point de raison de corrompre et de gaster les proportions, pour empescher qu'elles ne paroissent corrompues, et de rendre une chose défectueuse par l'intention que l'on a de la corriger.'
28. ibid., pp. 100 f.
29. op. cit., fol. 171 r.
30. op. cit., pp. 38, 66, 106.
31. op. cit., 717 f., 723.

Félibien draws the same conclusion. He believes the adaption of proportions to visual conditions to have been 'the reason that we find so many different measurements in the ancient Orders'.[32] Perrault was aware of this argument. He found that whenever he referred to the 'diversity of proportions on equally-approved buildings' as evidence against the uncritical assumption that everything in ancient architecture was made with good reason, the architects countered by pointing to the 'diversity of aspects which they imagine to have been the cause of this change of proportions'.[33] Most architects, he observed, 'want us to believe that the diversity found among ancient works must be attributed to this reason.'[34]

Perrault disagreed with this reasoning, but, at the same time, realized that even a well-founded modern theory of vision carried little weight with professional architects, as long as it was taken for granted that the ancients had conformed to Vitruvius's optical rules. It would, however, have been most difficult for him to disprove this assumption, had it not been for the good fortune that, while he was still working on the manuscript for the *Ordonnance*, Desgodets's outstanding work on Roman monuments was being prepared for publication.[35] The exact measurements, recorded by Desgodets, enabled him to include in the *Ordonnance* several pages in which he scrutinized a whole range of Roman monuments from this particular point of view.[36] He found that in some cases no change had been made where optical rules would have required it, in others that the change made was the opposite of what ought to have been done to comply with these rules, and that sometimes changes were made where, as far as optics and perspective were concerned, they were

32. *Entretiens*, p. 19.
33. *Ordonnance*, p. 109: '(Les architectes) ont voulu établir comme un fondement inébranlable, qu'il n'y avoit rien dans ces admirables restes qui ne fût fait avec grande raison; et quand on leur a objecté les diversitez des proportions dans des édifices également approuvez, ils l'ont attribuée à la diversité des aspects qu'ils ont supposé avoir esté cause de ce changement de proportions . . .'
34. ibid., p. 29.
35. Perrault acknowledges at the end of the preface (p. XXVII) his debt to Desgodets whose book, at that moment in the press, 'm'a servi pour sçavoir au juste les différentes proportions qui ont esté prises par cet Architecte avec une très grande exactitude.'
36. ibid., pp. 29, 98 ff.

completely unnecessary. 'Often,' he sums up, 'proportions are different in the same aspects, and then again they are the same in different aspects.'[37] His survey makes it evident, he declares categorically, that the ancients had no intention of changing the proportions according to different aspects and different dimensions. Sometimes changes had been made, but it would obviously be wrong to believe that optical reasons had been the cause, since 'they are not practised on the most approved buildings'. They are simply accidental, and this is also his final verdict: 'all the diversity has no other foundation than pure chance.'[38]

Perrault rightly expected opposition to his dissenting views. When in 1674, members of the Academy studied Vitruvius in Perrault's translation and when, in December of that year, they came across Perrault's first explicit note on optical adjustment, their reaction was the same as it had been when confronted with his peculiar views on beauty and custom: they were greatly puzzled. Even after reading the note once more the following week, they 'found so many difficulties' that they postponed a decision to another meeting, 'in order to have more time to think about it.'[39] Eighteen months later, when they had reached the sixth book with Vitruvius's remarks and Perrault's relevant lengthy notes on the subject, they again postponed further discussion until there should be a better attended meeting.[40] Another five years passed. Then, one week, members interrupted the study of Scamozzi's treatise, and 'by chance' (as the secretary words it) 'argued strongly' about Vitruvius's ideas on making adjustments for optical reasons. The 'chance' to air his views was no doubt seized by Perrault, who attended the meeting, and who could by now back his arguments with the extreme accuracy of Desgodets's measurements.[41] Discussions on the subject might also have

37. ibid., p. 109.
38. ibid., p. 29: '. . . toute cette diversité n'a point d'autre fondement que le hazard . . .'
p. 98: '. . . on ne doit point croire que ce soit un changement fait par des raisons d'Optique, mais seulement par hazard, puisque ces changemens n'ont point esté pratiquez dans les édifices les plus approuvez.'
39. *Procès-verbaux*, I, p. 87 (10 and 17 December 1674).
40. ibid., I, p. 119 (8 June 1676).
41. ibid., I, p. 311 (5 May 1681).

taken place on other occasions after the official closure of the meetings, since we are told by Desgodets that he 'had once (*autrefois*) heard this question of change of proportions being discussed in the Académie d'Architecture.' The wording of this remark and his absence from Paris make it unlikely that he referred to any of the meetings mentioned in the minutes.[42] 'Opinions were divided,' remarks Desgodets. The way in which he summarizes the arguments opposing change of proportions makes it evident that, on that occasion too, Perrault himself had argued his case. The discussion must have been lively, with the Director of the Academy, Perrault's most formidable opponent François Blondel, trying to refute him by using, we can be sure, the same arguments we meet some years later in his *Cours d'architecture*.[43]

Blondel begins the discussion by conceding that vision consists of 'two very different things', the image at the back of the eye and the judgment we make about it. However, to say that this judgment errs only rarely, is to take a too optimistic view of the faculties of the ordinary man, who may too often fall into an error similar to the one into which children fall when, incapable of rational thought, they believe that the stick seen under water is really broken.[44] People, advanced in age and thoroughly experienced, may be able to correct optical errors by referring to circumstances known to them in other ways, but it should never be forgotten that Vitruvius did not write for 'perfect persons', but formulated his rules of optical adjustment for the 'less enlightened people who, like himself, need some artifice to help them in correcting the errors

42. op. cit., p. 21. Having left Paris in September 1674 not to return before summer or autumn 1677, Desgodets cannot have been present at the first three meetings. He could have attended the meeting of 1681, but *autrefois* does not seem to refer to a meeting that, when he wrote the text, had taken place only a few months earlier. (The printing of the *Édifices* was completed in March 1682). Furthermore, the same passage appears already in a manuscript of the *Édifices* (Paris, Bibl. Nat., MS anc. franç. 381). Since the manuscript differs in some places from the published text, the passage must have been written some time before the final text was completed, which reduces even more the time that had elapsed since the meeting of 1681.

43. op. cit., pp. 715 ff. On the two preceding pages, Blondel 'quotes' in an abridged though fairly accurate form the arguments which Perrault had advanced in *Vitruvius*, pp. 204 f.

44. op. cit., p. 716.

of their senses.'[45] As to our ability to recognize correctly the shape of faces and size of persons at a high window, this may only be so at medium heights; at very great heights we could not judge if a face is round or long, not even whether it is a ball or a face.[46] To maintain that it is futile to enlarge the height of an entablature when resting on a tall column, and that, on the contrary, it should for the sake of apparent solidity be decreased is to criticize, for example, a monument as universally admired as the Three Columns on the Forum; this remark and other similar ones can only be explained by a wish to draw attention to oneself.[47] He, Blondel, is happy 'to conform to theory and practice of the great masters, ancient and modern, leaving to others, who by the force of their genius have risen high above the vulgar crowd, the pleasure which they derive from the eccentricity of their conceptions.'[48] He really does not wish to enter into a dispute whether the eye is deceived or not, because, he exclaims in exasperation, 'this discussion is too metaphysical for architects.'[49]

Perrault was rightly annoyed at these personal attacks, particularly as Blondel had declared at the beginning that, while claiming the right of academic liberty to dispute on controversial subjects, he 'had no intention of offending anybody'.[50] As to Blondel's dismissal of the whole subject as being too metaphysical, he did not believe that modern architects were incapable of reasoning, unless they had – as he, Blondel, had –

45. ibid., p. 717: '. . . nous pouvons toujours présumer en faveur de Vitruve, que ce n'est pas de ces personnes parfaites qu'il a entendu parler. Les règles qu'il donne sont pour des gens moins éclairés et qui, comme nous, ont besoin d'un peu d'art pour les aider à corriger les erreurs de leurs sens et les empescher de prendre les images apparantes pour les véritables.'

46. ibid., p. 721.

47. ibid., p. 718 f.

48. ibid., p. 719: 'Et pour moy . . . je me trouve plus assuré de me conformer aux raisonnemens et aux pratiques des plus grands Maîtres anciens et modernes, laissant à d'autres qui se sont par la force de leur génie élevés au dessus du vulgaire, le plaisir qu'ils ont dans la singularité de leurs opinions, dont ils peuvent goûter la douceur à longs traits, sans que je leur porte envie. Ils peuvent même avoir pitié de notre ignorance et de notre foiblesse et nous traiter de ridicules; Nous, dis-je' qui ne sommes pas capables de voir ce qu'ils voyent et de comprendre la force de leurs conceptions.'

49 ibid., p. 717.

50. ibid., p. 716.

'a too great veneration for the ancient architects.'[51] Perrault's great disappointment, however, was his obvious failure to achieve the success he had hoped for when making known what he had thought were original ideas: the mechanics of the built-in visual judgment had obviously not been understood at all, owing, it seems today, to a breakdown in communication between the scientist and the artist, indicating surprisingly that the gap, ever to be widened, made its first appearance as far back as the seventeenth century, when progress in science was gaining speed.[52]

Blondel did not understand the significance of Perrault's everyday examples and the bearing they had on vision and on the particular problems under discussion, but he knew, of course, that Perrault was better qualified than he was to examine a process which, after all, was a physiological one. It was safe to assume that Perrault's arguments contained some substance of truth, therefore, having done with the polemical possibilities of the dispute, he proceeded to examine the problem more seriously. He admits that reason, or common sense, judges 'the size of objects to be a good deal different from that represented in the eye', yet still insists that in cases where the object is placed at some distance from the eye, it would be wrong to leave it in 'its natural size without adding something to its proportions'.[53] He thus arrives at a solution typical of French classical thought, namely that 'the measure which should be given to the parts according to different situations and distances should be something between the appearance of the distant object in our eye . . . and its natural size.'[54] Having stated this, he examines ancient and modern

51. *Vitruvius*, p. 206.
52. ibid., p. 206: 'Cette manière de répondre me fait comprendre que le dessein que j'ay eu en communiquant au public la pensée qui m'est particulière sur le changement des proportions n'a pas eu le succez que je m'étois proposé; parce que mon intention n'estant point de me *singulariser*, comme on dit, mais seulement d'obliger les sçavans à m'instruire sur une question que je croyois n'estre pas sans difficulté, je voy qu'il semble qu'on ne me veuille rien répondre de raisonnable, de peur de faire tort à l'autorité des anciens, que l'on prétend estre au dessus de toutes les raisons.'
53. op. cit., p. 723.
54. ibid., p. 723: '. . . la mesure qu'il faut donner (aux parts d'un édifice) selon les différences des situations ou des distances, doit tenir un certain milieu de grandeur entre l'apparance que l'espèce d'un objet éloigné figure dans nostre oeil . . . et l'étendue naturelle du même objet.'

monuments and finds his notion of the middle way confirmed. Whereas Vignola, a century earlier, had still hoped to determine the exact measure of adjustments 'through the fine rules of perspective', Blondel has to admit that he 'does not know the rules that should be observed so as to find exactly and right away this mean between the effect of optical rules and that of natural proportions', yet expresses the hope that through further research 'this secret may in time be discovered'.[55] He obviously fails to understand that the point Perrault had wished to drive home was the futile and even harmful effect of any adjustment, full, half, or of any other degree.

This unyielding adherence to the principle of optical adjustment remains almost inexplicable until a certain quotation from Vitruvius, which Blondel repeats again and again, makes one suspect that an issue of greater consequence is at stake. In this remark Vitruvius stresses the importance of the architect's discriminating judgment in the execution of optical adjustment. Blondel quotes the sentence at the opening of his discourse on the change of proportions, repeats it when, in the course of his argument against Perrault, he selects various passages from Vitruvius that all emphasize the architect's *force d'esprit*, *jugement* and *connaissance*, and finally closes the whole discussion by quoting it once again.[56] Obviously, he attached great significance to this sentence by which Vitruvius declared that optical adjustment 'dépend plus de la vivacité de l'esprit et du génie de l'architecte, que des règles que l'on puisse donner'. At least, this is what Blondel read into 'haec autem etiam ingeniorum acuminibus, non solum doctrinis efficiuntur'.[57] However, different attitudes result in significantly different interpretations, as is proved by Perrault's translation of the same passage, which is closer to the Latin text. Blondel changes Vitruvius's plain statement that acumen is *also* needed in a

Lomazzo, *Trattato dell'arte della pittura, scultura e architettura*, Milan, 1584, p. 77, had already recommended 'la mistura di queste due proportioni', that is 'alla cosa secondo se, e secondo l'apparenza'.

55. Vignola, op. cit., Preface.
Blondel, op. cit., p. 726.
56. ibid., pp. 704, 722 (quoted in full in Appendix IV, 1), 726.
57. Vitruvius, VI, ii, 4.

phrase that gives unqualified preference and considerably greater importance to acumen than to doctrinae, whereas Perrault lays as little emphasis on the imponderable quality of the architect's judgment as was compatible with the Vitruvian text and translates: 'C'est en cela que l'esprit et la doctrine sont fort nécessaires.'[58]

The basic difference between Perrault's and Blondel's attitudes is brought into the open when their dispute turns to a special case, that of the Arc de Triomphe du Faubourg St Antoine, which Perrault had designed (Pl. 17). Blondel accuses Perrault of not practising what he preaches, since he has placed on top of his arch an equestrian statue of thirty feet, instead of the six or seven feet that would have been its natural proportion.[59] To this Perrault replies what he had already asserted ten years earlier when discussing oversize statues placed at great height, namely that he gave the equestrian statue of the King this colossal size, not in order to allow for any optical foreshortening, nor to give by this contrivance the impression of a statue of ordinary size, but precisely in order to make it appear colossal.[60] Blondel, while accepting this explanation, thought he had cornered his opponent by pointing out that, in this case, Perrault himself obviously believed 'that colossal figures in this situation and at this distance make a better effect than figures of natural size'. Perrault ought to admit, he demands, that on the same grounds an oversize entablature 'does better in certain situations and distances than one of ordinary height', and that generally 'architectural parts make a more agreeable effect in certain sizes when placed in a certain way than they would make if the proportional relation between them were different'.[61] With these arguments Blondel had strayed far from the

58. *Vitruvius*, p. 204.
59. op. cit., p. 719.
60. *Vitruvius*, pp. 205 D (already in 1st ed.), 205, E (addition of 2nd ed.), *Ordonnance*, p. 110.
61. op. cit., p. 719: 'Ils (that is to say, Perrault) ont donc crû que des figures Colossales faisoient, dans la situation et l'élognement de celles-ci, un meilleur effet que des naturelles: Et par la même raison ils devoient estre persuadez qu'un Entablement d'une hauteur extraordinaire . . . fera mieux dans une certaine situation et un certain élognement qu'un Entablement d'une hauteur ordinaire: Et qu'ainsi les parties d'Architecture font un effet plus agréable sous certaines mesures lors qu'elles sont situées d'une certaine manière, quelles ne feroient si elles avoient une autre proportion entr'elles.'

ground on which the controversy had originally been waged; the reason
he puts forward for changing proportions has nothing to do anymore
with optical adjustment; he demands the changes on purely aesthetic
grounds.

When Perrault deals with the subject in the *Ordonnance*, he gives as an
additional justification for his oversized statue the fact that it is in the
right proportion to the 'mass of the building' (that is, to the arch itself),
in the same way as the small figures lower down are in the right proportion to the columns on which they stand. He makes this point without,
it seems, realizing that he thus comes close to conceding that changes
may be called for, not for optical, but for aesthetic reasons.[62] To Blondel,
in any case, this was an important point which, no doubt, had always
been present in his mind while arguing with Perrault about optical
adjustment. 'The principal aim for architects and sculptors,' he wrote in
this connection, 'is to arrange the parts of their works in such a way that
they shall please.' This, however, would not come about 'if they always
made use of the same proportions in all sorts of situations and distances'.[63]

The inadequacy of human vision is for Blondel only one of several
reasons for advocating deviation from normal proportions. He deals
with the other reasons too, showing that proportions are affected by the
difference to be met with in the height of stories, the thickness of columns,
by the varying ratio of height to width of a building and, by the

62. *Ordonnance*, p. 110: '. . . il faut que cette Statue soit posée sur quelque chose qui ait rapport
à sa grandeur. . . . C'est ce que l'on a observé à l'Arc de Triomphe du Fauxbourg Saint Antoine,
où la Statue Colossale du Roy est posée au haut sur le massif de l'édifice . . . car ce massif sert
comme de Piedestail à la grande Statue, qui est beaucoup plus grande que celles qui sont sur les
Colonnes de l'Ordre, lesquelles luy sont proportionnées de mesme que la grande Statue l'est au
massif.'

Similarly, ibid., p. 32, when, in support of his proposal to give certain mouldings the same
proportions in all columns, he points to the fact that 'à mesure que la Colonne s'allonge dans les
Ordres délicats, ces parties, quoique les mêmes en grosseur, deviennent ou du moins paroissent
plus délicates à proportion de la hauteur de la Colonne'.

63. op. cit., p. 721. The view that the aim of art is to please was generally held at the time. For
parallel trend in literature see D. Mornet, *Histoire de la littérature française classique 1660–1700*,
Paris, 1942, pp. 154 ff. and Peyre, op. cit., p. 102, citing Molière's well-known saying: 'La grande
règle de toutes les règles est de plaire.'

distinctive character of the Orders.[64] They all interact and, together with changes called for by optical reasons, produce what Blondel repeatedly calls the admirable *variété* and *diversité*, a response similar to one coming from Philibert de l'Orme who, noticing all measures of ancient buildings to be unlike each other, found them, nevertheless, 'very beautiful and admirable to look at.'[65] Perrault, too, stressed the great variety of measures among ancient monuments, but he turned it into an argument for attaining hard and fast rules for the proportions of the Orders. Writers like Blondel, or architects like de l'Orme, reacted differently: they saw in the variety of measurements a sign of great vitality, akin to that of a living organism, and admired the wisdom and skill with which ancient architects had mastered the intricate tasks of their art. Adjustment seemed to them important, but, of course, it meant adjustment of rules, and the wish to define these rules was, naturally, a strong motive for their enquiries into architectural theory. All architectural writers stressed, at one and the same time, the importance of well-defined rules and of exercising discrimination in applying these rules, and insisted that, in order to choose the right proportion among the great variety of approved examples, the judgment of an experienced architect was needed.[66]

The circumstances which call for modifications to established rules, are described in the most general terms, even when the writer deals with Vitruvius's specific recommendations for optical adjustments. Architects are asked to 'have regard to the situation and the circumstance' and not to forget that things change 'according to the various aspects and distances from which they are seen'. Sometimes it is just the 'size, the situation and the distance,' or – more generally still – 'the work in hand' that calls for the 'force de leur esprit et la lumière de leur jugement', as Félibien expresses it. In another place, he reminds architects that they must know

64. op. cit., pp. 256 f., 312.
65. Blondel, op. cit., II, pp. 17, 710, 727.
de l'Orme, op. cit., fol. 211 r.: '... de toutes les mesures que j'ay remarquées aux édifices antiques, je n'en ay trouvé qui fussent semblables, ains tousjours différentes: et toutes fois les édifices estoient très-beaux et admirables à la veue.'
66. For complete quotations see Appendix IV.

'by optical rules and natural reasons the effect that each part is going to have according to where it is placed', thereby clearly indicating that adjustment for optical reasons is only one of many instances that require expert handling. A categorical statement by Philander, which Blondel cites in a fairly accurate translation, embraces every possible circumstance: 'les mêmes proportions ne font pas partout les mêmes effets.' Not only are the circumstances under which changes have to be made described in terms that apply to almost any occasion, but the phrases that indicate the ends to be achieved are equally general. Modifications of proportions are demanded 'in order to give to buildings a fine appearance and beauty', to lend them *commodité* and *grâce*, or in order to make them 'pleasant to look at and to prevent the eye from encountering something to which it may take offence'. These remarks, typical of the architectural literature of the time, make it evident that purely aesthetic considerations were behind the demands for making adjustments – far removed from the limited aim of correcting visual shortcomings. Aesthetic judgment, too, was, as we have seen, at the root of Blondel's remark about 'the better effect' of an over-sized equestrian statue, and to the same category belong all the other examples with which he hoped to refute Perrault: the extraordinary height of the balustrade at Caprarola, the size of the orb on the lantern of St Peter's, and the excessive size of the drum of the Val de Grâce.[67]

It seems that the only writer who was conscious of the difference that exists between adjustments made for optical and those made for aesthetic reasons, was Roger de Piles. One of his notes to Dufresnoy's *L'art de peinture* contains observations on the Column of Trajan in Rome that can only be understood in this way.[68] This monument with its spiral band of reliefs had become one of the favourite examples for those intent on

67. For documentation of this particular aspect, the importance attached to the expert judgment of the architect, see Appendix IV.

68. Roger de Piles, 'Remarques sur l'art de peinture de Charles Alfonse Du Fresnoy in C. A. Dufresnoy, *L'art de peinture*, Paris, 1668.

proving that the ancients had practised optical adjustment. It was thought that they had increased the actual size of the uppermost reliefs in relation to that of the lower ones so as to make all the reliefs *appear* to have the same size.[69] (Pl. 29). Whereas all other observers saw – probably with satisfaction, since it seemed to prove their case – that all the reliefs, including the uppermost ones, appeared to the eye to be of equal size, de Piles thought he had perceived that the top reliefs were larger, which, he points out, is an 'effect contrary to perspective'. He is aware of the rule according to which the reliefs should have this increased size, but although this rule is expounded in books on perspective, it is, for all that, in no way a rule of perspective, 'because it is only made use of when thought to be opportune.' Yet, even if all reliefs were made of equal size, he continues, they would not run counter to perspective 'and it can, therefore, be said with better reason that there is a rule of *bienséance* in perspective which assists vision and makes objects more agreeable to the eye.' He believes that on this basis 'rules of *bienséance* could be established'.[70] In the same year that de Piles wrote these lines, Colbert ordered the sculptor Girardon to have castings made of the reliefs; they arrived in Paris three years later.[71]

69. See, for instance, the remarks made by Chantelou, *Journal du voyage en France du Cavalier Bernin*, Paris, 1930, pp. 274 f. also Charles Perrault, *Mémoires*, p. 78.

70. op. cit., pp. 94 f.: 'Dans la Colonne Trajane nous voyons que les Figures les plus elevées sont plus grandes que celles d'en bas et font un effet tout contraire à la Perspective, puisqu'elles augmentent à mesure qu'elles s'éloignent. Je sçay qu'il y a une Règle, qui donne le moyen de les faire de la sorte; et quoy qu'elle soit dans quelques Livres de Perspective, elle n'est pas pour cela Règle de Perspective, puisqu'on ne s'en sert que lors seulement qu'on le juge à propos: car si par exemple les Figures qui sont au haut de la Colonne Trajane, n'estoient que de la mesme grandeur de celles qui sont au bas, elles ne seroient pas pour cela contre la Perspective; et ainsi l'on peut dire avec plus de raison, que c'est une Règle de Bienséance dans la Perspective, pour soulager la veue, et pour luy rendre les objets plus agréables. C'est sur ce fondement général que dans la Perspective on peut pour ainsi dire établir des Règles de Bienséance, quand l'occasion s'en rencontre.'

71. Clément, op. cit., V, p. 289.
Charles Perrault, *Mémoires*, p. 78.
Comptes, I, p. 548.
Blondel, who, one can be sure, had originally subscribed to the erroneous view about the size of the upper reliefs, adds to his quotation of Perrault's note on optical adjustment (p. 715) a sentence in which Perrault is supposed to cite the uniform size of all reliefs as additional proof that the ancients did not use optical adjustment. In fact, it is only in the *Ordonnance*, p. 100, that Perrault uses this argument.

Charles Perrault – accompanied, no doubt, by his brother, both eager
to disprove the theory of optical adjustment – measured the casts and
found, what they expected to find: the reliefs were, indeed, all of the
same size. Thus, one piece of evidence, invoked in support of optical
adjustment, had failed. De Piles had been proved wrong too – yet, his
arguments held good just the same, whether in this instance the top
reliefs had been increased in size or not: adjustments had been made in
the past and were made all the time for what he called *bienséance*; they
had nothing to do with optical corrections.

Proportions, then, can and ought to be changed. Yet, though imagination and judgment are needed when choosing the right proportion for
the particular work, they can move only within certain limits. The rules
remain effective, branding any transgression beyond these limits as
licence, a hideous crime in the eyes of the classical architect. The permissible limits were narrow, sometimes cut so finely that the modern
eye has difficulties in noticing them at all, but for the architect trained
in the classical tradition they were real tolerances, which allowed him
to create true works of art.[72] The beauty and organic life of classical
style rested on these slight deviations from the canon, and to make use
of them at the right place, in the right manner needed great experience.
The judicious handling of these adjustments was the touchstone by
which to evaluate the work and its artist. No wonder that architects set
great store by this freedom, restricted though it was: its limitations may
even have enhanced its value. That architects thought indeed along these
lines, is testified by Perrault himself. 'The majority of architects,' he comments on one occasion, 'believe that the aim of architecture consists in
knowing how to change proportions, with discretion as they call it, taking
into account the different circumstances of the various aspects and various
sizes of buildings;' they even maintain, he notes another time, that 'the
judicious handling of this change of proportions is one of the most
exquisite aspects of their art', and talk about it 'as if it does them the

72. For examples of permitted tolerances, see Appendix V.

greatest honour'.[73] According to Desgodets, the architects themselves told Perrault that 'the whole talent of an architect consists in being able to manage this change well, which must be put into practice at all times'.[74]

The slightly sarcastic tone, in which Perrault relates these sentiments, indicates that he failed to understand what the architects were referring to, much as Blondel failed to understood Perrault's physiological arguments. Once again, the difference between the two sides is brought out by the different way in which Blondel and Perrault render the Vitruvian text. Vitruvius wrote that adjustments should certainly be made, so that the building 'may seem to be rightly planned and the elevation may lack nothing' (which is Granger's translation of 'uti id videatur recte esse formatum in aspectuque nihil desideretur').[75] Blondel, who in this instance keeps fairly close to the text, conveys the meaning that owing to adjustment nothing less than perfection is achieved ('Je ne crois pas que l'on puisse douter qu'il ne faille augmenter ou diminuer les mesures ... et par ce moyen faire ensorte qu'il ne manque rien à leur perfection'), whereas Perrault, straying this time far from the text, makes Vitruvius say that adjustments are necessary as long as essential things remain unaffected ('Je ne crois pas que l'on doive douter qu'il ne soit nécessaire d'ajouter ou de diminuer en changeant les proportions ... pourveu que l'on ne touche point aux choses essentielles').[76]

Blondel's translation is in line with the general belief that the ultimate refinement of architecture depends on the wise application of adjustments.

73. *Ordonnance*, p. 29: 'La pluspart des Architectes croyent, que le fin de l'Architecture consiste à sçavoir changer les proportions avec prudence, ainsi qu'ils disent, ayant égard aux différentes circonstances de la diversité des Aspects et des grandeurs des édifices.'

Vitruvius, p. 204, note 3: '... la plus grande partie des Architectes et des Sculpteurs ... tiennent que la pratique judicieuse de ce changement des proportions est une des choses des plus fines de leur art.'

Ordonnance, p. 96: 'Les Architectes en parlent comme de ce qui leur fait le plus d'honneur, et prétendent que c'est dans la pratique des règles qu'ils ont pour cela, que consiste l'excellence de leur Art.'

74. op. cit., p. 21.
75. Vitruvius, VI, ii, 4.
76. Blondel, op. cit., p. 704.
Vitruvius, p. 204.

This conviction provides, I think, the clue to the eagerness with which architects seized on those passages where Vitruvius advocated corrections for optical reasons. Here seemed to be offered a rational explanation for a somewhat vague notion which in its effect, though difficult to define, was yet remarkable, bringing forth qualities as essential as *grâce* and the *je ne sais quoi*. The theory of adjustment was welcomed as being based on the science of perspective, which had lost little of the fascination that artists of the Renaissance had felt for it; it was welcomed, too, because architects hoped that the prestige which they enjoyed by being able to claim a scientific basis for architecture, would be enhanced through a rationalization of a practice that was still dominated by rule of thumb. For this reason, with Blondel as their spokesman, they reacted so sharply when Perrault rejected the theory outright. His stand was definite and uncompromising. He calls, as mentioned before, the change of proportions 'a bad practice', an 'abuse', not only useless, but *vicieux*, and believes that 'there is no reason at all for distorting and spoiling proportions'. Optical adjustment is 'not a good cure for an alleged fault', therefore, 'proportions must not be changed.'[77] Although these and similar remarks are unambiguous, they could be thought, being made in pursuance of his psychological and physiological arguments, to apply only to the specific case of optical adjustment. However, in the opening paragraph of the chapter that deals with 'the abuse of change of proportions' he gives his verdict in terms that are unmistakably directed against the concept of adjustment in general, revealing the reason for his opposition and, at the same time, bringing into the open the whole aim of his book. I shall, he declares, 'finish this treatise with a paradox, just as I began it with another which also relates to the change of proportions. Because, in the preface, I have tried to show that, since most architectural proportions are arbitrary and do not belong to the number of things that have a positive and natural beauty, there is nothing that could prevent one from making some changes to the established proportions and from being able to invent

77. see above notes, 24, 25, 27 on pages 77-78.

other proportions that are just as beautiful. Now, in this place, I maintain that, once these proportions have been regulated, they must not be changed any more and made different in different buildings for optical reasons and for the difference of aspects which they may have.'[78] The contrast between this point of view and the credo of the architects could not be more pronounced.[79]

It is no wonder that they were alarmed. Their ability to make use of permissible limits and their skill in adapting measurements to the specific task in hand were their passports to the status of an artist; more than that, it represented a degree of artistic freedom which, at a time when art was subjugated to stringent rules, they were anxious to retain. Understandably, they opposed any attempt at extending the realm of fixed rules still further.

Thus, what seemed to be a dispute about an abstruse problem, turns out to be a conflict of basic importance: the clash between the artists, jealously guarding any degree of freedom they can claim, and a scientist, expert in quite different fields, who, being primarily interested in the theoretical superstructure of architecture, is eager to bar from an important part of this architecture a diversity that to him seems random and meaningless.

Two years after the publication of the *Ordonnance*, Colbert's successor, Louvois, asked architectural experts for their opinion on Perrault's Arc de Triomphe. At an extraordinary assembly, attended by Blondel,

78. *Ordonnance*, p. 96: 'Chapitre VII. De l'abus du changement des Proportions . . . Cet examen est ce que j'ay intention de faire dans ce Chapitre, afin de finir ce traité par un paradoxe, comme je l'ay commencé par un autre, qui appartient aussi au changement des Proportions. Car j'ay tasché de faire voir dans la Préface, que la pluspart des Proportions de l'Architecture estant arbitraires, et n'estant point du nombre de ces choses qui ont une beauté positive et naturelle, il n'y a rien qui doive empescher qu'on ne fasse quelque changement aux Proportions établies, et qu'on n'en puisse inventer d'autres qui paroissent aussi belles. Et je prétens icy que ces proportions ayant esté une fois reglées, elles ne doivent plus estre changées et rendues différentes dans des Edifices différens, par des raisons d'Optique et de la différence des aspects qu'ils peuvent avoir.'

79. In the next century, the majority of architects still subscribed to the theory of optical adjustment. A few, however, probably influenced by Perrault's arguments, dissented, the more notable ones being J. Courtonne (*Traité de la perspective*, Paris, 1725, pp. 99 f., taken over verbatim by J.-F. Blondel, *L'architecture françoise*, Paris, 1752, I, p. 69.) and Pierre Patte (*Mémoires sur les objets les plus importans de l'architecture*, Paris, 1769, p. 77).

Bullet, Gittard, d'Orbay and Félibien, they pronounced a devastating
verdict. Before, however, giving a detailed list of countless faults, they
made a remark which was aimed precisely at the issue that had caused
their conflict with Perrault and pinpointed his lack of understanding
for the refinements of their craft: they rejected the proportions of the
central arch as unsuitable for the purpose, but in particular because 'it is
embedded and confined in such a way that it seems too narrow for its
height although *it has its legitimate measures.*'[80] In other words, Perrault
failed because he thought it unnecessary to adjust the proportions
'according to place and situation'.

80. *Procès-verbaux*, II, p. 98 (20 July 1685). The emphasis given to the last words in the remark
quoted is mine. On 12 December 1678 (ibid., I, pp. 255 f.) the same members had seen the design
and had approved the ratio of 1:2 'comme une chose conforme aux règles et aux bons exemples';
now, with the model before them, they thought adjustments were necessary.

CHAPTER IV

The Orders

IT is reasonable to assume that the preface of a book stands in meaningful relationship to its main part; that it either presents in general terms what is subsequently given a detailed treatment, or that it sets out the reason for dealing with the subject chosen. Those who believe that Perrault had proclaimed in the preface the artist's freedom and the relativity of taste, would find it difficult to explain why a dogmatic book on the five Orders is preceded by this particular preface. If, on the other hand, the interpretation advanced in the last two chapters is accepted, preface and treatise appear to be linked in a sensible way: the validity of the rules, which Perrault is now going to lay down, is reinforced by the arguments he had developed in the preface, or, as he himself expresses it, the preface gives the general reasons for justifying the liberty taken of proposing changes; the treatise itself, the detailed reasons for each particular change.[1]

What, then, does Perrault wish to achieve when taking on the intricate subject of the Orders? In the dedication to Colbert he calls the project 'quite bold and unusual' and speaks of the *nouveautés* the book contains; but then he claims nothing more startling than that 'those who should wish to put its rules into practice will find them of considerable usefulness, since they make things easy that so far had the habit of being troublesome.' They are troublesome because of 'the perplexing confusion in which modern authors have left the major part of what concerns the five Orders'.[2] His rules will be definite; they will also be easy to

1. *Ordonnance*, p. XXIII.
2. ibid., Epître: '. . . il y a apparence que les curieux . . . verront avec plaisir les nouveautez que ce Livre contient, et que ceux qui voudront pratiquer ses règles, trouveront une utilité considérable dans la facilité qu'elles apportent aux choses qui avoient de coutume de leur faire plus de peine . . . il falloit encore débrouiller l'embarras et la confusion où les Auteurs Modernes ont laissé la plus grande partie de ce qui appartient aux cinq espèces de Colonnes.'

remember,[3] or, rather, because they have the virtue of being simple, they can claim to be definite. This is the ever recurring theme: the facility with which his proportions can be remembered and applied.

Perrault distinguishes three manners in architecture: 'the *Ancienne* which Vitruvius has taught us, the *Antique* which we study in Roman monuments, and the *Moderne* on which we have books written during the last 120 years'.[4] The manner he would like to see re-established is the first, which we would call the Greek style, known to him only through Vitruvius.[5] Its inventors, so he claims, had achieved perfection by applying simple proportions, which were based on whole figures.[6] Why, later-on, architects gave up these easy proportions and, instead, adopted 'fractional and difficult' ones, is incomprehensible to him.[7] When recommending ratios expressed in whole numbers, he is, however, not motivated by any thought of establishing a proportional system which, based on a scale of interrelated numbers, would reflect, in some mysterious way, those embodied in the laws of nature. This idea, much alive during the preceding century and taken up again in his own time, was alien to Perrault's predominantly rational way of thinking. In a preliminary chapter, dealing with the two different manners of arriving at the proportions of the Orders, he makes his position clear.

Two methods, he explains in this chapter, have been used by architects 'for establishing the proportional dimensions of those parts that make up the columns'.[8] The module, usually half the diameter of the column, is the

3. ibid., p. XXVI: He hopes that through his book he may be the cause 'que l'on donne aux Règles des Ordres d'Architecture la précision, la perfection, et la facilité de les retenir qui leur manquent'.
4. ibid., p. 8.
5. ibid., p. XXII: '. . . ce que j'avance de nouveau, n'est point tant pour corriger l'Antique que pour tascher de le rétablir dans son ancienne perfection.'
6. ibid., p. XXI: '. . . y ayant grande apparence que les premiers inventeurs des proportions de chaque Ordre . . . les ont faites actuellement justes . . .'
7. ibid., p. XXI: '. . . je ne sçay pas, et ne croy pas aussi que l'on puisse sçavoir, les raisons qui ont porté les Architectes à suivre des proportions rompues et difficiles, sans nécessité, et d'affecter de changer les anciennes qui estoient aisées estant de nombres entiers.'
8. ibid., p. 3.
On these two methods see P. H. Scholfield, op. cit., pp. 22, 39 f.

unit common to both, as far as the major parts of the column – base, shaft, capital, entablature – are concerned; but, whereas one method retains this module for recording the sizes of smaller parts also, dividing it for that purpose into usually thirty smaller units or minutes, the other method gives up, at this point, the modular unit altogether. The method then adopted is to divide the major member into as many equal units as is most convenient and share them out among the smaller parts in the required proportion. Perrault had become familiar with the second method and its advantages through his work on Vitruvius. In a note to Vitruvius's text, he points out that with the first method increasingly smaller details can, by necessity, only be expressed in awkward fractional figures:[9] the second method, on the other hand, by its process of division into equal units and by repeating this process in a sequence of successive subdivisions, operates with whole numbers only. The reason why he prefers a method which expresses proportions in simple ratios is not that it always relates the whole to its parts; this, he says, gives no visual enjoyment, since the eye is not receptive to any kind of correlation except that of well-ordered symmetry. What attracts him to this method is 'the ease it offers to the memory for retaining the measurements'.[10] Of the two methods, the modular one is, no doubt, inferior as a proportional system, but it is not so much its imperfection as the awkwardness of its application that caused Perrault to reject it. His comments on the so-called attic base and on the different ways in which the two systems deal with it make that evident.

The method of successive subdivisions prescribed by Vitruvius for this base is, so runs Perrault's argument, simple and clear. 'Once we know that the third part of the attic base gives the size of the plinth, the fourth that of the lower torus, and the sixth that of the upper one, it is almost

9. *Vitruvius*, p. 90, note 23.

10. *Ordonnance*, p. 4: He prefers the method used by the ancients 'non pas tant à cause qu'elle suppose toujours le rapport d'un tout à ses parties; car je ne croy pas qu'il résulte rien de là qui puisse estre agréable à la veue, n'y ayant proprement que les rapports d'ordre ou d'égalité qui la satisfassent, parce que les autres rapports ne luy sont pas mêsme sensibles. Mais ce que je trouve de meilleur dans la manière des Anciens, est la facilité qu'elle donne à la mémoire pour retenir les mesures . . .'

A similar remark on p. V.

impossible to forget the proportions of this base.' When, however, the
dimensions are given in modular minutes, they are harder to memorize.
'It is not the same,' Perrault continues, 'with 10, 7½ and 5 minutes with
which one measures the parts of this base, because the relation which these
numbers have among each other are not known,' since it is not obvious
that '10 is the third, 7½ the fourth and 5 the sixth part of the thirty minutes
that make up the total height of the base.'[11] This advantage would be
even more pronounced if the final subdivision of the attic base would be
made into seven parts, instead of the six usually prescribed. This would
lead, as he had remarked already in his *Vitruvius*, to the ridiculous result
of having to mark the size of one of the small fillets as 1 1/14 of
a minute.[12] This is not quite as far-fetched as it sounds, since Blondel,
undisturbed by the futility of it, works out modular ratios with great
accuracy, quoting, for instance, the height of the Doric entablature as
being 3 19/24 and that of the Corinthian cornice as 1 29/84 modules![13]

Blondel's procedure is an extreme case. His treatise on the Orders,
consisting of an endless number of dimensions often expressed in un-
wieldy figures, may very well have been an additional reason for Perrault
to discard the system of modular units when dealing with smaller parts,
and to aim at a simplified system. However, his assertion that modern
architects 'always use identical minutes' applied only to those authors
who, like Desgodets, were recording ancient monuments, or were,
for the sake of comparison, reducing the Orders of various authors to a
common denominator, as did Fréart and Blondel.[14] Not that he pretended
to introduce something new: on the contrary, he claimed to re-establish
the simple proportions of an original style which had only been abandoned by modern architects because they were unable to record the odd
measurements of ancient buildings in any other way. Yet, in his opinion,

---

11. ibid., p. 4.
12. *Vitruvius*, p. 90, note 23. The final division into seven parts is adopted, for instance, by
Alberti, Bullant and Mauclerc.
13. op. cit., I, pp. 44, 109. Similarly awkward figures are used by Scamozzi and Abraham Bosse.
14. Perrault had, no doubt, Fréart's and Blondels' treatises in mind when remarking (*Ordonnance*,
p. XIV) on the method used by modern architectural writers.

the right conclusion to be drawn from these irregularities was to assume that these buildings 'were obviously not the true originals'.[15] These words allude to a striking phrase from Fréart's widely-read book, in which the author pleaded that those wishing to study the Orders should first go to the source before examining the books written by modern authors, 'because the best books that we have on the subject are the works of the ancient masters that we see still standing'.[16] Perrault had already in the preface dealt with this argument, rejecting it outright. The few sentences of his reply are like an outline of the way in which he intended to proceed when composing his Orders. Assuming, he reasons, that 'the works we have of Antiquity are like books from which we must learn the proportions of architecture, then they are not the originals produced by the first and true authors; but they are only copies, differing among themselves, of which some are true and correct in one thing, some in another, so that in order to restore in architecture, as it were, the true sense of the text, it is necessary to go and look for it in these different copies; being generally approved works, each of them must contain something true and correct, the selection of which must obviously be based on the regularity of divisions, expressed not in unreasonable fractions, but in easy and convenient ones, like those of Vitruvius.'[17]

Perrault finds proof for Roman monuments being 'copies' and not 'originals' in the frequently encountered minute deviations of their

15. *Ordonnance*, p. 4: 'Ce qui a obligé les Modernes à se servir toûjours des mêmes minutes, est le besoin qu'ils ont eu souvent de marquer des grandeurs qui n'ont point de proportion, ny avec la grandeur du module entier, ny avec celles des autres parties . . . et ils ont été obligez d'en user ainsi, à cause qu'ils ne se sont proposé de donner les mesures que des ouvrages qui nous restent des Anciens, qui apparemment n'estant point les vrais originaux, n'ont pu avoir la juste précision des proportions que les premiers Inventeurs leurs avoient données.'

16. op. cit., p. 4.

17. *Ordonnance*, pp. XXII f.: 'Car enfin ma pensée est, que si les ouvrages que nous avons de l'Antique sont comme des livres où nous devons apprendre les proportions de l'Architecture, ces ouvrages ne sont pas les originaux faits par les premiers et véritables Auteurs; mais seulement des copies différentes entre-elles, et dont les unes sont fidèles et correctes en une chose, les autres en une autre: ensorte que dans l'Architecture pour restituer le véritable sens du texte, s'il faut ainsi parler, il est nécessaire de l'aller chercher dans ces différentes copies, qui estant des ouvrages approuvez, doivent contenir chacun quelque chose de correct et fidèle, dont le choix doit apparemment estre fondé sur la régularité des divisions non rompues sans raison, mais faciles et commodes, telles qu'elles sont dans Vitruve.'

measurements from round figures; when, for instance, the plinth of a base, instead of being 10 minutes high, is half a minute higher or lower, or when the length of one of the columns of the Pantheon is 19 modules and $16\frac{1}{2}$ minutes instead of the round 20 modules.[18] There seems to be no reason why the 'first inventors' should have stopped short of the whole figures, nor why the architects who succeeded them should have made these changes, except that they did not notice them.[19] This, chance or negligent workmanship are the only explanations of which he can think.[20] The reason for the changes he is going to propose are, on the contrary, 'clear and evident', namely, as he does not tire of telling, 'the ease with which to make divisions and the ease with which to remember them'.[21]

The proportions Perrault prescribes, supposedly derived from an imaginary *ancien* style, do not differ basically from those set forth in numerous treatises of his own time and of the preceding century. Perrault's attic base, for instance, conforms to the proportions prescribed by Vitruvius; his and Palladio's base are identical.[22] It is, however, significant that of the two it is Palladio, the practical architect, who admits a variation: by changing two dimensions, he, in fact, offers two slightly modified versions of the base, one as described in the text, the other as presented in the design. This is not an isolated instance in Palladio's treatise: having divided the three parts of the Tuscan base in the ratio of $4 : 3 : 1$, he remarks that the smallest moulding 'can also be made somewhat smaller', which he then carries into effect in the drawing, with

18. ibid., pp. 4, XXI.

19. *Vitruvius*, p. 114, note 9: '. . . les Architectes qui ont changé ces proportions dans le théâtre de Marcellus et dans les Colisées ne l'ont point fait avec raison; mais seulement pour n'y avoir pas pris-garde.'

20. *Ordonnance*, p. XIX: '. . . les choses dont ils ne pourront trouver de raison . . . n'ont point d'autre fondement que le hazard et le caprice des ouvriers . . .' Similarly, p. XXI.

21. ibid., p. XXII: '. . . ceux que je propose se trouveront icy fondez sur des raisons claires et évidentes, telles que sont la facilité de faire les divisions et celle de les retenir.'

22. ibid., p. 45; Palladio, op. cit., I, p. 22; Vitruvius, III, v, 2.

If Perrault ever studied Palladio's treatise closely, he must have found the discrepancy between the dimensions of the attic base, as described in the text and as presented in the drawing, most disturbing. Because Palladio altered, on the drawing, the dimensions of two mouldings slightly, the simple ratios arrived at in the text by subdivision were lacking – the whole, as a consequence, not even adding up to the 30 minutes prescribed in the text.

the result that he once more abandons the ratio he had described. On another occasion, he introduces the base of the Corinthian Order, which is a variation of the attic base, with the advice that 'one can also vary some other parts, as is to be seen on the design.'[23] Blondel, aware that Palladio 'has in the details of his parts changed many things', assumes that he did it 'for the better effect'.[24]

Palladio is not alone in exercising some latitude in the application of his own rules. Often the measurements lack the precision one would expect in a treatise on the Orders: remarks, such as 'sometimes less' or 'sometimes more' qualify definite dimensions, and frequently, from the start, only approximate dimensions are given, being 'near to' or 'slightly less than' or 'a little more than' a round figure. Then again, size or proportion are definite, but the limits within which they are permitted to move are also specified.[25]

In the previous chapter it was shown that this comparatively flexible attitude was the outcome of the professional architect's experience and that in practice, modifications are always necessary in order to achieve the desired effect: this attitude was further encouraged by the variations observed on Roman monuments. For this reason, many writers, foremost among them Serlio and de l'Orme, published ancient fragments of the Orders, the proportions of which did not conform to their own rules laid down only a few pages before, the difference being at times considerable. A French writer, after having given his rules for the Doric Order, refers his readers to Serlio's relevant chapter with its numerous ancient examples 'so that they can choose what is most pleasant to them', and commends the two variations he himself gives of almost every part of the Orders as being both 'in accordance with correct and perfect proportions'. Bosse, too, publishes two alternative sets of Orders, one

23. op. cit., pp. 19, 42 (Appendix V, 6, 8).
This is further evidence for a trend in Palladio's work noted by Wittkower, op. cit., p. 140, note 3.
24. op. cit., p. 119.
25. For documentation of this attitude, dealt with in this and the following two paragraphs, see Appendix V.

with the height of the entablature being a fifth of that of the column, and
the other a fourth, so as 'to give, if possible, general satisfaction', since
'taste and opinions differ regarding the proportions of the main members
of the Orders'.[26]

Compilations, such as Fréart's and Blondel's books, include the proportions adopted by various modern authors, which, naturally, are not
identical with the proportions the reader has been led to consider the
norm, in Fréart's case the examples taken from antiquity, in Blondel's
case the Order he calls Vitruvian. Blondel, treating all examples as being
of equal validity, declares that he 'thought the reader would like to see
here the opinions (of Vignola, Scamozzi and Palladio), so as to leave the
choice to the judgment of those who will have to use' the particular
Order to which he was referring, and Fréart, although critical of at least
some authors, sees the advantage of reducing the various designs to a
common denominator because it gives 'everybody the liberty of choosing
among them as he fancies and of following whichever of the authors . . .
he wishes, because they are all commonly approved.'[27]

As all writers on the Orders, with the exception of Vignola, thought
it necessary to modify and vary their rules to some extent, it is most likely
that they were in agreement with a warning, voiced by de l'Orme, not to
rely too much on precepts and general rules for the proportions, measurements and ornaments of columns, and likely also that they all endorsed
Aristotle's dictum, quoted by de l'Orme in this place, namely that 'men
of experience succeed even better than those who have theory without
experience'; this was endorsed especially, one suspects, by those whose
professional work brought them into contact with Perrault.[28]

It is against the background of this attitude, undogmatic and open-
minded considering the restraints imposed by classical principles, that
Perrault's attempt to arrive at fixed rules must be judged. The rules he

26. Mauclerc, see Appendix V, 18; Bosse, see Appendix V, 31.
27. Blondel, see Appendix V, 33; Fréart, see Appendix V, 25.
28. op. cit., fol. 195 r. Aristotle's remark (in W. D. Ross's translation) from Metaphysics, 981 a,
14.

lays down are final and do not permit any variation. The three instances where he admits the possibility of a different measurement only underline, through their insignificance, the complete absence of more essential variations and the finality with which everything else is advanced. For that reason, it may not be amiss to show how trivial his three concessions are: he allows firstly, the curve of the flutings of the Doric Order to be somewhat shallower than the one selected by him; secondly, the guttae of its entablature to be round as well as square or triangular; and, lastly, the use of a certain kind of moulding 'because it conforms to the opinion of some people,' although he has prescribed a different one.[29] If one adds to this his advice that the filling of flutings, a doubtful feature in his opinion, 'should only rarely be made use of,' the number of occasions on which he swayed slightly from his usual decisiveness is complete. Everywhere else, throughout the ninety pages that make up the detailed description of the five Orders, it is the hard and fast rule that alone counts.[30]

The confidence with which Perrault presents his system is extraordinary. The positive tenor of his statements rests on his conviction that the method which produces these definite results is 'the best one can choose', 'the most reliable rule', the one he has taken as his guiding principle. It is somewhat disappointing to find that these glowing attributes refer to nothing more exciting than finding the mean between two extremes – the calculation of an average that would 'reconcile divers opinions and different examples encountered in architecture'.[31] However, this approach, prosaic, unimaginative and seemingly far removed from aesthetic considerations, is in line with Perrault's view that proportions are not the

29. *Ordonnance*, pp. 47, 50, 52.

30. ibid., p. 58.

31. ibid., p. 33: '. . . la médiocrité, que je considère comme la règle la plus certaine, pour concilier les opinions diverses et les exemples différens qui se rencontrent dans l'Architecture . . .'

p. 38: '. . . la médiocrité doit estre choisie comme la meilleure.'

p. 90: '. . . la médiocrité, que j'ay prise pour ma règle . . .'

In another place (p. 9), he compares his procedure to what 'les Jurisconsultes appellent le jugement des Rustiques, qui se donnoit dans les causes où les choses estoient tellement embrouillées, que les Juges les plus éclairez n'y pouvoient rien connoistre; ce jugement estoit de partager le différend par la moitié.'

cause of beauty: in addition, while statistics seem today a doubtful procedure for arriving at aesthetically satisfactory forms, this was not so in the seventeenth century. The mean then meant more than an arithmetical or geometrical term: its position between extremes was thought to coincide with perfection. It would be absurd to suggest that the idea of obtaining fixed rules by a method of averaging had for Perrault any metaphysical significance, but his thoughts were, no doubt, conditioned by a mental climate in which much of the thinking of an incomparably greater mind than Perrault's was 'built upon the notion of two extremes, between which there must be a mean,' as has been said of Pascal.[32] His dictum 'rien que la médiocrité n'est bon' is echoed, though on a lower level, by Perrault's professed intention always to follow 'la médiocrité que j'ai prise pour ma règle'; and Descartes's maxim of choosing 'amongst many opinions, all equally received, only the most moderate ones . . . because these are always most suited for putting into practice and are probably the best, for all excess has a tendency to be bad', must, we feel sure, have met with Perrault's wholehearted approval.[33] Thus, when he suggested the application of the mean as a solution for the reigning confusion in architectural proportions, his contemporaries not only recognized it as a familiar notion, but as one that had value and significance.

It must, however, be admitted that Perrault goes about his task with little method or care. In order to arrive at the mean measurements of the major members of the Orders, he devises a number of tables which list examples taken from ancient monuments and from architectural treatises, from Vitruvius, Serlio, Vignola, Palladio, Scamozzi and a few others. The selection, however, is arbitrary: authors and buildings which are present in one table do not appear in another, the total number in

32. Borgerhoff, op. cit., p. 114.
33. Pascal, *Pensées*, No. 378, *Oeuvres*, XIII, p. 288. See also *Pensées*, Nos. 69–72, 381.
    Descartes, *Discours de la méthode*, *Oeuvres*, ed. Ch. Adam and P. Tannery, Paris, 1902, VI, p. 23.
    In a letter to Conrart, Charles Perrault speaks of 'cette médiocrité si souhaitable et si recherchée' and maintains 'qu'on ne doit pas me blâmer si je me la suis proposée, et si quelquefois j'ai refusé de m'élever pour ne me pas écarter de cette route moyenne que j'ai choisie.' (cit., Rouger, *Contes de Perrault*, p. XLV.).

each table and for each Order varies considerably, some, it seems, presenting a fair selection, others only an unconvincing assortment. Another quite extraordinary feature is the little attention he pays to accuracy, especially in the first part of the treatise. Some mistakes, it is true, are due to printer's errors, but, since a long list of errata corrects misspellings and mutilated text, a less careless author would have noticed, and included in his list, wrong figures and names, equally evident and misleading. Other errors are just due to negligence. In some cases, Perrault must have gone wrong when copying measurements marked on Desgodets's engravings and, at times, when transposing figures from his own notes. He is also careless in arranging the tables; the thoughtless misplacing of a dividing line leads in one table to devastating results: a number of records assembled there are thrown into great disarray, with the size of Vignola's particularly tall entablature badly affected; it is listed as too low by two whole modules. Perrault is so little troubled by this patent mistake, or so completely unaware of it, that he carries the wrong size into the text. In another table, he lists the sizes given by modern authors for the heights of pedestals, but forgets that he had already supplied the same information in a preceding table and consequently fails to notice the difference between the two sets of figures, due to mistakes in both tables; here rectification to establish correspondence was certainly needed.

Another set of mistakes is connected with Perrault's main source for the measurements of ancient buildings, *Les édifices antiques de Rome* by Desgodets. He probably became aware of this work only after he had partly completed his manuscript. Seeing the great quantity of detailed records which Desgodets had brought back from Rome, he considered them a welcome corroboration of his main thesis, that of the random variety of ancient monuments, and decided to incorporate the new material into the existing text. However, once again he is not too scrupulous in this work; the seams of various interpolations are more noticeable than was necessary; references in the text to the original tables were not rectified when the new information was inserted into

them and, as a consequence, they have become meaningless. The many
new measurements now available also prompted him, in one or two
instances, to introduce a manner of arriving at the mean different from
the one already described in the manuscript. In these cases, Perrault
troubled neither to remove from the text the first manner, nor to give
an explanation for a duplication that was obviously unnecessary, since
both ways led to the same result.

The mistakes so far dealt with are numerous and, at times, of some
magnitude. They are, however, of little consequence and prove only
that Perrault worked in an extremely perfunctory manner: since he did
not set out to find the average of all measurements listed, but was only
concerned with the establishment of the mean between two extremes,
the correct figures would in the end have made no difference, provided
that the figures at the low and high end of the scale were correct.

Perrault does not always aim at arithmetical accuracy when working out
the mean; at times he is satisfied with a measurement that 'is approx-
imately equidistant from the extremes.'[34] However, more often than not,
he wants to establish the precise mean. If in these cases mistakes occur that
affect the extremes – and they do on a few occasions – then it is difficult to
believe that the wrong figures are due to negligence and not to intentional
'rectification'. For instance, only by changing Palladio's clearly marked
dimension of two modules into three was he able to arrive at a mean of
four modules for the pedestal of the Tuscan Order, and only by somewhat conveniently mistaking the feet, by which Desgodets had marked a
certain dimension, for modules did he achieve the expected mean of the
Ionic pedestal. When, in another table, a high extreme of 44 required a
low extreme of 40 minutes in order to arrive at a mean of 42, and when
we then see him change a clearly marked figure in Fréart from 39 to 40,
so as to eliminate an inconveniently low extreme, it is once more not
unreasonable to question his good faith. Finally, when he concludes
from a correct total of 10 modules 5 minutes that this is a figure 'of which
one half amounts to 4 modules 20 minutes', this being the figure he

34. *Ordonnance*, p. 10; also p. 27.

requires for the mean, one wonders then which is more astounding: his indifference to accuracy or his trust in the reader's lack of attention.[35]

This complete disregard for basic arithmetic, this careless attitude that does not trouble about accuracy, and this cavalier manner that changes figures when required, point to one conclusion: Perrault devised the system of proportions first, and only then arranged and selected the comparative figures of ancient and modern Orders in such a way as to provide the required mean. He did not proceed the other way round. As we shall see, in his choice of proportions he kept to a middle way, avoiding all extremes, but the semblance of arithmetical accuracy is an afterthought, no more than a veneer with which he hoped to give his work an impressive finish. Reading his text and then glancing through his tables, noticing the errors and inaccuracies, one has the distinct impression that Perrault is so strongly convinced of the correctness and reasonableness of his proportions that he takes little trouble about the score of detailed measurements from which, so he pretends, the proportions proposed by him have been derived. He was always fascinated by devising a theory, or as he called it, a system, which would resolve intricate problems, but was little concerned, except in his anatomical research, about subjecting these theories to rigorous tests. The attitude that made him present comprehensive theories on subjects such as elasticity, weight, transparency, the origin of life and the function of the soul, without the support of a solid base of experimental research is not unlike the one that made him treat the evidence for his architectural system in such a perfunctory manner.

We shall, therefore, leave this somewhat deceptive part of his theory, from which nothing of positive value can be gleaned, and proceed to look closer at his proportions and the kind of Orders they produce. The first part of the book deals with 'things common to all Orders,' that is, the pedestal, the column and the entablature, and also the rate of diminution and projection applicable to these parts. A first, conventional, chapter introduces the five Orders and their different characters; the

35. see Appendix VI for a more detailed account of these mistakes.

second deals with the two ways of determining proportions, the 'Vitru-vian' and the modular system, of which we have already spoken. In the chapters that follow he discusses the proportions of the parts just men-tioned, separately and in detail.

It soon becomes apparent that simplification and unification are his main objectives; simplifying the set of proportions, which at various times and in various forms had been proposed in numerous treatises, and unifying those measurements that normally differ from Order to Order or, where distinction is desirable, confining the differences at least within regular progression. Not that this orderly and unifying principle was absent from the proportional rules normally followed. All those who had written on the Orders adopted the Vitruvian rule which prescribed one module as the height of all bases, a size to which the architects of the ancient monuments had, to a great extent, kept. Similarly, there existed general agreement about the dimensions of the capitals: one module for the Tuscan, and the Doric, two modules and one sixth for the Corinthian and the Composite, the Ionic being placed in a separate category. Naturally, Perrault made no changes in these measurements, where standardization had already been achieved, although he regrets 'the somewhat cumbersome proportions' which, for the Ionic capital, he cannot avoid prescribing.[36]

For a few other features an overall regularity was proposed by at least some authors. Palladio and Scamozzi maintained a constant ratio between the base and the cornice of the pedestals, and Vignola, with other writers following him, fixed the height of the entablature throughout the five Orders to one fourth of that of the column; this nevertheless, meant that, with the length of the column increasing, the entablature differed in height from Order to Order. Finally, the progression in the modular height of the columns generally tended to proceed by fairly regular, though rarely identical, steps.

The essence of proportional systems is, of course, regularity; but, as their authors could choose from a wide range of acceptable ratios and

36. *Ordonnance*, p. 31.

were thus able to change them from one part to the next within the same
Order and, even more so, for the same parts of different Orders, they
achieved orderly integration without sacrificing that degree of differentiation which alone infuses the likeness of an organism into the Orders.

In Perrault's eyes this diversity is a fault; a blemish he seeks to remove
by introducing uniformity to a far greater extent than ever tried before.
With this aim in mind, he contrives simple, easy rules that are to control
three important aspects: progression of the columns, progression of the
pedestals, and height of the entablature.

Progression of the columns, that is, the difference in the height of the
column of one Order, including base and capital, from the height of the
next Order, should be in whole numbers. Here, however, he encounters a
difficulty, for the only method by which this could be achieved without
transgressing classical boundaries, was by using the one adopted by
Serlio. He started with 12 modules for the Tuscan Order and proceeded
with four steps of two modules each, which led finally to the 20 modules
of the Composite Order. This, however, meant an exceptionally short
Tuscan column, and Perrault, no doubt, rules this out as offending his
principle of adherence to the middle way. His solution to the problem is
quite ingenious. At that time, the module commonly used was equal to
half the diameter of the column. Perrault proposed a new, smaller
module, equal to only a third of the diameter. The reduction has the
effect that one and a half new modules take the place of one normal
module.[37] A progression, then, that starts with a Tuscan of the still
acceptable size of $14\frac{2}{3}$ modules and proceeds via 16, $17\frac{1}{3}$ and $18\frac{2}{3}$ to the
20 modules of the Composite produces, when converted into new
modules, a tidy progression from 22 to 30 with intervals of two new
modules between each Order.[38] (Pl. 30).

This device proved helpful also for achieving a regular progression for
the pedestals. Vignola had already laid down the uniform rule for making

37. He explains the *petit module* on p. 5, comparing it in a 'Table des Modules' with the other
two kind of modules.
38. *Ordonnance*, pp. 6, 11 f.

the height of the pedestals a third of that of the column. This ratio, applied to Perrault's own range of columns, did not conform with his desire for regularity, but, when applied to a range from 12 to 20 modules, in other words to Serlio's range, a scale emerged that showed, again when converted into his new modules, the heights of the pedestals to move in equal steps of one module each, from six modules of the Tuscan to ten of the Composite pedestal.[39]

It is hard to believe that Perrault seriously hoped to succeed in displacing the time-honoured module of half a diameter by his new modules. That he nevertheless proposed it, shows how important regularity was to him. He himself had not much use for his new *petit module*, after it had helped him out on these two occasions. He still mentions it here and there, but more often than not quotes the normal *moyen module*, or both figures at the same time.[40] On the whole, the regularity that he had achieved was brought about by nothing more than some kind of arithmetical trick. The actual proportions of column and pedestal were not basically changed by this device. When, however, he deals with the entablature, the third principal part of the Order, the situation is different. He still gives the size proposed by him in *petits modules*, although there was no need for this, since a measurement carried out in normal modules would also have resulted in a whole figure. In this instance, the new scale was, therefore, of no consequence; but what Perrault has to say about the entablature and what to suggest, contains, indeed, some real innovation.

The proportion of the entablature, he argues, ought to be the best regulated of all, but, in fact, we find a disturbing variety. 'There is hardly a building, ancient or modern, where this proportion is not different.' The architects of ancient monuments had the sound idea of rectifying the very low entablatures they saw on buildings conforming to Vitruvian precepts; but by overdoing this correction, they produced tall columns with 'entablatures of a height that seems unbearable' and

39. ibid., pp. 6, 15 ff. Whether Perrault intentionally applied his scale to Serlio's range, it is impossible to say.
40. for instance, ibid., p. 39.

sinned against what Perrault considers one of the principal architectural rules, that of apparent solidity. 'Nothing is more destructive to the beauty of a building than to observe proportions among the constituent parts that are contrary to what should establish this solidity, for instance when these parts seem incapable of supporting what they carry.' Modern architects, he explains, have tried, in their turn, to correct these excessive faults, but they never went to the root of the trouble, the lack of apparent solidity. With these particular components of the Orders, solidity depends, naturally, on the weight of the entablature and the strength of the column. The weight of the entablature is dependent on its height, but the strength of the column depends on its thickness, not on its height. For that reason, it is fundamentally wrong to relate the height of the entablature to the height of the column: it has to be related to its diameter.[41]

Perrault's proposal ensures that the appearance of solidity is taken care of automatically, since the smaller the circumference of the column, the lighter the entablature will be. It has the further advantage that the height of the entablature can be expressed in precise units, the same for all five Orders: twice the diameter of the column. This means that his entablatures will be of four normal or six *petits modules*, a measurement that 'is equidistant from the extremes to be found on ancient monuments'.[42]

The improvement no doubt most important to him was the regularity thus achieved and the ease with which the uniform size of the entablatures could be remembered. Significantly, only towards the end of the book, as an afterthought, does a point which he had overlooked mentioning in the appropriate place occur to him, namely that this uniform measurement is necessarily accompanied by varying ratios of column to entablature, because the columns increase in height from Order to Order. Since in his opinion, 'the eye is not even receptive' to these ratios, he apparently prefers the definite and equal size of the entablature to a uniform ratio as

41. ibid., pp. 7 f.
42. ibid., p. 9.

proposed by 'the three most famous authors who have written on architecture,' namely Vignola, Palladio and Scamozzi.[43] He indicates that these authors have been satisfied with approximate ratios. Although this is not correct (and somewhat disingenous of him to suggest), he is, nevertheless, right in pointing out that under his rule the ratio, admittedly, does change, but that it changes automatically at a steady rate. It is typical of his whole approach that, unable in this case to avoid figures that vary from Order to Order, he takes pride in having conceived a scheme by which the ratio of entablature to column is at least 'always decreasing equally by one third'.[44] It can be assumed that the 'three most famous authors' were, in contrast with him, well satisfied with having to cope, within bounds, with an amount of variety that enhanced the individual character of each Order.

As for Perrault, not even the regularity so far brought about satisfied him. One of his occasional remarks could serve as a motto for his eager efforts to achieve standardization. He had noticed that the dimensions of a moulding, which appeared on all Orders, was, in the Ionic Order, because of its special character, clearly defined. 'I cannot see any reason,' is his reaction, 'for changing (this dimension) in any of the other Orders.'[45] Equally revealing is the reason he gives, in a different context, for believing his method to be preferable to the ones commonly used by other authors. They vary the proportions of identical parts from Order to Order, making, for instance, architrave and frieze equal in size in one Order and not in another, whereas 'if we follow the third (that is, his) method, we shall always make them equal'.[46] He

43. ibid., pp. 111 f.
44. loc. cit.,: '. . . la proportion de l'Entablement allant toujours diminuant également d'un tiers de la hauteur de tout l'Entablement dans chaque Ordre, à mesure qu'il est plus léger et plus délicat.'
   Vignola prescribes a ratio of 1:4 for all five Orders; Palladio and Scamozzi retain this ratio for the Tuscan and Doric, but reduce it to 1:5 for the taller Orders.
45. ibid., p. 33: 'Mais ce qui me détermine davantage à cette proportion de l'Astragale du haut des Colonnes, est celle qui est reglée dans l'Ordre Ionique, où il doit estre égal à la largeur de l'Oeil de la Volute . . . car cette proportion estant déterminée dans cet Ordre, je ne voy point de raison de la changer dans les autres.'
46. ibid., p. XVI.

will not rest until other features, apart from the three already considered, have fallen into line; until they, too, are subjected to simple proportions, identical wherever possible. No author had ever aspired to such a high degree of regimentation. The three parts that compose the pedestal, the three that form the entablature, the mouldings that mark the upper and lower limits of the column's shaft, and the degree of diminution and of projections are all given proportions or dimensions that are definite and uniform with the occasional exception only, of the Doric and the Tuscan.[47]

Even here he does not stop: having been successful in regulating the progression of the total height of the pedestal, he is now going to apply the same principle to the details of its base and cornice. Just as the length of the column increases in proportion to the more refined and delicate character of the Order, so it is with 'the mouldings (which) also become less crude as their numbers increase at a steady rate, the base of the Tuscan pedestal having two mouldings, the Doric three, the Ionic four, the Corinthian five and the Composite six. In the same way, the cornice of the pedestal has three mouldings in the Tuscan, four in the Doric, five in the Ionic, six in the Corinthian and seven in the Composite.'[48]

Standardization, however, continues. There does not seem to be any reason why only the number of mouldings should grow in an orderly fashion; the same could be done for the number of units into which the height of base and cornice of the pedestals are to be divided, those units on which the proportional ratios of these mouldings are based. The greater the number of mouldings, the finer must be the gradation of the division. Again, we have the same arrangement – an increase in even steps. This time, the scale for the number of units into which base and cornice should be divided moves from six to ten units for the base, and

47. In all Orders, the proportions of base to die to cornice of the pedestal are as 2:5:1; of architrave to frieze to cornice of the entablature (the Doric excepted) as 6:6:8; the projection of the cornice of the entablature (again the Doric excepted) is fixed at 48 minutes, thus equalling its height, the diminution of all columns (except the Tuscan) at 4 minutes, the thickness of the moulding at the lower end of the shaft at 3 minutes, that of the upper end at $3\frac{1}{3}$ minutes (ibid., pp. 18 f., 7, 30, 22, 32, 39.).
48. ibid., p. 36.

from eight to twelve for the cornice. Perrault illustrates the somewhat complicated scheme by a line drawing, explaining that 'the arabic figures are for the number of parts by which base and cornice are divided; the Roman figures for the number of mouldings of which each base and each cornice are composed,' and obviously considers the sequence of these figures so important that he reproduces the same diagram in each of the five chapters that deal with the details of the Orders[49] (Fig. below).

To proceed further in this drive for rigid uniformity would, one feels, lead to the negation of everything that marks the beauty of the five Orders. In comparison with Perrault's inflexible products, with dimensions

Tofcan.   Dorique.   Ionique.   Corinthien.   Compofite.

Perrault, Diagram of proportional system for pedestals. From *Ordonnance*.

49. ibid., pp. 36 f.

and proportions brought into strict order, the classical Orders, as we know them from the writings of other authors, seem to be filled with a life of their own. In spite of being subjected to the discipline of rules, they preserve, in each of the five variations, a good measure of individuality.

The regulations concerning base and cornice of the pedestal have taken us already into the second part of the book, where Perrault deals with the minutiae of classical doctrine. Before following him on this tortuous route we may like to pause and reflect on a different aspect arising from the proportions he has proposed so far.

Many authors of books on architectural theory had been practising architects: it would not be surprising to discover that, when using the Orders on their own buildings, they did not adhere pedantically to dimensions and proportions laid down in their writings. Various practical and aesthetic considerations would always call for adjustments. We have seen that most architects, in fact, considered that the skill of a good architect consisted in adjusting the rules when circumstances demanded it. In this respect, Perrault's case was different. 'Once these proportions have been regulated, they must not be changed and rendered differently on different buildings.' We have quoted this decisive dictum before.[50] When, therefore, measurements which he prescribed in his book are at variance with those found on a building with which his name has been connected, then the discrepancy is of some consequence. This is not the place to go into the vexed question of the authorship of the Louvre Colonnade; only as far as conclusions can be drawn – and have, in fact, been drawn – from the conflict between theory and practice, will it concern us here.

The Corinthian Order of the Colonnade differs in three major measurements from the Corinthian Order of the *Ordonnance*: the column, including base and capital, is 21 modules high instead of $18\frac{2}{3}$; the capital is higher by more than a quarter, and the entablature has a height of over

50. ibid., p. 96 (see above chapter III, p. 93, note 78.).

5 modules instead of Perrault's uniform measurement of 4 modules[51] (Pl. 31). These differences are of a magnitude that has caused recent authors to acclaim them as important supporting evidence for their case against Perrault's authorship.[52] The discrepancy between building and book gives, indeed, rise to grave doubts, yet the situation is not quite as clear cut as these critics would have it.

The design of another monument, the Arc de Triomphe at the Porte St Antoine, is ascribed to Perrault. (Pl. 17). Whereas the controversy about the identity of the architect responsible for the Louvre Colonnade broke out during Perrault's lifetime, with the Perraults on one side and Le Vau and d'Orbay on the other, and while it never ceased to be waged, his authorship for the Arc de Triomphe has never seriously been challenged. Not only was he thought to be its designer by both friend and foe alike, and not only is it the only building for which he acknowledged full responsibility publicly – that is, in print as distinct from private communications made by him or his brother Charles – but it was also he who was blamed by the assembled members of the Academy for the numerous shortcomings of the design.[53] Yet, the measurements of the Corinthian Order of the Arc de Triomphe are identical with those of the Colonnade, only the capital being slightly lower, though still different from the one proposed in the *Ordonnance*. A recent writer, highly critical of Perrault, concluded that either d'Orbay was responsible for the design (an untenable assumption in view of his presence at the meeting of the Academy just mentioned), or that Perrault borrowed heavily from Le Brun's similar design.[54] Even if that should have been so, Perrault still identified himself with the work: for that reason, it seems

51. The measurements of the Colonnade were taken in the eighteenth century by Patte, *Mémoires sur les objets les plus importans de l'architecture*, Paris, 1769, Pls. XVIII ff., and confirmed fifty years later by Baltard, *Paris et ses monuments*, Paris, 1803, I.

52. Laprade, op. cit., pp. 324 ff.
Armand Sigwalt, *Une mystification de Charles Perrault*, Paris, 1948.

53. see above p. 94. In *Vitruvius*, p. 20, note 2, he speaks of the 'peu de largeur que je donnois à l'empatement (de l'Arc de Triomphe)', and p. 205, E of the statue 'que j'ay mis au haut de l'Arc de Triomphe.'

54. Laprade, op. cit., p. 326 and App. Al. For the possible cause of the similarity between Perrault's and Le Brun's designs see above p. 24.

extraordinary that, throughout the *Ordonnance*, he never refers to these, for him, unusual proportions. He mentioned the arch, especially in connection with the dispute about the size of the equestrian statue, but the measurements of its Order, so much in excess of everything he proposes in the book, are not referred to at all. It must not, of course, be forgotten that the *Ordonnance* was written thirteen years after the design had been submitted. At that time, 1668, Perrault had only started on the translation of Vitruvius, a task from which, as a by-product, his own ideas on architectural theory gradually emerged. At this early period, Perrault may still have followed Vignola as the most popular author in France with whose rules the measurements of the Arc de Triomphe and the Colonnade to a great extent agree. It is possible that in the intervening years he had changed his views on the 'correct' proportions of the Orders, and might not have wanted to draw attention to a patent contradiction that would only have led to awkward discussions. Whatever may have been the reason, one conclusion can be drawn from all this: neither the fact that the measurements differ from those published in the *Ordonnance*, nor the fact that they are not referred to in the book, could in themselves lend support to the arguments against his claim to have designed the Colonnade.

The problem of the Colonnade is more complex. Perrault does refer, in the *Ordonnance*, to the unusual proportion of one part of its Order, the capital.[55] It is true that he cites it in a different context, as proof for his postulate that proportions are not founded on an absolute canon of beauty; yet, it indicates that he is not averse to exposing the singularities of this Order. Furthermore, he specifically mentions the Louvre, when, in a note to Vitruvius, he discusses the motif of coupled columns, and gives some basic dimensions: the diameter of the column, the size of the intercolumnation, and the span of the architrave connecting column with wall.[56] He never alludes, however, to the Order as such, neither

55. *Ordonnance*, p. XI.
56. *Vitruvius*, p. 79 E. The information about the size of the architrave is an addition to the second edition.

when he deals, in the first part of the *Ordonnance*, with the Orders in general, nor when, in the fourth chapter of the second part, he discusses the Corinthian Order in particular. This strange omission was already noticed by Pierre Patte, an architect writing in the next century. He had measured the Colonnade carefully and was struck by the fact that 'the proportions which he (Perrault) proposes (in the *Ordonnance*) in no way agree with those of the building'[57] (Pl. 31). He thinks it only natural to expect that Perrault, in the book, 'would propose as model his Corinthian Order of the peristyle of the Louvre, which had been so successful,' but, strangely enough, this is not the case.[58] Another instance of Perrault's peculiar behaviour disturbs him just as much. The columns have been given a slight swelling in the lower third, a feature not only uncommon in Perrault's time, but one he had expressly rejected, first in the *Vitruvius* and again in the *Ordonnance*.[59] 'It is surely strange,' wonders Patte, 'that after these remarks Perrault has not informed us of the reasons that induced him to give this swelling to the columns.'[60] Patte is clearly puzzled about the inconsistency between what Perrault, the architect, built, and what Perrault, the author, wrote; but, being convinced of his authorship of the Louvre, he quickly restores his peace of mind by concluding that 'it is only too common to see architects contradict themselves in this way'.[61]

The Colonnade had been measured some seventeen years earlier by another architect, J.-F. Blondel, who believed as fervently in the genius of Perrault, the architect, as Patte did.[62] Blondel remained unaware of the difference between these measurements and those theoretically proposed by Perrault, but, in the course of his description of the Louvre, he

---

57. op. cit., Chapter VIII: 'Description historique de la Colonnade du Louvre.' (pp. 319 ff.) On Patte see Mae Mathieu, *Pierre Patte*, Paris, 1940, specially pp. 137 ff.

58. op. cit. p., 338.

59. *Vitruvius*, p. 82, note 25; *Ordonnance*, p. 24. In chapter VIII, p. 112, he lists the swelling as a permissible *abus*.

60. op. cit., p. 335.

61. ibid., p. 338.

62. J.-F. Blondel, *L'Architecture françoise*, Paris, 1752, IV, pp. 9 ff. The measurements are given on pp. 41 ff.

reproduced a document that, coupled with his own explanatory remarks, goes some way to account for Perrault's failure to refer to the puzzling discrepancy. Blondel published Perrault's grand plan (of about 1671) to complete the Louvre by connecting it with the Tuileries, a plan he had found in the two now-destroyed volumes in which Charles Perrault had collected his brother's designs. Attached to this plan was a *mémoire*, written by Perrault himself, of which the part describing the Colonnade reads (in Blondel's reproduction and retaining the lacunae of his text) as follows: 'The principal façade towards St Germain l'Auxerrois is composed of a great *avant-corps* in the centre, of two wings, and of two pavilions at the corners . . . The basement is thirty feet high; above these wings are two peristyles, having each 14 columns; these columns are Corinthian and isolated . . .' At this point, Blondel adds this surprising note: 'We have been forced to leave some lacunae in Perrault's description and to make some changes in the text, which we have found in some respects obscure and, moreover, not in agreement with the majority of measurements which we took most accurately, before we entered upon the present description.'[63]

Thus, at the time when the total completion of the Louvre was being planned, that is, in 1671 or soon after, but in any case at a time when the main structure of the Colonnade had been completed, Perrault described it with measurements different from those actually used. It seems that the most likely explanation is that he did not know them. On the other hand, he must have taken from somewhere the details and measurements that puzzled Blondel. I would suggest that the obvious source was a plan that was readily available to him, namely his own design, submitted, about four years earlier, to the committee of which he was a member. It is possible that Perrault was not even aware that the measurements on the building itself were different from those on his own plan, and that,

63. ibid., p. 11, note t.: 'Nous avons été obligés de laisser quelques lacunes dans la description de *Perrault* et de faire quelques changemens dans le texte que nous avons trouvé obscur en certains endroits, ne se rapportant pas d'ailleurs avec la plupart des mesures que nous avons prises exactement sur les lieux avant que d'entreprendre la description que nous en donnons.'

for this reason, he had not thought it necessary to verify them.[64] Another piece of evidence points, I think, to the same conclusion. We have mentioned that Perrault referred to the sizes of intercolumnation and to the span of the architraves. That was in 1673: a decade later, in the second edition of *Vitruvius*, he changes these figures – from 12 feet to 11 feet (in two places, so it cannot be due to a printer's error), and from 'plus de douze pieds' to 'près de douze pieds'.[65] The puzzling thing is that the second set of figures is wrong.[66] Why Perrault altered what had been right, is impossible to say. One conclusion can, however, be drawn from this strange behaviour: it displays a degree of uncertainty about measurements affecting vital proportions that is incompatible with the image of Perrault as the architect of the Colonnade, in full control of planning and execution. (Pls 31, 32). Yet, there cannot be any doubt that Perrault as member of the *petit conseil* assisted in the initial planning of the Colonnade. On the other hand, the evidence on which our conjecture (and it is not more than that) is based, suggests that he took no active part in the subsequent phases leading to the final design.

From the interpretation of the relevant evidence it would follow that the two contestants for the authorship of the Colonnade might have both genuinely believed that they had spoken the truth: Perrault, when he told Leibniz that 'it is according to (his) design that the work is being done at present' – a design of which it is impossible to say how far it contained features which, through their originality, influenced others – and d'Orbay, when he told Boileau that he would prove 'with plans on the table that it is the design of the famous Monsieur Levau that is being followed for the façade of the Louvre'.[67]

64. This explanation agrees with that given by Tony Sauvel, op. cit., *Bulletin Monumental*, 1964, pp. 345, ff. He believes that, when in 1668 the condemnation of Le Vau's southern front necessitated changes in the plan of the eastern façade, the plan then adopted was not, as Perrault may have believed, his own of 1664, but Le Vau's of 1667. For the changes made to the plans in 1668, see Hautecoeur, *Louvre*, pp. 171 f.

65. *Vitruvius*, 1st ed.: p. 76, note 3, p. 205, note 7; 2nd ed.: p. 79, E, p. 217, note 7.

66. It is also strange that the correct figure of 12 feet is given by Charles in *Parallele*, I, p. 175, his *Mémoires*, p. 87, and in the mémoire attached to their plan for Ste Geneviève (Petzet, op. cit., p. 95.).

67. Leibniz, op. cit., p. 235; Boileau, *Oeuvres*, III, p. 302.

To return to the *Ordonnance*; its second part deals, chapter by chapter, with each of the five Orders, separately and in great detail. The various types of bases, the flutings of the shaft, the five kinds of capitals, the three members of the entablature, the sequence of divisions and subdivisions which ensure well balanced proportions of these parts – Perrault methodically discusses all these, and a score of other details. Next to proportions, he is interested in what he calls the character of the Order; the number and shape of mouldings, that is, the profiling, as well as the purely decorative elements. With the help of his *Fréart* and *Desgodets*, he scrutinizes the Orders of modern architects and of ancient monuments and assembles a whole range of examples – their dimensions, their shapes, their peculiarities. The method remains the same throughout the five chapters so that it may suffice to quote, as a typical specimen, his examination of the Corinthian capital.[68] (Pl. 33).

The total height is considered first. The size he has adopted is that of the diameter of the column plus one sixth. 'In antiquity it is sometimes lower by one seventh . . . as can be seen at the Temple of the Sybil in Tivoli, a size according to Vitruvius. At other times, it is taller, as on the Temple of Vesta in Rome and on the Frontispiece of Nero where it exceeds the diameter of the column by about two sixths. Then again, it has the size which I give it, as on the Porticus of Septimius and on the Temple of Jupiter Tonans. In some cases it is only slightly lower, as on the Pantheon, at the Three Columns, on the Temples of Faustina, Mars the Avenger, the Porticus of Septimius (*sic*) and on the Arch of Constantine, in other cases it is somewhat higher, as at the Thermae of Diocletian. Modern writers are also divided, since some give it the same size as I do – Palladio, Scamozzi, Vignola, Viola, Delorme – while other writers, such as Bullant, Alberti, Cataneo, Barbaro, and Serlio, make it according to Vitruvius.' Next, he turns to the parts that make up the capital and subjects them to the same scrutiny. There are monuments where the thickness of the abacus is only one eighth of the total height of the capital, 'the one of the Forum of Nerva coming within a third of a minute to the

68. *Ordonnance*, pp. 73 ff.

size I give it.' The leaves on the capital, he finds, are sometimes those of the acanthus, at other times of the olive, mostly with five incisions, but also with three and four; sometimes the two rows of leaves are of equal height, but examples exist where one is higher than the other. The rose in the centre of the abacus varies considerably, either different in shape with differently formed leaves and pistils, or different in the degree to which it projects over the abacus. Thus it goes on, for every detail the examples being quoted. He may deal with a question that is clearly of some consequence, such as the ratio between the three parts of the entablature or the number and proportions of the fasciae making up the architrave, or he may judge with much fastidiousness whether a certain moulding should be in the form of an astragal, or an ovolo, or a fillet; whatever the point to be settled, whether significant or trivial, he presents a documentation of the infinite variations that is as thorough as the measurements recorded in the two textbooks enable him to be.

To deal with a wide range of details is traditional for the class of books to which the *Ordonnance* belongs. What is remarkable is Perrault's perseverance and methodical procedure. Others cited ancient monuments either in support of, or as exceptions to, the rule they wished to establish, but nobody before him had delved into the jungle of formal and proportional modifications with quite so much enthusiasm. He does so for two reasons; in the first place, he is thus able to give ample proof for his assertion that beauty does not depend on exact proportions, since the recorded variations have been taken from buildings all recognized as of equal aesthetic value or from the Orders of equally respected great masters of architecture, and in the second place, the wide range of these measurements makes it possible for him to find the right proportion by applying once more his method, which is 'the best one can choose' – namely of taking the middle way.

This time, however, Perrault does not aim at arithmetical accuracy; he is satisfied with choosing a dimension that holds, more or less, to the centre. Sometimes he merely lists the many ancient and modern examples, and records to what extent they differ from the proportions, shapes or arrangements he has prescribed, but frequently he makes a definite selection, naming a specific monument or particular author he has decided to follow. He chooses different models for different details. One monument is the model for the architrave, another for the sequence of mouldings of the cornice, another again for the height of the larmier, another for that of the cyma, one type of moulding is identical with the one used by Palladio, the next with the one described by Serlio, a detail of a cornice follows one author, the flutings of a column another. 'Among all these differences,' he writes after having shown the various ways in which the profiling of the Tuscan capital had been done in the past, 'I have chosen the manner of Vitruvius,' and it is again Vitruvius that he follows in the design of the Tuscan and attic base, in that of the Ionic capital, and in the projection of the Doric capital and the proportions of its architrave.[69] Equally as often it is a modern author who provides the model he is going to adopt. 'I have imitated Serlio in making architrave and frieze of equal height' is his comment on the Tuscan entablature, while its cornice 'is closely related to that of Vignola'[70]; in another instance, he follows Alberti who, among a whole range of authors and monuments cited, 'keeps to the middle way,' whereas the character of the Corinthian base of the pedestal 'is taken from Palladio who has imitated that on the Arch of Constantine'.[71] When he reaches the last three Orders, the number of monuments to choose from increases. For a detail of the Ionic capital he names as his model the Colosseum, for other details of this Order the Theatre of Marcellus and the Temple of Fortuna Virilis.[72] The proportions of the Corinthian cornice he takes 'from the cornices of the Pantheon which is the most approved work of the Corinthian Order', while for the Composite Order he forms the base according to the Arch of Titus and the architrave and cornice according to those of the Frontispiece of Nero.[73] (Pls 34–37).

69. ibid., pp. 38, 40, 41, 45, 49, 50.
70. ibid., p. 41.
71. ibid., pp. 64, 69.
72. ibid., pp. 61, 64, 65.
73. ibid., pp. 78, 90.

The choice Perrault has is wide. Every page of Desgodets's book with its measured drawings, or of Fréart's book with its comparison of ancient with modern Orders, would offer him variations of the one he would choose, from negligible to more important differences. True to his guiding principle he selects what 'keeps to the middle between two extremes'. With these words, often repeated, he rejects the 'excessively ornate' pedestal of the Column of Trajan as well as Palladio's extremely plain one, and decides to match the even character of Scamozzi's Tuscan pedestal.[74] He is in broad agreement with Vignola's Tuscan cornice, because it, too, 'keeps to the middle between the extremes of delicacy . . . which Scamozzi gives it, and that of too great simplicity which Serlio has adopted.'[75] Choosing between the 'extraordinarily small' projection of Alberti's Doric capital and the 'excessively great' projection of the Colosseum, he decides to follow the 'ordinary proportion' with a projection of $37\frac{1}{2}$ minutes which, besides conforming to Vitruvian rules, is the one adopted by the architect of the Theatre of Marcellus and also by Barbaro and Serlio.[76] It is the same on every occasion. He always prefers 'proportions (that) are in the middle between the different excesses of the Ancients and the Moderns', between 'too much ornamentation and . . . too great simplicity', and is always intent on keeping 'at an equal distance from the extremes that are to be found in ancient works'.[77]

'Extreme' and 'excessive' are for him mostly those features that are indicative of the 'baroque' trend in Roman architecture. The massing together of a great number of mouldings, typical of this style, evokes in him only the impression of 'strange confusion'.[78] A cornice having modillions as well as dentils, an arrangement meant to give it a richer appearance and encountered on many Roman monuments, is rejected

74. ibid., p. 38.
75. ibid., p. 41.
76. ibid., p. 49.
77. ibid., pp. 76, 84, 9.
    Pascal in 'L'Esprit géométrique', Oeuvres, IX, p. 289, had said: 'Ce n'est pas dans les choses extraordinaires et bizarres que se trouve l'excellence de quelque genre que ce soit.'
78. ibid., p. 56.

because 'this great pile of ornaments causes a confusion disagreeable to look at'.[79] His reason for being critical of an Ionic entablature with modillions in place of dentils is not so much its bewildering aspect as that it tends to confuse the distinct character of the five Orders, 'the modillions being the characteristic feature of the Corinthian and the Composite, just as the mutulae are those of the Doric, and the dentils those of the Ionic.' It offends his sense of order, apart from the fact that Vitruvius 'only admitted a plain dentil for this Order'.[80] He also disapproves strongly of the way in which some architects join frieze and architrave, welding them together, as it were, by ending the frieze in a concave moulding, called a *congé*. Although he can think of only two Roman monuments that show this feature, Palladio and Scamozzi adopted it in spite of its 'bad effect'.[81] What is even worse, these two architects made the plinth of the base of the Doric column join the cornice of the pedestal again by a *congé*. Through this extraordinary arrangement, for which no example in antiquity exists, 'this essential part of the base is in effect abolished and destroyed'; an offence of such magnitude that he includes this practice in the list of abuses with which he concludes his treatise.[82] To the small number of *abusi*, listed by Palladio in his *Quattro Libri*, he adds a few others; among them the practice, typical of the Baroque, of making columns and pilasters 'penetrate and intermingle with each other', an abuse of which even Palladio, he regrets to say, was guilty once, as was also the architect of the Pantheon, who departed from 'exact regularity' when allowing two half-pilasters to form an angle.[83]

Seeking the middle way, Perrault rejects what is irregular, such as the Ionic Order of the Temple of Concord, 'irregular in all its parts,' and the 'most irregular' cornice of the Arch of Constantine.[84] 'Very unusual' too,

79. ibid., p. 78. He also rejects (pp. 47 f.) those Doric columns, mentioned by Vitruvius, which instead of normal flutings have twenty canted angles, because of the 'confusion désagréable à cause de la difficulté qu'il y a de rendre la séparation des deux faces assez visible et assez distincte.
80. ibid., pp. 66, 78.
81. ibid., p. 77.
82. ibid., pp. 46 f.
83. The *abus* are dealt with in Chapter VIII, pp. 112–124. The reference to Palladio on pp. 113 f.
84. ibid., pp. 66, 70.

according to him, is the narrow spacing of modillions in Scamozzi's Corinthian cornice. While admitting that this spacing is advantageous 'when columns are coupled in porticos', he nevertheless concludes: 'because the character of this cornice is too far removed from the ordinary . . . I do not believe that it could be employed without taking too great liberties,' a judgment that has also some bearing on the problem of his authorship of the Colonnade.[85] Irregularity being suspect, it is not surprising to see his choice occasionally being determined by what is customary – choosing the attic base because 'it is the one most commonly in use';[86] a proportion, accepted by all modern architects, because he had thought that he 'could not go wrong in following these great masters'[87]; and the exceptional degree of diminution of the Tuscan column because one should 'make allowance for custom which is one of the principal laws of architecture.'[88]

This, then, is what Perrault offered in his treatise: the five Orders in a sequence of great regularity, not marred by any extravagant features, securely balanced between the too little and the too much, and composed of simple and easily recalled proportions. As with all attempts at standardization, Perrault expected his standardized Orders, once they had been accepted, to be rigidly adhered to. Because the norms he presented were not based on the whim of individual taste, but on the rational method of determining the average among proportions and measurements of works of indisputable beauty, he felt confident that unprejudiced people would accept them and recognize that this was the only way of arriving at 'something fixed, constant and decided in architecture.'[89] One may ask, however, if this was his aim, how it can be reconciled with his often-repeated statement that the proportions proposed by him are nothing more than probable. He speaks of 'the probability of the mean proportion'

85. ibid., pp. 80 f.
86. ibid., p. 45.
87. ibid., p. 71.
88. ibid., p. 21.
89. ibid., p. XV.: '. . . afin que d'une façon ou d'autre on eust quelque chose de fixe, de constant, et d'arresté dans l'Architecture, du moins à l'égard des proportions des cinq Ordres.'

and of keeping to the middle as the only way 'for establishing a fixed
rule with some probability'.[90] Does he not contradict himself by stating
that 'if we cannot say that this proportion is the true one . . . it should
at least be regarded as the probable one based on positive reason'?[91]
Calling proportions *probables* and *vraisemblables* and, at the same time,
expecting them to be *fixes* and *constantes* remains, I believe, unintelligible
until one considers what Perrault, the scientist, understood by these
terms. I submit that, in this instance, Perrault transferred a term with
which he was familiar as a scientist, to the aesthetic context, and not only
the term but also its special meaning.

In common with other leading scientists of the seventeenth century,
he is convinced that in natural science the true causes are hidden from us.
'It is impossible to arrive at a perfect knowledge of things,' he declares
in the introduction to his *Essais*.[92] A few years later, he is even more
sceptical, and considers the best results we can achieve in this field to be
those that make us see more clearly the reasons why we cannot know the
cause of natural phenomena. 'I never tire of repeating on all occasions,
because I wish everyone to be as convinced of it as I am . . . that we do
not seek anything in this science other than what we can reasonably hope
for, and this amounts only to the probability of knowledge.'[93] This was
said towards the end of his life; but already twenty years earlier, in the
first programme for the Academy of Science, he had expressed the
warning that 'probability is usually the only result of reasoning in

90. ibid., p. 31: '. . . ces diversitez opposées peuvent établir la probabilité de la proportion
médiocre . . .'
    p. 9: '. . . on ne peut faire autre chose pour établir une règle certaine avec quelque probabilité
que de tenir le milieu . . .'
    91. ibid., p. XVII: 'En sorte que si l'on ne peut pas dire que cette proportion soit la véritable . . .
elle doit du moins estre reputée vrai-semblable, puisqu'elle est fondée sur une raison positive . . .
also p. XIV: 'mais même qu'il . . . n'y a point, à proprement parler, dans l'Architecture de proportions véritables en elles-mesmes; il reste à examiner si l'on en peut établir de probables et de
vray-semblables fondées sur des raisons positives . . .'
    92. *Essais*, I, Preface.
    93. ibid., IV, p. 2: '. . . je ne me lasse point de répeter dans toutes les occasions, parce que je
souhaite qu'on en soit autant persuadé que je le suis . . . qu'on ne cherche point autre chose dans
cette Science que ce que l'on en doit raisonnablement espérer, et qui se reduit à la seule probabilité
des connoissances.'

scientific research'.[94] Probability is for Perrault, as it was for his friend Huygens, his colleague Cureau de la Chambre, and his contemporary Hartsoeker, the highest degree of certainty it was possible to achieve in this field.[95] Although the knowledge based on it is, he declares, 'only the very imperfect shadow' of the knowledge God has reserved for himself, yet, so he professes triumphantly, 'it surpasses in *noblesse* and beauty all other human knowledge.'[96] He attached, I believe, this meaning and this value to the term *probable* when he applied it to architecture, where it was senseless to look for true proportions, because, in contrast with the truth of God's creation, they did not exist. To arrive at probable proportions was an achievement of which to be proud.

The examination of the treatise itself confirms the conclusion reached after having studied its preface: neither the tenor of the treatise as a whole, nor a single proposal in it indicates any desire on Perrault's part to set the trend towards greater artistic freedom. On the contrary, the limits within which the Orders can move are narrowed, and with the Orders,

---

94. Académie des Sciences, *Registre* (1667), I, fol. 24: '. . . la probabilité qui est d'ordinaire le seul effet du raisonnement dans la recherche des choses naturelles . . .'

95. Cureau de la Chambre, *Le système de l'âme*, Paris, 1665, Preface: 'J'ay seulement cherché le vray-semblable . . . et au lieu de démonstrations qui sont inconnues en ces matières, je me suis contenté de conjectures et de raisons probables.'

Huygens, *Traité de la lumière*, Leyden, 1690 (according to Huygens's statement in the preface, discussed in the Academy already in 1678), *Oeuvres*, XIX, p. 454: 'Il est possible toutefois d'y arriver à un degré de vraisemblance, qui bien souvent ne cède guere à une évidence entière.'

Similarly in his letter to Pierre Perrault, *Oeuvres*, VII, p. 298.

Nicolas Hartsoeker, *Conjectures physiques*, Amsterdam, 1706, pp. 1 f.: 'La Nature travaille par des voyes et des ressorts si cachez, qu'il est impossible à l'esprit humain de pénétrer ses plus profonds secrets: ainsi l'on est presque toujours obligé de se contenter d'une simple probabilité.'

96. *Essais*, IV, p. 2: '. . . bien que (les connaissances) ne soient que l'ombre très imparfaite de celles que l'Ouvrier même de la Nature a voulu se réserver, elles ne laissent pas de surpasser en noblesse et en beauté toutes les autres connoissances humaines.'

On the 'probabilisme de Perrault' and the parallel tendency in Huygens's scientific attitude see Alberto Tenenti, 'Claude Perrault et la pensée scientifique française dans la seconde moitié du XVIIe siècle' in *Hommage à Lucien Febvre*, Paris, 1953, II, pp. 303 ff., and J. Barchilon, op. cit., pp. 30 ff.

For the general scientific outlook at this period, of which Perrault's statements are a reflection, see J. Roger, op. cit., pp. 201 f., and R. H. Popkin, *The History of Scepticism from Erasmus to Descartes*, Assen, 1964, in particular chapter VII on 'Constructive or mitigated Scepticism' where reference is made to the 'formulation of a theory which could accept the full force of the sceptical attack on the possibility of human knowledge . . . and yet allow for the possibility of knowledge in a lesser sense as convincing or probable truths about appearances.'

necessarily the scope of the total architectural composition. Uniformity, order, and the middle way – these were Perrault's tenets. He was, through his brother and through his own work for the Crown, closely connected with the Establishment and was, no doubt, conversant with the general aims pursued by those who were part of it. The wish for order and unity, clarity and simplicity, was as strong among men of science as among those who looked after the affairs of state. Any move to restrain the individual's freedom of choice, to strengthen the unifying force, would be welcomed and considered a move in the right direction.

It was not expediency alone that caused Perrault to dedicate his book on the *Ordonnance des cinq espèces de colonnes* to Colbert; the first servant of the absolute state was a suitable person to receive it. (Pl. 39).

CHAPTER V

The Sequel

VEN if the foregoing interpretation of Perrault's aim in writing his book is thought to be reasonable, it does not necessarily follow that its readers recognized what he had been aiming at. Although the many controversial and challenging statements were no more than means by which to reach the ultimate goal, they tended to conceal this goal.

The review, which we are now going to undertake, will show that, for this and other reasons, the book was not generally a success, at least not until, very much later, the evaluation of his unconventional remarks turned full circle.

We shall examine the response to Perrault's theory by contemporary and succeeding writers. While the influence of his proportional rules – or the lack of it – will not detain us unduly, we shall review at some length those writings in which, in some way or other, reference is made to Perrault, or which contain ideas that may have been derived from him; in particular we shall take a close look at a treatise whose author made ample use of Perrault's text; we shall also try to answer the question of whether a link exists between Perrault's ideas and those prevalent in the aesthetic literature of the eighteenth century. Among the writers dealt with in this review, three stand out from the rest. They are François Blondel in the seventeenth century, Charles Etienne Briseux in the eighteenth century, and the German art historian, Cornelius Gurlitt, in the nineteenth century. They are the only authors who undertook a critical interpretation of Perrault's ideas, examining his statements on beauty, proportions, custom and the right to make changes. Finally, we shall explain why Gurlitt's interpretation, although diametrically opposed to the one offered by Blondel and Briseux, failed equally to give a true account of Perrault's ideas and aims.

FRANÇOIS BLONDEL'S CRITICISM

The second part of Blondel's *Cours* appeared almost simultaneously with Perrault's *Ordonnance*. Having dealt in the first part with the Orders in general, Blondel now widened the scope of his treatise to include the whole apparatus of classical architecture – columns, this time in great detail, pedestals, pediments and pilasters, intercolumniation and superimposed Orders, door and windows, vaults and domes, bridges and staircases – in short, everything that a professor of architecture was supposed to teach his students. Then, in the final two books, he felt free to deal with basic problems, of which the question of optical adjustment was one. There remained another, even more important, the climax of the whole course: proof that beauty was dependent on proportions.

Blondel reviews in detail Vitruvian precepts and those of modern masters, analyses ancient and modern buildings, and considers Ouvrard's and St Hilarion's proportional systems. They all confirm his conviction that the eternal laws of nature are valid for proportions also; that only by applying regular proportional measurements have architects 'created all the beauty they intended to give to their works'.[1]

The only writer who had expressly challenged this belief was Perrault.[2] Blondel knew of Perrault's forthcoming book, but since at that time it was available only in manuscript, he was in no position to quote from it.

1. op. cit., Book V., chapters I–XIII, pp. 727–761. The quotation on p. 754.
2. Blondel refers on p. 755 to some 'Architectes, qui ont acquis de la réputation,' who do not believe that knowledge of proportions is useful to them, since 'les règles de Théorie ne servent qu'à les embarasser et à émousser, pour ainsi dire, la pointe et le vif de leurs inventions, l'esprit n'agissant jamais plus heureusement que lors qu'il est affranchi de toutes sortes de servitude, et que l'on lui laisse une entière liberté pour ses productions'. In Blondel's opinion, this attitude only leads to 'des nouveautez bigearres et des caprices extravagants'. It is difficult to know whom Blondel had in mind, but it was certainly not Perrault. In the first place, he refers to him by name when, later on, he deals with his views, and, secondly, he would be the last person to honour Perrault by elevating him to the rank of 'architect of repute'. But, above all, Perrault had never spoken against rules, nor advocated unrestrained freedom or believed beauty to be 'un pur effet du génie'.

However, there were Perrault's notes in his editions of Vitruvius, and they already contained views, as Blondel points out, which were far removed from those held by Vitruvius himself.³ Blondel cites *in extenso* a passage in which Perrault had outlined his main argument: that proportions have no beauty that can be called *réelle, convaincante* and *nécessaire*, and that they please and are thought to be beautiful only through seeing them continually in company with other kinds of beauty which have these qualities.⁴ Although Perrault had not yet taken up the uncompromising position maintained in the *Ordonnance*, this passage was radical enough to disturb Blondel considerably. His opposition was absolute.

Blondel fills many pages to prove that proportions call forth a beauty that is real and natural.⁵ His reasoning is in no way original: it amounts to a reiteration of the classical faith and, as so often happens in these matters, what requires proof, is assumed. He cannot understand how anyone can seriously believe that proportions are not *convaincantes*, when everybody approves of them the moment he perceives them, or how it can be said that they are not *nécessaires* when everybody knows that without them, the graceful beauty of a building would disappear. Perrault's views seem to him so preposterous that he feels inclined to doubt his sincerity.⁶ Nevertheless, he thinks that they need serious refutation, so he sets out to disprove them. He shows – or rather asserts – that, while custom certainly affects the palate, it cannot possibly have any influence on our aesthetic enjoyment which, on the contrary, is real and natural.⁷ Meeting Perrault on his own ground, he demonstrates how in physics the inductive method had been successful in establishing 'stable and constant principles' and that the same method, applied to architecture, has the same result.⁸ If long observation establishes that on buildings

3. ibid., pp. 761 f.
4. ibid., p. 762. Blondel gives in this place a slightly condensed, but otherwise correct quotation of Perrault's note in *Vitruvius*, p. 105, note 7.
5. Chapters XIV–XVI, pp. 761–74.
6. ibid., p. 762: 'Quoique cette pensée soit singulière et extraordinaire, et que j'aye beaucoup de panchant à ne la pas croire absolument véritable, je n'ay garde néanmoins d'entreprendre de la réfuter.'
7. ibid., p. 765 f.

which please, certain proportions are always encountered which are never present on buildings which shock, then, Blondel concludes, 'I cannot see that anyone should be surprised if I pronounce boldly that these proportions are the cause of beauty and elegance in architecture and that as a result a stable and constant principle can be established.'[9] As for Perrault's assertion that the real cause of beauty must be looked for in the accompanying qualities, such as richness of material and precise workmanship, this, in Blondel's opinion, is obviously false. It is disproved by buildings made from ordinary material and lacking any ornament. In spite of their plain, simple aspect we derive from them surprisingly great pleasure and this for no other reason than for 'the great accuracy of their measurements and proportions'.[10]

In the course of these arguments, Blondel quotes Perrault as saying that proportions 'cannot be seen and, therefore, cannot be the cause of a sensible effect such as the pleasure which beauty gives us.' He also rebukes Perrault for making people who value proportions look ridiculous by alleging that they attribute the cause of beauty 'to this imaginary proportion, give it gratuitously a despotic authority over the movements of our soul and make us submit to its commands'. These quotations – not to be found in his *Vitruvius*, nor in the *Ordonnance* – probably come from one of

8. ibid., pp. 768 ff.

9. ibid., p. 771.

10. ibid., pp. 772 f. As an example for beauty in simplicity he cites S. Sabina (*sic*) in Padua as mentioned by Wotton (op. cit., p. 12).

The same point had already been made by Alberti (*De re aedificatoria*, VI, 5), and repeated by Daviler, *Les Oeuvres d'Architecture d'Anthoine Le Pautre*, about 1691, p. 38, where the following remark may be directed against Perrault: 'Il y a enfin des personnes qui s'imaginent que le merveilleux d'un édifice ... est causée par l'abondance des ornemens et la rareté de la matière, sans faire réflexion qu'il n'y a que les belles proportions qui impriment le respect ... dans les esprits intelligens, et que plusieurs Eglises de Naples, avec la profusion de l'or et des marbres, sont inférieures en beauté à celle de Sainte Justine de Padoue avec la simple blancheur de ses murs.'

Desgodets, *Cours d'architecture*, Paris, Bibl. Nat. Estampes Ha 23, fol. 299, also refers to S. Giustina, as does J.-F. Blondel, *L'architecture françoise*, Paris, 1752, I, p. 59, adding as a further example the *Observatoire* (which he accepts as Perrault's work), although on the preceding page he had reiterated François Blondel's criticism of Perrault's view about beauty dependent on richness of material.

It is ironic that two designs for which Perrault's authorship is acknowledged, one for the Observatoire and the other for the Temple of Jerusalem, are simple to the extreme.

the *mémoires* which Perrault, according to Charles, had written for the *petit conseil*.[11]

These are the main points of Blondel's 'refutation.' His whole case takes up considerably more space, but since, within the framework of classical architecture, his arguments are self-evident, there is no need to recount them in detail. What must be stressed, however, is the earnestness with which Blondel attempts to give a reasoned reply to the core of Perrault's theory and the fact that he devoted three long chapters to that purpose. This must surely have been of great importance to Perrault, who had the opportunity of reading the *Cours* before preparing the second edition of his *Vitruvius*. It comes then as a surprise to find that Perrault does not refer to these chapters at all.

His total indifference to Blondel's lengthy remarks is extraordinary. It becomes puzzling when one realizes that in other instances Perrault seizes with obvious delight the opportunity of being able to reply to Blondel's criticism: a long addition doubles the length of a note in which he had advocated the use of coupled columns; this, he says, was done in answer to 'Monsieur Blondel (who) in his learned lectures on architecture, from which he has composed a *Cours*, utilizes three whole chapters, namely the 10th, 11th and 12th of the first book of its third part, in order to show that the habit . . . of doubling columns is a licence which should not be permitted.'[12] Similarly, he enlarges his note on the bad effect produced by optical adjustments and deals at length with Blondel's counter-arguments.[13] However, when Blondel attacks his views on proportions, he does not respond. Not even the fact that in this instance Blondel refers

---

11. op. cit., p. 768: 'Mais ils se mocquent de tout ce qui se dit de la proportion, *parce*, disent-ils, *que l'on ne la voit pas, et partant qu'elle ne peut pas estre la cause d'un effet sensible, comme est celuy du plaisir que donne la beauté.*' (cf. *Ordonnance*, p. V.)

p. 767: '*il faut au contraire que nous en aillions chercher la cause ailleurs, et l'imputer si nous voulons, comme a fait Vitruve et la pluspart des autres Architectes, à cette imaginaire proportion, en luy accordant volontairement une autorité despotique sur les mouvemens de nostre âme, en nous soumettant à ses ordres, et renonçant à tout autre plaisir qu'à ceux que nousfinous figurons recevoir d'elle.* (Blondel's italics). On Perrault's *mémoires* for the *petit conseil* see above p. 24.

12. *Vitruvius*, p. 79, E. He also adds a new note (p. 64, note 26) in reply to a point made by 'Monsieur Blondel dans la troisième partie de son Cours d'Architecture.'

13. ibid., p. 205, E.

to him by name, nor the oblique reference to his contempt for common opinions or to his affected *singularité*, provokes him into coming to the defence of his own case.[14]

Is it then possible that Blondel may, after all, have been right in doubting Perrault's sincerity? He knew him, of course, personally and must have discussed the subject with him on many occasions. Why, then, does Perrault refrain from taking up the challenge and from replying to Blondel's rejection of his singular views? Why is Perrault silent in this instance – Perrault who obviously loved arguments and as little liked admitting defeat as anybody else? In the *avertissement* to the second edition of *Vitruvius* he had made the explicit statement that as to his particular views 'far from having retracted them in this edition, they are now confirmed by new reasons which have occurred to him, it so happening that the objections which were raised had no other effect than to make him think further about these things and to convince him more and more of the truth of his first ideas.'[15] This is correct regarding the expanded notes on optical adjustment and coupled columns, but is not borne out by the way in which he dealt with the notes concerning proportion, musical harmony and custom, which were reprinted in exactly the same form in which they first appeared eleven years earlier, as if the three long chapters in Blondel's *Cours* had never been written.[16] This strange attitude is difficult to explain except on the basis of the interpretation of Perrault's theory outlined in the preceding chapters. It seems to me that only this interpretation is consistent with his behaviour, and that this behaviour in its turn strengthens the likelihood of the interpretation's being correct.

We have shown that Perrault did in no way 'despise' proportions, as

14. op. cit., p. 763: '... par mépris des sentimens ordinaires, ils en ayent voulu prendre de singuliers ...'

15. 'Pour se qui est de plusieurs opinions particulières, que l'Auteur avoit avancées dans ses Notes avec quelque défiance, dans la crainte de ne les avoir pas assez examinées; bien loin qu'elles soient retractées dans cette Edition, elles y sont confirmées par de nouvelles raisons qui luy sont venues dans l'esprit, estant arrivé que ce qu'on luy a objecté n'a point eu d'autre effet que de le faire penser davantage à ces choses, et le persuader de plus en plus de la vérité de ses premières pensées ...'

16. ibid., p. 105, note 7 (this is the passage quoted by Blondel in full), p. 106, note 12.

Blondel suggested.[17] On the contrary, he thought them to be an essential part of the art of building and wished to see their measurements fixed. Others had tried to do the same, but only Perrault realized that nobody would ever have enough authority to impose rules as long as it was generally believed that absolute proportions existed. Perrault wished to shake this belief. For this reason, and for this reason alone, he excluded proportions from the positive qualities and called them 'arbitrary'; in other words assigned them to a class which could be controlled by human agencies. A controversy with Blondel on this issue would have led him into an impossible position: he would either have had to disclose the reasons for the stand he had taken, in which case, at least in the eyes of his opponents, his sincerity would be questionable, or he would have had to reject Blondel's arguments and this would have meant having to reject, at the same time, principles on which the classical style was based – the only style which he recognized.

Thus, Perrault's reluctance to enter into a discussion becomes understandable. Furthermore, it helps to clarify the meaning Perrault attached to the term 'proportion'. As for Blondel, he took proportion in its widest sense: as ratios consisting of two or three magnitudes with the help of which the whole and its parts had been composed. His chapters on Palladio's buildings, on those of modern and ancient times, and in particular his analysis of the Pantheon, make this abundantly clear.[18] However, is this the kind of proportions which Perrault had in mind when he speaks of their arbitrary character, asserting that they could be different without in any way affecting the beauty of the building? Compared with the clear definitions given in Blondel's *Cours*, those of the *Ordonnance* are less explicit.

Speaking of proportions, Perrault often gives examples that refer to detailed, not general, proportions. Thus, it is by the commonly accepted ratio between capital and column or, less specifically, the proportions of 'the parts of the Orders' that he illustrates the influence of custom.[19] When

17. op. cit., p. 763.
18. ibid., Chapters VI–IX (pp. 738–54).

he wants to prove that proportions have no absolute value, he makes the point that for the beauty of a building it is of no great importance that 'in the Ionic Order, for example, the height of the dentil of the cornice is precisely equal to that of the second fascia of the architrave' and, in another place, finds his view that proportions are not the cause of beauty confirmed by the fact that the columns of the Pantheon and those of the Temple of Castor exceed round figures by odd minutes which, if omitted, could not possibly have any detrimental effect.[20] He is obviously irritated by the seriousness with which these proportional measurements were being treated by the majority of architects who 'are convinced that the monuments would loose all their beauty if a single minute had been taken away from or added to any of these parts,' whereas, in fact, the precision of proportions, such as 'the thickness of an astragal, the height of a *larmier* or the greater or lesser measurement of a dentil,' does not make up the beauty of ancient buildings.[21] These passages, and others of a similar nature, point to the conclusion that Perrault's unorthodox pronouncements on proportion were meant to apply only to the limited field of the Orders. Against this, however, must be ranged the occasions when he speaks of proportions in general terms, when, for instance, rejecting the musical analogy, he refers to 'the proportions which must be observed in architecture', and when, in another context, he remarks that 'a building pleases because of its proportions'.[22] The clearest statement that he intended proportions to be understood in the widest sense occurs when he derides architects for believing that 'the beauty of the Pantheon,

19. *Ordonnance*, pp. VIII, X.
20. ibid., pp. XV, XXI.
21. ibid., p. XVII: '... cependant la pluspart des Architectes sont persuadez que ces ouvrages auroient perdu toute leur beauté, si une seule minute avoit esté ostée ou adjoutée à quelqu'un des membres ...' p. XX: '... la grosseur d'un Astragale, la hauteur d'un Larmier, ou d'un Denticule plus ou moins grande; la précision de ces proportions n'estant pas ce qui fait la beauté de l'Antique ...'
22. ibid., p. III: 'Cela fait connoistre quel fondement peut avoir l'opinion de ceux qui croyent que les proportions qui doivent estre gardées dans l'Architecture sont des choses certaines et invariables, telles que sont les proportions qui font la beauté et l'agrément de la Musique ...'
p. VI: '... la difficulté est seulement de sçavoir si ... ce qui fait qu'un Bastiment plaist à cause de ses proportions, n'est pas la mesme chose que ce qui fait qu'un habit à la mode plaist à cause de ses proportions ...'

for example, consists in the ratio of the thickness of its walls to the enclosed space, of its width to its height and hundred other things of whom . . ., if they were perceptible, one cannot be certain that they could not be otherwise without being displeasing.'[23]

On balance, it seems that Perrault did not differentiate between two kinds of proportion, and that he was aware that whatever he said of one would apply equally to the other. Blondel's charge was serious because he understood Perrault's paradoxical statements to affect a basic principle of architecture, not just comparatively insignificant features of the Orders. If Perrault had meant to refer only to these, he could have silenced Blondel by clearing up the misunderstanding, but, no doubt, he thought – rightly – that proportions are indivisible and preferred to leave the field to Blondel.

The few writers who, in the next century, commented on this dispute agreed with Blondel's reading. 'As for me,' said Soufflot in a lecture given in 1739 to members of the Academy in Lyons, 'I always inclined more towards the opinions of Monsieur Blondel than those of Monsieur Perrault, at least regarding the proportions in general and even with regard to a number of detailed proportions.'[24] Recapitulating the arguments of the dispute, the younger Blondel and Briseux implicitly accepted François Blondels' interpretation: they, also, believed that Perrault's strictures were aimed at the whole framework of proportions.[25]

If Perrault had not gone further than making a distinction between positive and arbitrary qualities of beauty, there would hardly have been much opposition, notwithstanding the denigrating connotation of the term *arbitraire*, but to include proportions among the class of arbitrary beauty

23. ibid., p. V: '. . . la plupart des Architectes . . . veulent qu'on croye que ce qui fait la beauté par exemple du Panthéon, est la proportion que l'épaisseur de ses murs a avec le vuide du Temple, celle que sa largeur a avec sa hauteur, et cent autres choses, dont on ne s'apperçoit point, si on ne les mesure, et par lesquelles, quand on s'en appercevroit, on ne seroit point asseuré qu'elles ne puissent estre autrement sans déplaire.'

24. *Mémoire sur les proportions de l'architecture*, (1739), Lyon, Bibl. de l'Académie, MS 194, fols. 132–8 (reproduced in M. Petzet, *Soufflot's Sainte Geneviève*, Berlin, 1961, pp. 131 ff.).

25. J.-F. Blondel, *L'architecture françoise*, I, pp. 58 f.; *Cours d'architecture*, Paris, 1771 ff., III, pp. 10 ff. Ch.-E. Briseux, *Traité du Beau essentiel dans les arts*, Paris, 1752 (see below pp. 168 ff.).

was unheard of.[26] Never before had the direct link between proportion and beauty been questioned in this outspoken way, nor was it to be done again, except seventy years later by Burke, whose statement that 'proportions are not the cause of beauty' which formed an integral part of his sensationalistic theory, was equally categorical and equally futile.[27] No wonder that the reaction to Perrault's *paradoxe* was sheer incredulity. It was simply not possible, it was thought, that he really meant what he had said about proportions. Inwardly he must have known that he was in the wrong, and must have felt how absurd it all was. Probably he had said it in the heat of the argument, and, as often happens to a scholar engaged in a dispute, was loath to retract once he had asserted it. A less indulgent view was that only his spirit of contradiction could have induced Perrault to fight one of the most elementary architectural notions, and only sheer obstinacy could have made him hold on to it; a stubborn attitude that was no credit to him.[28]

26. For the roots of this distinction in Platonic thought, see B. Bosanquet, *A History of Aesthetic*, New York, 1957 (1st ed. 1932), p. 33.

27. E. Burke, *A Philosophical Enquiry into the Origin of our Idea of the Sublime and Beautiful*, (1757) ed. J. T. Boulton, London, 1958, pp. 91 ff.

28. E.-L. Boullée, *Architecture Essai sur l'art*, Paris, Bibl. Nat. MS 9153, fol. 72 r f.: 'J'ai rencontré d'habiles gens qui m'ont objecté ... que, surement, Perrault pensait autrement qu'il ne l'avait fait paraître.' (Boullées' treatise was first published by Helen Rosenau, London, 1953, and recently, with annotations, by J.-M. Pérouse de Montclos, Paris, 1968. Both editions give the pagination of the original manuscript).

Soufflot, op. cit., fol. 132 v: '... les sçavans ont quelque fois ... la mauvaise qualité de ne vouloir point se retracter de ce qu'ils ont une fois avancé bien qu'intérieurement ils sentent leur tort et agissent conséquemment aux principes contre lesquels ils déclament.'

fol. 135 v: 'Ce n'est donc pas sans raison que des architectes ont quelquefois changé les proportions légitimes de l'architecture et l'on ne peut pas conclure de ces différences que les proportions soyent chimériques, lorsque l'on veut examiner les choses du bon costé et bannir tout entestement.'

M.-A. Laugier, *Essai sur l'architecture*, Paris, 1755, p. 108: '... la nécessité des proportions ... que M. Perraud (*sic*) n'a combattue que par esprit de contradiction. Il sentoit toute l'absurdité de son paradoxe qu'il n'a soutenu que par pur entêtement.'

p. 260: 'M. Perrauld (*sic*) qui a soutenu le contraire, ne l'a fait que par esprit de contradiction; et il a montré sur ce sujet un entêtement qui ne lui fait pas honneur.'

Briseux, op. cit., pp. 65 f.: If one examines what Perrault said about proportions, one will be convinced 'que sa conviction intérieure y étoit opposée'.

When the first volume of Charles Perrault's *Parallèle* had been published, which contained many of Claude's arguments, it was also thought that he took his work 'comme un jeu d'esprit par lequel il avoit appuyé des paradoxes qu'il estoit fort éloigné de prendre pour des véritez.' (*Journal des Sçavans*, 1689, p. 9).

With these sweeping statements, Perrault's unorthodox opinions were brushed aside. Reading the Preface today, one expects to hear of a lively discussion taking place between those who accepted Perrault's views as a new and progressive programme and those who rallied to the defence of classical doctrine. This certainly did not happen. It is true that, in the middle of the century, the younger Blondel took up François Blondel's case, that another influential writer, Pierre Patte, commented in detail on some of Perrault's ideas and that, at the same time, an English architect, about whom more will be said at a later stage, drew much information from the *Ordonnance*; but it is only Briseux – to whom we shall also return – who saw the controversy between Blondel and Perrault as an issue of such vital importance that he made it the focal point of his whole treatise.[29] Yet, far from presenting the general reaction, Briseux's book was the exception: on the whole, Perrault's challenge to orthodox opinion was not taken up.

Most frequently, the *Ordonnance* was looked at and commented upon as nothing more than another book on the Orders. A distinction may be seen in the fact that Perrault's name was often added to the names of those who made up the usual list of authoritative writers on the Orders. In this way, it happened that Blondel and Perrault were at times listed in close proximity as writers on architectural theory of equal expert knowledge, without so much as a hint at the divergent views which separated them. The apparent similarity between their treatises was, in fact, sometimes so predominant in the writer's mind, that both were credited with pursuing the same aim, that of the establishment of definite proportions. 'Vitruvius,' wrote Patte in 1755, 'Palladio, Scamozzi, Serlio, Perrault, François Blondel and numerous other authors have in turn made attempts to fix the beauties of this art by trying to define immutable proportions.'[30] Later in the century, another writer spoke of 'Palladio, Blondel, Perrault and a few others' as having all taught that only exact ratios between the

29. J.-F. Blondel, *Architecture française*, 1752, I, pp. 56 ff., *Cours*, III, Chapter I.
Pierre Patte, *Mémoires*, 1769, pp. 76 ff.
30. *Etudes d'architecture*, Paris (1755), p. 2.

principal parts could produce an aesthetically satisfying composition, thereby simply ignoring the implications of Perrault's peculiar and seemingly contrary views.[31]

Occasionally, however, the Ordonnance is specifically mentioned. One of the first reviews reads:

'The book which Monsieur Perrault made public last year under the name of *Ordonnance des Cinq Espèces de Colonnes selon la méthode des Anciens* contains a method infinitely easier to apply to the five Orders than all the other methods, because here the parts consist of invariable measurements; they are either the same in all Orders, such as the entablatures which have throughout a height of two diameters, or they proceed by equal differences, such as the columns which advance by two-thirds of a diameter from Order to Order and the pedestals which advance only by one third. He was mainly engaged on conceiving measurements of the architectural Orders based on the mean between the greatest and the smallest to be found on ancient monuments and in architectural books. This he has done very successfully.'[32]

This was written in 1684 by François Blondel, by the same man who, only one year previously, had made his censorious remarks in the *Cours*! The dual aspect of the *Ordonnance* comes out clearly. Confining his comments this time to the main part of the treatise, Blondel readily made them as appreciative as they had been critical when he considered exclusively Perrault's general ideas.

Cordemoy, writing at the beginning of the next century, was also in two minds about the *Ordonnance*. On the one hand, he called it 'perhaps the only book from which the workmen derive some benefit', because Perrault provides them with 'a sure and easy rule for the measurements and proportions of each Order', but, on the other hand, rejected Perrault's

---

31. *Recueil de quelques écrits relatifs à un ouvrage périodique sur les arts libéraux qui n'a point été publié*, London and Paris, 1776, p. 40.

32. L. Savot, *L'architecture françoise des bastimens particuliers ... augmentée dans cette seconde édition ... des notes de Monsieur Blondel*, Paris, 1685, p. 341, note b.

An account of the *Ordonnance* was given already in the *Journal des Sçavans* of 26 July 1683, and was mentioned by Germain Brice, *Description nouvelle ... de Paris*, The Hague, 1685, II, p. 145.

exposition of principles as 'too long-winded, involved and somewhat obscure'. Obviously, he had little use for the Preface, yet great admiration for the sections that deal with the Orders.[33] One can be sure that the Director of the Academy in Rome also had the main part of the *Ordonnance* in mind, when, a few years earlier, he recommended it as 'the best book in its genre'.[34] By the middle of the century, its evaluation had not much changed. J.-F. Blondel found Perrault's method 'as clear as it is clever', the treatise itself – somewhat reservedly – to be 'not without merit', then, having included it in a list of books recommended for the study of architecture, thought it advisable to add this critical observation, the only one among seventeen entries: 'a work less esteemed than his commentaries (on Vitruvius), although its system deserves attention'.[35]

Even though the merit of the book was sometimes recognized, Perrault's rigid system was not taken up by the profession, at least not in France, the only exception being Cordemoy who was not an architect. Single features were occasionally recommended.[36] Comparatively important was one arising from a decision by members of the Academy in 1701 that 'the height of the entablature ... could be determined by the diameter of the column by always giving two diameters to the entablature.'[37] The minutes do not, however, record Perrault's name who, we have seen, had been the originator of this innovation. His other innovation, the *petit module*, was completely ignored in French architectural literature, again with the exception of Cordemoy who, quoting Perrault

33. De Cordemoy, *Nouveau traité de toute l'architecture*, Paris, 1714, p. 2.
Cordemoy's explicit rejection of Perrault's theoretical notions as too involved was noted by D. Nyberg, 'The "Mémoires critiques d'architecture" by Michel de Frémin,' *Journal of the Society of Architectural Historians*, XXII, 1963, p. 220, note 17, but was ignored by R. D. Middleton, 'The Abbé de Cordemoy and the Graeco-Gothic Ideal,' *Journal of the Warburg and Courtauld Institutes*, XXV, 1962, pp. 278 ff.
34. *Correspondance des Directeurs de l'Académie de France à Rome*, publ. by A. de Montaiglon, Paris, 1888, II, p. 253 (9 August 1696).
35. *L'architecture françoise*, II, p. 57, IV, p. 5; *Discours sur la nécessité de l'étude de l'architecture*, Paris, 1754, pp. 83 f.
36. For instance by Sébastien Leclerc, *Traité d'architecture*, Paris, 1714, p. 60, and J. Dolivet. *Nouveau traité des cinq ordres d'architecture*, (1711), London, Brit. Mus., MS Harley 6337, fols. 15 ff.
For Perrault's influence on English writers on the Orders, see below p. 154, note 85.
37. *Procès-verbaux*, III, p. 124.

extensively in this connection and even reproducing the relevant table, stated that he certainly followed his way of measuring.'[38] Hardly anyone else did. Briseux refers contemptuously to the total rejection of Perrault's Orders by all architects; a remark which, it seems, came near the truth.[39]

Once the arbitrary character of proportions was established, the matter of proportional rules could, in Perrault's opinion, be settled, once and for all, by a purely rational method. It is hardly surprising that nobody conceded this. All writers, those who preceded Perrault as well as those who came after him, were convinced that the 'lawgiver' had not yet arrived. Some hoped, like Perrault, that through their own system they might assume this rôle, but the majority probably agreed with Patte's observation that 'nobody had yet sufficient authority for making laws that would be kept inviolably, the reason being either the difficulty of finding rules which in themselves possess evident truth ... or the impossibility of subjecting the human spirit to decisions which are not based on principles derived from nature.'[40]What is needed, argues another writer, is a co-operative effort through institutions such as the Académie d'Architecture; they may succeed where a single person is always bound to fail.[41] The same consideration had caused members of the Academy in January 1689 to interrupt the reading of the *Ordonnance* which had occupied their time for seven consecutive weekly meetings.[42] Although they had many reservations concerning the Preface, believing it to be unsuitable for the instruction of architectural students, they had read it to

---

38. op. cit., pp. 5 f., 248 ff.
Frézier, without adopting it, mentions that 'quelques-uns n'en ont pris que le tiers sous le nom de petit module.' (*Dissertation sur les ordres d'architecture*, Strasbourg, 1738, p. 18).
39. op. cit., p. 2.
The ease of Perrault's system seems to have appealed to amateurs. Apart from Cordemoy and Dolivet, there was a mathematician, Charles de Neuvéglise, who, dealing with the Orders, adopted 'les mesures et les proportions de Monsieur Perrault comme celles qui nous ont parues les plus faciles ...' (*Traité ... de toutes les mathématiques*, Trevoux, 1700, p. 111); and P. Delaroche, (a priest according to Soane, *Lectures on Architecture*, 1929, p. 42), who also 'followed Perrault pretty close ... chusing the little module' (*An Essay on the Orders of Architecture*, London, 1769, p. 6.).
40. *Etudes*, p. 2.
41. C.-A. Guillaumot, *Remarque sur un livre intitulé Observations sur l'architecture*, Paris, 1768, pp. IV f.
42. *Procès-verbaux*, II, p. 173.

the end;[43] only when they reached the fourth chapter, dealing with the height of the entablature, they stopped and never again resumed the reading. Instead, in twenty meetings extending over the next seven months, they tried to 'regulate . . . those proportions which they consider the best to be followed.'[44] In other words, what upset them more than any of Perrault's bizarre opinions and wherein they saw the greater threat, was his audacity in usurping their function – the definition of the proportional rules for the five Orders.

It is remarkable how little interest the book aroused considering its challenging nature. One reason for the lack of response may have been Blondel's refutation, which, far from stimulating further discussion, may have made people feel that these ideas had been adequately dealt with, and that no more needed to be said.[45] However, an additional, and quite likely major, reason for disregarding the *Ordonnance* and especially its preface was Perrault's fame.

He was the architect of the Louvre Colonnade. It is true that there had been heated argument about this attribution. Boileau's spirited backing of d'Orbay's and Le Vau's claim had brought some people over to their side,[46] but they remained a minority, in time vastly outnumbered by those who firmly proclaimed Perrault's authorship. For many succeeding generations the Colonnade was the image of French classical spirit at its best. It was seen as an authoritative building, a masterpiece not only of French architecture but of the human spirit, as illustrative of the age of Louis XIV as of Perrault's talent; its columns were believed to be the most beautiful imaginable, its entablature equal to the best remains of antiquity – to quote but a few of the many eulogies given.

43. ibid., II, p. 171.
44. ibid., p. 174.
45. An echo of the dispute about coupled columns in Daviler, op. cit., p. 2. A few years later, come, from a rather unexpected quarter, critical comments on Blondel's case and Perrault's views in a book by a German professor of Mathematics (Johann George Wagner, *Probe der sechsten Säulen-Ordnung*, Breslau & Leipzig, 1728, pp. 16 ff.).
46. For instance, Pierre Nativelle, *Nouveau traité d'architecture*, Paris, 1729, Pl. 41; J. Courtonne *Nouveaux essais sur l'architecture*, (ca. 1733), Paris, Bibl. de l'Institut, MS 1032, fols. 43, 50; Pierre Alexis Delamaire, *La pure vérité*, (1737), Paris, Bibl. de l'Arsenal, MS 3054, p. 142.

Even when faults are noted – and this happens already in the eighteenth century – it is still regarded as 'the triumph of architecture', as 'skilful in construction, admirable in the ordonnance and sublime in the arrangement of ornaments'. It is only natural that Perrault as the creator of this truly outstanding building – 'the only one to give posterity a high idea of the reign of Louis XIV' – was acclaimed as one of the great architects of genius who 'from time to time rise above the customary routine of ordinary artists and produce by intuition masterpieces'. An artist as great as Perrault could, when necessary, depart from rules in order to achieve that elegant gracefulness 'which charms and delights, whereas cold correctness and scrupulous observation of these rules chills the spectator's feeling'.[47]

No wonder that, seen against the artistic sensitivity with which Perrault was credited as the architect of the Colonnade, his theoretical statements regarding proportions and optical adjustment seemed strangely inconsequent and almost meaningless. As was shown in a previous chapter, the discrepancy between what Perrault taught and what he practised did not remain unnoticed, but nobody, with the exception of his opponent Briseux, drew the conclusion and questioned his rôle as an architect. It is important to keep in mind that, whatever doubts modern scholars may have about Perrault's architectural activity, his fame as the creator of the Colonnade was at that time well established, lasting for centuries and spreading throughout Europe. As a historical fact, whether justified or not, this fame was effective; one of its effects being that, dazzled by the brilliance of the Louvre, his questionable theories were more often than not disregarded.[48]

47. The laudatory remarks, typical of the praise lavished on the Louvre, have been extracted from the following writings: Florent Lecomte, *Cabinet des Singularitez d'Architecture* . . ., Paris, 1699; J.-F. Blondel, *Architecture françoise*, II, p. 37, *Cours*, III, p. 66, IV, p. XLVI; La Font de Saint-Yenne, *L'Ombre*, p. 101; Saint-Yves, *Observations sur les arts*, p. 150; Laugier, *Observations sur l'architecture*, 1765, p. 79; P.-J. Antoine, *Série des colonnes*, 1782, p. 24.

48. It is significant for the overpowering effect of Perrault's fame that when the younger Blondel deals with, and rejects, his theory of beauty by accompaniment, he points in the next sentence to the Colonnade as one of the buildings that disproves that 'superficial' view (*Cours*, III, pp. 11 f.).

FRÉZIER

There is, however, one treatise on the Orders where, it seems, Perrault's ideas found an echo. Its author, Amédée François Frézier, was an officer in the *Corps du génie*, an engineer engaged on inspecting and building fortifications, not an architect.[49] He was best known as an expert on the science of stonecutting, an intricate subject on which he had written a voluminous standard work. Because of his profession, he was never elected to be a member of the Academy, yet, his knowledge of architecture, both in practice and in theory, was considerable, and when he took upon himself the task of criticizing the writings of amateurs such as Cordemoy and Laugier, he was able to present the point of view of the profession with authority. His own *Dissertation sur les ordres d'architecture*, published in Strasbourg in 1738, was, for all its unconventional statements, firmly grounded in the long tradition of books on the Orders.

There cannot be any doubt that Perrault influenced him. Frézier is the only French author who, in the controversy about Perrault's subversive statements on the cause of beauty, sides with him, at least partially. In a critical review of Briseux's book in which Perrault had been attacked, he declares that he is 'halfway with Perrault regarding the inadequacy of proportions to establish true beauty'.[50] When further on in the same review, but now dealing with Laugier, he remarks that he 'would without hesitation say that beauty is arbitrary', it seems obvious that Perrault had found a disciple.[51] Later in the review, Frézier refers, for a more detailed discussion on these views, to his earlier *Dissertation*. A study of this treatise makes it evident that the apparent similarity between Perrault's and Frézier's viewpoints does not reach down to basic principles.

Frézier was as much concerned about the influence of custom as Perrault had been. It is with buildings as with clothes, he declared: to

49. For biographical data, see P. du Colombier, 'Amedée François Frézier,' *Festschrift für Karl Lohmeyer*, Saarbrücken, 1954, pp. 159 ff.
50. *Mercure de France*, July 1954, p. 14: 'Quoique je sois de moitié avec Perrault sur l'insuffisance des proportions pour établir une beauté *réelle* . . .'
51. ibid., pp. 21 f.

provide protection is recognized as a basic need, but as to the graceful form of attire 'it depends to such an extent on the habit of seeing things shaped in a certain manner that whatever does not conform to the fashion becomes intolerable and ridiculous.'[52] Thus, Frézier, following Perrault's lead, related custom to beauty. For Perrault, however, the force of custom was a fact which had to be accepted whether one liked its effect or not, and beauty, as affected by custom, was for him a basic quality, beauty in its widest sense. When Frézier speaks of beauty in this connection, he means, as it were, the outer-skin of things, and sees the influence of custom as a harmful process which blocks the way to his ultimate goal, the establishment of what he calls *architecture naturelle*.[53] Custom should, in Frézier's opinion, be resisted, even in cases where 'the *abus* has prevailed to such an extent over the rules of reason that the eyes have become accustomed to it and architects endorse and approve it'.[54]

In order to emphasize his point, he makes observations which, if taken out of context, appear to express undiluted relativism. Our decoration, he argues, lacks *beauté réelle* because our custom and fashion are neither constant nor universal. 'The people of East and West, of North and South have their own customs in the matter of buildings and have decorations according to their own taste: are we the only people who have received the best taste and common sense as their share?...What a difference there is between the buildings of the ancient Greeks and Egyptians and those of the Mohammedans who succeeded them in the same country...what a difference between the Gothic buildings seen in such great numbers in France and the Low Countries and those built by Frenchmen to-day! Were our ancestors right? Are we? That is a question which is not easier to decide than the one which could be debated about the different manner of our dresses.'[55] These are radical views indeed, and

52. *Dissertation*, p. 5.
53. ibid., p. 52: 'pour moi (je) m'attache toujours à l'imitation de l'Architecture la plus naturelle.' p. 8: 'S'il est donc quelque règle universelle pour les Ordres, elle ne peut être fondée que sur l'imitation de l'Architecture naturelle.' also pp. 32, 51.
54. ibid., p. 11.
55. ibid., p. 5.

vividly expose the complete absence of anything comparable among
Perrault's pronouncements. In fact, Frézier had as little intention of
advocating relativism in matters of art as Perrault had; his object was
to demonstrate that, lacking sound principles, we deviate from true
beauty as easily as other people. His remarks are meant as a weapon with
which to combat the pitiful results of custom and fashion; that is, the
Rococo decoration of his own time and the excesses of the Roman
Baroque.[56]

On another level, the process is the same: Perrault and Frézier start
from similar conceptions, but take different routes. They were both
'Moderns'. Already in 1709, Frézier ridicules the notion that we should
be content to imitate the Ancients because to surpass them appears to be
impossible;[57] he too points to the variety of proportions among ancient
monuments and modern treatises. Whereas Perrault makes this diversity
the basis for his system of average proportions, Frézier takes it as
proof that no firm rules can be derived from these measurements,
since for any fault, a precedent can be found in antiquity.[58] Turning away
from 'this variety of taste and opinions', he seeks to be guided by the only
principle that is truly independent – that of function. Every rational
being, he declares, must agree with the maxim 'that the purpose each
thing is intended for, according to its nature, should be one of the
principal reasons on which to found the beauty of buildings.'[59] This
sentence is taken word for word from one of Perrault's commentaries
on Vitruvius.[60] Perrault mentions function in other places too; in his
first formulation of the two classes of beauty he includes fitness among

56. ibid., pp. 6 ff., particularly the second paragraph on p. 7 where he concludes, after having
listed all the extravagant features of Baroque architecture: 'Au milieu de cette variété de goûts et
d'opinions, ne sera-t-il pas permis d'établir quelques principes . . .?'

57. *Journal de Trévoux*, September 1709, p. 1620.

58. *Dissertation*, p. 59: 'Certainement si les exemples des monumens antiques autorisent les
desseins d'Architecture, il n'est sorte de défaut qui ne se trouve autorisé.'

59. *Journal de Trévoux*, 1709, p. 1636: 'Il est bon ici de faire attention à une maxime d'Architecture
de laquelle tout homme raisonnable doit convenir: *Que l'usage auquel chaque chose est destinée selon
sa nature, doit estre une des principales raisons sur lesquelles la beauté des édifices doit estre fondée.*' (Frézier's
italics).

60. *Vitruvius*, p. 214, note 6.

the positive qualities and, speaking in another place as an anatomist, he realizes that 'the perfection of everything depends on the relation it has to the end for which it is made'.[61] Yet, in the *Ordonnance* he discarded the conception of function; it does not form part of his theoretical system. Frézier took his cue from Perrault, but for him function remained, throughout his long life, the great guiding principle to which everything else had to submit.

However, he confined the functional test and the establishment of firm proportions to the major parts, realizing that for the smaller parts an almost infinite number of variations are possible so that it would be senseless 'to pass the time with these punctilious precisions to which architects wish to subject us'.[62] In contrast, Perrault insisted on 'punctilious precision' and would never have subscribed to Frézier's concession of 'leaving to architects the liberty of making use (of these combinations)'.[63] This was probably the reason why Frézier went only half-way with Perrault.

In justification of the changes proposed by him, Frézier quoted 'a modern author' as saying that 'we have as much right to change the thoughts of the Romans as they had to alter the Orders of the Greeks.'[64] He, Frézier, approves of this maxim which, however, he believes many people will condemn because 'it seems to deliver the architectural Orders to the capricious whim of architects'.[65] There had been so many notions common to Frézier's and Perrault's treatises that it comes as a surprise to find that this 'modern author' is François Blondel.[66] It would

---

61. ibid., p. 217, note 8; p. 12, note 13; *Mémoires . . . des animaux*, preface: '. . . la perfection de chaque chose dépend du rapport qu'elle a à la fin pour laquelle elle est faite.'

See, however, E. R. de Zurko, *Origins of Functionalist Theory*, New York, 1957, p. 69, who takes the view that Perrault's contribution to functionalism is important.

62. *Dissertation*, p. 17.

63. ibid., p. 57.

64. loc. cit.,: 'Nous avons autant de droit, a fort bien dit un Auteur moderne, de changer les pensées des Romains, que ceux-ci en ont eu d'alterer les ordres des Grecs.'

65. loc. cit.,: 'On se récriera, sans doute, sur une maxime qui semble livrer les Ordres d'Architecture au caprice des Architectes.'

66. Blondel, op. cit., p. 250:'.'.. nous n'avons pas moins de droit de changer les pensées Romains, que les Romains en ont eu d'alterer celles qu'ils avoient receues des Architectes Grecs.'

have been more to the point, it seems to us, to have quoted Perrault's reference to Hermogenes, whose innovation figured so prominently in his dispute with Blondel, than Blondel's remark occasioned by the comparatively unimportant subject of a design for a French Order. It is possible that Frézier sensed Perrault's inconsistency in pleading for the right to make changes and, at the same time, proposing a rigid proportional system. Frézier's aim was more in line with Blondel's and was consistent with classical doctrine: to arrive at rules based on common sense without imposing unnecessary restrictions. No doubt, Perrault's writings prompted Frézier, but the goal he set himself was different from the one which Perrault sought.

The conception of the dual nature of beauty on which Perrault's case greatly depended, became one of the leading topics in the aesthetic literature of the next century. The names signifying the different types of beauty varied of course, but, whether one class was related to *idées*, the other to *sentiments*, whether absolute beauty was opposed to comparative, intrinsic to relative, or whether it was divided into two, three or, by Diderot, even into five classes, the aim was invariably the same: to save the conception of beauty as an absolute value from the threat of being undermined by the constantly growing awareness of the relativity of taste.[67] The majority of the authors probably did not even know of Perrault's theory, and only in isolated cases have we some indication of Perrault's being a possible source.

A book in which Perrault's theory of transference was taken up is Père André's influential *Essai sur le beau*, first published in 1741 and running into many editions.[68] André divides beauty into *beau essentiel*, which is absolute, *beau naturel*, which is independent of human opinions, and 'a type of beauty . . . which is *arbitraire*'.[69] While this may be reminiscent of Perrault's classification, only the fact that André, who was mainly interested in moral and aesthetic questions of a general nature,

67. see W. Herrmann, *Laugier and 18th century French Theory*, London, 1962, Appendix III.
68. I have used the edition of 1770.
69. *Essai*, p. 6.

starts his investigation by applying his system to architecture, justifies the conjecture that the initial impetus came from Perrault. It is true that in an introductory chapter André makes 'regularity, order, proportions and symmetry' the attributes of the supreme kind of beauty, of the *beau essentiel*, but these terms signify universal ideas in the Platonic sense.[70] When he deals with a subject as specific as the art of building, he assigns the proportional rules of the Orders to the *beau arbitraire*.[71] These rules, André observes, are sometimes disregarded by great architects, in which case they commit, strictly speaking, a fault; but since this fault is embedded in an otherwise beautiful work of art 'we give it, seeing it so well accompanied, a beauty in its own right which, in fact, it only derives from its accompaniments,' and admire it 'by the force of habit' even when encountered in a second-rate work.[72] André restricts this process of transference to licences inspired by the genius of the great artist, whereas Perrault sees it as affecting arbitrary beauty as a whole. Nevertheless, since André mentions this particular effect only when dealing with art and architecture, it is most likely that he adopted it from Perrault.[73]

The association of ideas, on which 'beauty by accompaniment' is based, played no further part in André's hierarchical structure of beauty. In England, on the other hand, the theory, first outlined by Locke, had been adopted and developed by a succession of writers of whom Gerard, the author of an *Essay on Taste*, was the first after Perrault to apply it to

70. ibid., p. 9.

71. ibid., pp. 30 f.

72. ibid., pp. 34 ff.: 'On commence ordinairement par les plus belles (parties des ouvrages de l'art) . . . et si l'on en rencontre quelqu'une qui s'écarte un peu de la règle, on la voit si bien accompagnée, qu'on lui donne en propre une beauté qu'elle ne tire que de ses accompagnemens. C'est un défaut . . . mais l'objet où il se rencontre, est un l'ouvrage de l'Art . . . son défaut changera bientôt de nom et d'idée . . . Qu'il arrive ensuite que l'on rencontre ce même défaut dans quelqu'imitation . . . l'idée du beau qu'on y avoit attachée, se reveille . . . Autrefois l'on avoit admiré ce défaut dans l'original par le mérite emprunté de ses accompagnemens; et en vertu de cet agréable souvenir, on l'admire encore, quoiqu'isolé dans sa copie, par la force de l'habitude, qui prévient la réflexion.'

73. André's book was very influential. Diderot thought highly of it ('le système le plus suivi, le plus étendu et le mieux lié que je connoisse,' *Encyclopédie*, sub Beau); even a hundred years after its first edition, the *Essai* was still much valued (Victor Cousin, *Cours de philosophie*, Brussels, 1840, p. 201).

aesthetics.[74] Gerard's arguments differ from Perrault's. According to him, objects are considered beautiful because, among other reasons, they are connected in the mind 'with agreeable ideas of any sort', as, for instance, a green field through its association with fertility.[75] The point Perrault wished to make was that by accompaniment we not only transfer the quality of one object to another, but, more importantly, take the cause for what in fact has been the effect, and that, furthermore, we should free ourselves of this 'prejudice' and take note of the true state of affairs. Hume, who made a thorough examination of cause and effect, and the way in which the mind necessarily associates the one with the other (what he calls 'customary contiguity'), dealt with the psychological and epistemological aspect of the problem. It was only when Henry Home, Lord Kames, looked, a few years after Gerard, at this interaction in relation to aesthetic experience that Perrault's specific notion was reflected in English aesthetic thought.[76]

Kames, appreciating that 'the train of our thoughts . . . will be found of great importance in the fine arts,' notes that 'the beauty of the effect, by an easy transition of ideas, is transferred to the cause; and is perceived as one of the qualities of the cause.'[77] By this he means that the beauty inherent in the perfect utility of an object is transferred to the object itself, although it 'has no beauty in itself', just as Perrault asserts that the beauty inherent in a richly-adorned, magnificent and symmetrical building is transferred to its proportions, although 'their beauty has nothing real'.[78] When, in an introductory chapter, Kames deals with the fact, by then well-known, that 'an agreeable object makes everything connected with

74. Alexander Gerard, *An Essay on Taste*, London, 1759.

75. ibid., p. 43.

76. Henry Home, Lord Kames, *Elements of Criticism*, Edinburgh, 1762. I have used the ninth edition of 1817.

77. ibid., I, pp. 15 f., 179.

78. ibid., p. 179: 'the utility of the plough, for example, may make it an object of admiration, or of desire; but why should utility make it appear beautiful? A natural propensity . . . will explain that doubt: the beauty of the effect, by an easy transition of ideas, is transferred to the cause; and is perceived as one of the qualities of the cause. Thus a subject void of intrinsic beauty appears beautiful from its utility.'
Perrault, *Vitruvius*, p. 105, note 7.

it agreeable', he concludes his supporting evidence by pointing out 'that the respect and esteem, which the great, the powerful, the opulent, naturally command, are in some measure communicated to their dress, to their manners, and to all their connexions.'[79] This sounds familiar; it recalls Perrault's observation that 'the esteem we have for the merit and fine grace of courtiers makes us like their dress and manner of speech.'[80] Perhaps it is just coincidence; but remarks made by Kames in another context prove that Perrault's arguments were known to him.

Kames distinguishes between intrinsic beauty, which is 'ultimate', and relative beauty.[81] His analysis shows that, in spite of similar terminology, his classification has little in common with Perrault's. Not only does Kames relate relative beauty exclusively to function, but, above all, he sees proportions, together with other classical conceptions, as attributes of intrinsic beauty. Nothing would have been more abhorrent to Perrault's way of thinking than Kames's statement that 'we are framed by nature to relish proportion'.[82] Absurd is, in Kames's opinion, the opposite view according to which the pleasure we derive from proportions is not inborn; this, Kames points out, had been asserted by Perrault, who 'is the only author who runs to the opposite extreme; maintaining that the different proportions assigned to each order of columns are arbitrary, and that the beauty of these proportions is entirely the effect of custom.' Kames's reaction to this paradoxical view is similar to that of Soufflot, Laugier and so many others. 'This betrays,' he continues, 'ignorance of human nature, which evidently delights in proportion as well as in regularity, order, and propriety. But without any acquaintance with human nature a single reflection might have convinced him of his error, that if these proportions had not originally been agreeable, they could not have been established by custom.'[83] Now, the 'Perault' (*sic*) whom he quotes is Charles, not Claude, and the book

---

79. ibid., I, pp. 59 ff. The last quotation on p. 62.
80. *Ordonnance*, p. VIII.
81. op. cit. I, p. 179.
82. ibid., II, p. 413; similarly I, p. 182.
83. ibid., II, 414 f.

referred to is the *Parallèle*, not the *Ordonnance*, yet, even so, Perrault's ideas had found an echo in an important book of classical aesthetics, although it is a critical echo and brought about only through his brother's more famous book.[84]

Among English architects the situation was, of course, different; they knew Claude's writings while those of Charles lay outside their sphere of interest. The English edition of *Vitruvius* (in its abridged form) appeared for the first time in 1692; that of the *Ordonnance* in 1708. The *Ordonnance* was not translated into any other language but English, a sign of the comparatively close link between the two countries. Perrault's fame as an architect may have been one reason for the publisher's selecting this particular work. Possibly a more convincing consideration was the fact that the Ordonnance was a book dealing with the Orders in a simple, easily understandable manner. The publication of a great number of practical books on the Orders during the second quarter of the eighteenth century shows that in England – different from the situation in France – a new interest in this subject had emerged. Thus, the part of the *Ordonnance* that dealt with the Orders is likely to have had a greater influence in England than it ever had in France.[85] In addition, as the evidence provided by two major English architectural treatises shows, a genuine interest in Perrault's ideas existed – an interest that was stronger than in France itself. This may have been simply a matter of the prophet being honoured save in his own country, but I suspect the deeper reason must

84. *Parallèle des anciens et des modernes*, Paris, 1688, I, pp. 136 ff. (Kames quotes from the edition of 1693).
Charles makes ample use of his brother's arguments, including, for instance, the 'Court' simile (I, p. 140). However, there are differences in emphasis, the most notable that Charles considers arbitrary to be inferior to positive beauty (p. 139). See on this the remarks by Max Imdahl and H. R. Jauss in their valuable facsimile edition of the *Parallèle*, Munich, 1964, pp. 78, 58 ff.). On the whole, Charles's exposition is much cruder than Claude's. Typical in this respect is the different notion they both have about the transference of qualities: for Perrault it is a psychological phenomenon of great significance, for Charles nothing more than 'une heureuse contagion' (p. 140).
85. I am indebted to Eileen Harris for drawing my attention to this trend in English architectural literature and to the likelihood that Perrault's book on the Orders was for this reason of greater value to the English than to the French reader. In particular, his method of dividing and subdividing the lesser members of the Orders into equal parts must have appealed to writers whose books were meant to give simple instructions to common builders. However, as we mentioned

be looked for in the particular trend of English thought. Locke's empiricism had created an awareness of problems to which some of Perrault's ideas seemed to be related; an affinity that must have been felt increasingly strongly as Berkeley and Hume developed Locke's conceptions further.

WREN, CHAMBERS AND WARE

A tract written by Perrault's great contemporary Christopher Wren contains passages that recall Perrault's notion of the dual nature of beauty. We have no evidence that the two men met when Wren visited Paris in 1665, but as soon as his books were available in England, Wren became familiar with Perrault's views. In this tract, found among his papers, Wren wrote that 'there are two Causes of Beauty, natural and customary.'[86] He then explains that natural beauty derives from 'geometry, consisting in Uniformity (that is Equality) and Proportion'. This clearly contradicts Perrault's classification. The difference between the two deepens when Wren declares that of the geometrical figures the most beautiful are the square and the circle, the parallelogram and the oval, and straight lines in preference to curves. This is far removed from Perrault's positive qualities, and I suspect that even Wren's notion of equality had little in common with the kind of symmetry which Perrault had called 'a very apparent thing'.[87]

---

before, this proportional system had been used by almost every author preceeding Perrault. Batty Langley specifically states that his system of proportioning by equal parts had been 'composed from the Masters of all Nations'. (*The Builder's Compleat Assistant*, London, s.d., Part III, headings to lectures IV ff.). Nevertheless, the systematic way in which Perrault applied this method singled him out and, no doubt, impressed his English readers. As far as I can see, in only few cases are the divisions into equal parts applied by English authors identical with those proposed by Perrault, and, with the exception of Gibbs, the process of continuous divisions described by them is considerably more complicated than Perrault's. Furthermore, the effect of Perrault's book seems to have been restricted to the adoption of this particular proportional method. Ware excepted, no writer applied Perrault's extreme standardization. All followed the traditional way when dealing with the progression of columns and pedestals, with the height of the entablature, with diminution and projection. In all these cases they adopt the variations which had been established by Vitruvius and the 'great masters' of the Cinquecento.

86. *Parentalia*, London, 1750 (Reprint by Gregg Press, 1965), p. 351.
87. *Ordonnance*, p. VII.

Wren comes nearer to Perrault's text when he defines customary beauty as 'begotten by the Use of our Senses to those Objects which are usually pleasing to us for other Causes, as Familiarity or particular Inclination breeds a Love to Things not in themselves lovely.' Even here it seems strange, if the *Ordonnance* were the source, that Wren did not take up Perrault's most original conception, the transference of the aesthetic value from positive to arbitrary beauty. Furthermore, for Wren, but not for Perrault, natural was superior to customary beauty; the former providing 'the true Test', the latter 'the great Occasion of Errors'. This should be compared with Perrault's view that 'knowledge of the arbitrary beauties . . . alone distinguishes the true architects from those who are not.'[88]

Wren may have been impressed by the poignant way in which Perrault defined the dual nature of beauty, but it is difficult to see that Perrault could have inspired him by the content of his argument alone. It is more likely that Wren was influenced, particularly in the category of natural beauty, by neo-Platonic thought.[89]

On another level a comparison between the two men is obviously called for. They both shared a keen interest in anatomy, dissections, physiology, physical sciences and mathematics; Wren discussed scientific problems with the men who later formed the Royal Society, Perrault with those assembled in the Académie des Sciences. Yet Wren, though never loosing interest in these matters, changed his profession to become a great architect. His course in life shows that a similar, decisive turning

88. ibid., p. XII.
89. On the question of Perrault's influence on Wren, see V. Fürst, *The Architecture of Sir Christopher Wren*, London, 1956, p. 174 and note 1023. Fürst believes it to be 'beyond reasonable doubt that Wren was endorsing Perrault's thoughts to the point of verbal coincidence' and that he copied directly from the English translation of the *Ordonnance*; E. F. Sekler, *Wren and his Place in European Architecture*, London, 1956, pp. 53 ff., stresses the differences and believes Wren's ideas to be rooted in Platonic and Vitruvian ideas; Kerry Downes, *Hawksmoor*, London, 1959, pp. 25 f., takes up a position somewhere in the middle between these two views; Wren's most recent biographer, Margaret Whinney, *Wren*, London, 1971, p. 202, sees the importance of Wren's remarks 'not, however, solely connected with his knowledge of French thought, but chiefly in its clear indication of his reverence for the rules of geometry and of proportion.' Similarly already Zurko, op. cit., p. 73 and Scholfield, op. cit., p. 76.

point was missing in Perrault's career and that in comparison with Wren, Perrault's pursuit of architectural practice lacked depth.

We know that, later in the century, the foremost English architect, Sir William Chambers, certainly studied Perrault's theory.[90] Among notes made by him in preparation for lectures (which, however, he never delivered), there is one on which he jotted down the page references of passages in Perrault's books that were relevant to the problem of beauty and proportions.[91] As a result, Chambers composed a text, preserved in different versions, in which he opposes two basic dogmas: one 'first stated by Perrault who asserted that the forms and proportions of the Orders of Architecture . . . owed all their power to habit, that they had at first been adopted not as having any Intrinsic merit, but because they hapned to be associated with other positive Qualities,' and the other dogma which is held by people whose 'number is great, but their opinions are Various. Some maintaining that beauty Consists in fitness or propriety others that it consists in Variety, Novelty, Harmonic relations, particular undulating lines, Triangles, Geometrical or Arithmetical progressions, association of Ideas and no two are of the same opinion.'[92] Chambers's attitude is in marked contrast to that of, say,

90. Eileen Harris has dealt with Chambers's views on architectural theory in two papers: 'Burke and Chambers on the Sublime and Beautiful,' *Essays in the History of Architecture presented to Rudolf Wittkower*, London, 1967, pp. 207 ff., and 'The Treatise on Civil Architecture,' in John Harris, *Sir William Chambers*, London, 1970, pp. 128 ff.

91. Eileen Harris was the first to investigate these lecture notes and emphasize their importance. The notes are kept at the Library of the Royal Institute of British Architects. This particular one, numbered Cha 1/8 X6, reads as follows:

'Perault Vitruvius
Vide Preface P5 beauty no other Standard than fancy
See p. 12 note 13 See p. 106 note 12 on proportions
See 214 note 6 on beauty
See all Perrault's preface to the 5 Orders
Perault 5 Or pref VI do X do XI do XII
it must be observed that in Architecture there are two kinds of perfection the one positive the other undetermined under the first kind must be classed richness of materials grandeur of dimension accuracy and neatness of execution Symetry all which are universally perceived and universally approved of under the Second head may be Comprehended form proportion disposition etc.'

92. R.I.B.A. Cha 1/8 XIV and Cha 1/8 XIII.

Soufflot or the younger Blondel. They sided unhesitatingly with François Blondel; Chambers avoids a decision in the belief that the solution to this philosophical problem is as much beyond the capacity of human under- standing as the quadratur of the circle.[93] However, as another note shows, he, like the French architects, thought it wrong to conclude from the 'infinite number of proportions diametrically opposite to each other which never the less are equally beautiful, that proportion is not necessary to the Essence of beauty. . . .'[94]

The great variations found among ancient monuments proved to Chambers that true beauty lies beyond uniform rigidity. In this connec- tion, there is a revealing critical remark about Vignola, whose Orders, in a general way, he is inclined to take as models. Vignola, he observes, 'constantly adjusted his measures . . . supposing the deviations from them, in his antique models, to proceed rather from the inaccurate execution of the workmen, than from any premeditated design.' He, Chambers, on the contrary, thinks it 'prudent on every occasion, where the same circumstances subsist, to observe exactly the same proportions; notwithstanding they may in themselves appear irregular and uncon- nected.' For that reason, he 'measured with the utmost accuracy many antique and modern buildings.'[95] Perrault was of the same opinion as Vignola, namely that 'the first inventors of the proportions of each Order did not make them as we see them in ancient works, where they only approximate to these easily commensurable measurements, but that, in fact, they made them commensurable,' while Chambers through- out his treatise preferred the odd measurements he had observed on ancient monuments.[96] He, thus, belonged to those architects whose absurd faith in the efficacy of minute changes Perrault had ridiculed. The most telling example of Chambers's approach, so different from Perrault's,

93. ibid., Cha 1/8 XIII: 'I will not therefore either perplex you nor burden myself in Search of that which so many great Philosophers have not been able to find let us suppose it (is) placed beyond the reach of human understanding like the Longitude and Quadratur of the Circle.'
94. ibid., Cha 1/8 X.
1. *Treatise on the Decorative Part of Civil Architecture*, London, 1791, p. 107.
95. *Treatise*, 1759, pp. 18 f.
96. *Ordonnance*, pl XXI.

is the measure he allots to the Doric capital. Architectural theory had, since Vitruvius, fixed its height at one whole module. Chambers rejects this round figure; instead, he takes as models the Colosseum and the Theatre of Marcellus and adds another two minutes![97]

This empirical approach also makes him adopt the modular system down to the smallest detail, opposing 'the many who prefer the method of measuring by equal parts'. In his opinion, it is as easy to remember a set of modular figures as to recall the intricate system of divisions and subdivisions; 'all that is requisite in composing' a part of a column is to know its general proportions, and 'when a design is to be executed, it is easy to have recourse to figured drawings or prints.' The last words refer, no doubt, to the many books on the Orders then in circulation, but the fact that the Attic base serves him as an example links his remark with the relevant comments made by Perrault who also selected this base in order to prove the advantage of his 'easy' method.[98] Chambers may equally have been thinking of James Gibbs who, perhaps under Perrault's influence, had used the 'method of dividing Orders mechanically into equal parts' and, because it avoids fractions, had claimed it to be 'the easiest that hath yet been published'.[99]

Some of the notes among Chambers's papers touch on other subjects dealt with by Perrault. One note refers to musical analogy, which, like Perrault, he rejects.[100] Another note comments on the topic which was discussed by almost every contemporary writer, the classification of beauty. Chambers divides aesthetic sensation into two categories: one affected by 'particular qualities in Visible Objects that Act immediately upon the organs of Vision', such as dimension, quality of light and brilliancy of colour; the other category relating to 'Propriety, Proportion, Symetry, local Colours, Grace, dignity, imitation, Accuracy, or neatness

97. op. cit., p. 21.
98. ibid., pp. 10 f. *Ordonnance*, p. 4. For the general preference of proportioning by equal parts see above, page 154, note 85.
99. *Rules for Drawing the several Parts of Architecture*, London, 1732, p. 1.
1. *Treatise*, 1759 p. 14.
100. E. Harris, *Burke*, p. 210, note 26, is of the opinion that Chambers's 'distinction between sounds and visible objects is probably derived from Claude Perrault . . .'

of Execution, materials, fitness, perfection, distance,' all owing 'their
power Chiefly to the Ideas which we connect with them'. In other words,
he differentiates between physiological and psychological causes of aesthetic
perception. That this does not correspond to Perrault's distinction of
positive and arbitrary qualities is shown by the fact that symmetry,
accuracy of execution and materials, which Perrault considered as
positive, are attributed by Chambers, together with proportion and
grace, to his 'psychological' class, all of which 'are the result of reasoning
and arise from the Association of Ideas'.[101] There is one other point that
needs mentioning: whatever the difference in approach, Chambers took
Perrault's theory seriously and did not reject it out of hand. However,
it aroused his interest comparatively late, at a time when he was preparing
his lectures: in the first edition of his treatise, published more than a
decade earlier, his attention to Perrault's ideas is less pronounced. He
comes close to them only when considering 'the general proportion for
the Apertures', believing the universally-preferred proportion of height
to width to be due to habit, and 'that we may look for the origin of many
proportions in Architecture in the same source'. The pleasure they give
us must 'be ascribed either to prejudice, or to our habit of connecting
other ideas with these figures, rather than to any particular charm inherent in them', that is to say 'if the breadth be predominant, we are
struck with the ideas of majesty and strength; and if the height predomi-
nates, with those of elegance and delicacy.'[102] In addition to this passage
which, however, I believe to be influenced by contemporary English
thought on the association of ideas rather than by Perrault, only two
other issues connected explicitly or by inference with Perrault found a
place in the first edition: firstly, Perrault's method of measuring, which
he rejects, and secondly, his arguments against adjusting the diminution

101. R.I.B.A. Cha 1/8 VIII. The note is quoted in full by E. Harris, *Burke*, pp. 209 f. and *Chambers*,
p. 132. Mrs Harris, comparing Chambers's remarks with Perrault's, comes also to the conclusion
that 'inspired perhaps by Gerard, Chambers goes much further than Perrault in tracing virtually
everything, including "dignity, Accuracy and neatness of Execution, and materials", qualities
that Perrault regarded as positive beauties, to association.' (*Burke*, p. 211).
102. op. cit., pp. 64 f.

of columns according to their height, which he accepts.[103] The really basic problems arising from Perrault's dispute with Blondel did not engage Chambers's attention till after 1770 and only one of them eventually found its way into print.[104] This is the more remarkable, since only two years before the first appearance of Chambers's treatise a work had been published that relied to an extraordinary degree on Perrault's *Ordonnance*.

This work was Isaac Ware's *Complete Body of Architecture*, an ambitious undertaking, designed to discuss every aspect of architecture. The sections dealing with the Orders form only a part (though a substantial one) of the book.[105] While with most authors so far considered Perrault's influence remained doubtful or could only be deduced with some probability, it is quite certain that Ware wrote the chapters on the Orders with the *Ordonnance* next to him. There is not a section that deals with their parts, be it base, shaft, capital or entablature, into which Ware did not incorporate what Perrault had written on the subject. He either literally copied or closely followed Perrault's text, mostly shortening and occasionally paraphrasing it.[106] Ware does not disclose that what appears to be the result of his own research is, in fact, taken from another author. Only at the end, does he acknowledge his debt. Discussing 'General Proportions of the Orders', a section based entirely on Perrault's second chapter, he refers to Perrault's innovation of the *petit module* which, he says, 'we have followed even where we have been most obliged to that author, as we have been, in the greatest degree, on a multitude of occasions.'[107] He was, indeed, obliged to Perrault, and the occasions were

103. op. cit., p. 14: 'Perrault in his notes . . . endeavours to prove the absurdity thereof.'

104. op. cit., (1791), p. 107.

105. London, 1756. The Orders are dealt with under the heading: 'Of the Ornamental Parts of Buildings,' Part III, pp. 127–271.

106. The instances in which Ware followed Perrault's text (always that of the English edition of 1708) are so numerous that it must suffice to indicate the more extensive borrowings: Ware pp. 182 f., Perrault, pp. 70 ff. (Ionic capital); Ware pp. 198 ff., Perrault pp. 85 f. (Corinthian capital); Ware p. 209, Perrault pp. 78 f. (Corinthian pedestal); Ware pp. 227 ff., Perrault pp. 94 f. (Composite capital).

107. op. cit., p. 267. Occasionally, Ware names Perrault in the preceding sections (f.i. pp. 157, 185, 189, 191, 195, 219), but in these cases the reference is confined to recommending a detail proposed by Perrault and is in no way distinct from frequent references to other authors.

many: from the detailed documentation about the great variety of measurements and forms, from the uniform rate of diminution and the progression of columns and pedestals by equal steps down to a host of specific proportions and observations.

Ware compiled his work from many sources. Tracing them is of no interest except to reveal his lack of originality. Yet, he is more independent in thought than his inclination to appear in borrowed plumes would suggest. For this reason, especially in the present context, his treatise is instructive. It confirms an observation, made already when discussing Frézier's book, that notions about the influence of custom and chance, prejudice and fashion, can be combined with views different from those held by Perrault.

'Palladio,' declares Ware, 'has done it best.' Of all authors he 'is understood to be the best and greatest'.[108] It is not surprising to hear an author close to Burlington's circle preferring Palladio to any other architect; besides, within the confines of architectural theory this was the traditional view, firmly established by Fréart's and Blondel's authoritative treatises. However, the rôle Ware assigns to Palladio, notwithstanding his admiration for him, is peculiar. He considers Palladio's rules for the Orders to be 'too narrow and too strict a confinement . . . useful in the highest degree to the common architect,' but not to the 'bolder spirit'.[109] For the 'person of real genius . . . one would wish no system of rules had been laid down for any particular proportions.'[110] But, since his book caters for the amateur and builder as well as for the professional architect, he will set out for each Order, in the first place Palladio's rules – 'the most authentick with the common race of builder'[111] – and, then, 'for the use of him who has judgment and imagination . . . on each head mention

108. ibid., pp. 152, 131.
109. ibid., pp. 140 f.: 'The single proportions described by Palladio are too narrow and too strict a confinement. They are useful in the highest degree to the common architect, and therefore we shall on every occasion deliver them; and as they are the best that have been established, we shall deliver them only: but to enlarge the view for the bolder spirit, we shall on each occasion deliver also the practice of the antients in its extent.'
110. ibid., pp. 134 f.
111. ibid., p. 147.

the greatest variations that the antients have taken . . . and hence establish . . . a mean or middle proportion between them.'[112] It is at this point that Perrault's book became so useful to Ware. Perrault had done all the spade-work for him, having assembled innumerable variations throughout the text. But Perrault's book meant more to him than a handy collection of figures: the whole idea of calculating the mean appealed to him.

He does not propose the mean 'in opposition to Palladio's rules', but as an alternative. Generally, a few lines are sufficient for dealing with Palladio's proportions, while considerable more space is taken up for ancient variations and the mean derived therefrom, a part that is invariably based on the *Ordonnance*. Since the source for the mean proportion is practically never indicated, the extraordinary situation arises that the reader of the most comprehensive book on architecture in the English language is completely unaware that the alternative proportions described at such length in this book are those of a French author.

Although Ware devotes so much space to Perrault's unified system of simple proportions, his basic outlook is different. Like Perrault he stresses the great variety brought to light by a study of ancient remains, like Perrault he makes it the basis for his calculation, but for Perrault the result – the mean – is an end in itself by which he overcomes this disturbing variety and thus arrives at something stable. For Ware, the mean is an exponent of the great variety; it does not overcome, but embraces it. It is one of the many alternatives from which the truly great architect is able to choose. The right way of instructing the student is to 'let him know what are the rules established by the most authentick writers, and what is the extent taken in variation by the antients, and what is the mean of that compass either way. Having these assistances before him, let him . . . determine as these architects did, what was best and

112. ibid., p. 135. 'We shall not,' he continues, 'propose this in opposition to Palladio's rules, but deliver it for the architect of genius to study and to compare with them.' Similarly p. 131: 'We shall therefore deliver (Palladio's) as the general and received authentic proportion in each order; but, upon a general review of the several remains in which that order is preserved, we shall add what is the mean or middle proportion of the several parts, calculating from them all.'

most noble, not in general, but in the present instance.'[113] Perrault is exasperated by the disorder of ancient variations, Ware is full of admiration for the scope it offers: for Perrault it is a sign of careless negligence, for Ware a sign of artistic mastery, and he never tires of paying tribute to the subtle skill of the ancient architects. Almost every time he has given Palladio's proportions and has calculated the mean from ancient and modern variations, he ends with a warning not to adhere too strictly to the exact rule. Each time he does so, the gulf that separates his attitude from that of Perrault widens. Their respective treatment of the Corinthian architrave may serve as an example. Perrault first states clearly the proportions he has chosen for it and then lists the many examples of which they form the mean.[114] Ware follows Perrault's text closely, citing the same examples (including those of Palladio and de l'Orme), but ends with a piece of advice that undoes everything at which Perrault had aimed: 'Both proportions are beautiful, both authorized by rule and by the antient remains: the architect may therefore take either of these, or the medium between, or any other proportion from one extreme to the other . . . It is thus of the other (variations); we have delivered a middle measure, on either side of which the architect may indulge his genius with variation; for the antients, who are his oracles, have done the same.'[115]

By insistently reminding the architects of their right to make selections between equally-valid measurements, Ware succeeded in producing a book which, in spite of being filled with extracts from the writings of others, has one outstanding merit: its main theme, pervading the whole treatise, is the notion of classical freedom. It is a notion that belongs, as has already been shown in a previous chapter, to the credo of classical doctrine, a notion that was generally accepted. Ware explains it, however, in greater detail and with greater perception than any writer before

113. ibid., p. 143.
114. *Ordonnance*, pp. 76 f.
115. op. cit., p. 204. After having followed Perrault closely when dealing with the frieze of the Composite Order (p. 233), Ware adds that the reader 'has a vast field before him for the indulging of his genius . . . let him see all and . . . select with discretion.'

him. It is his foremost ideal. 'We find there is great liberty, and why do we not take it? Let us be as bold as the antients, but first let us be judicious. Let us understand how far we may vary, and then not fear to do it.'[116] Modern architects, he believes, follow the ancients too scrupulously. They themselves knew that beauty was not restricted to one particular proportion, 'hence they indulged their genius in its regulated flight, and from that liberty produced those several great works in the same order, which are all beautiful, though extremely different one from another.'[117] The beaten path is, no doubt, the safe one, 'but he who is worthy to be called an architect, will not condescend to follow the practice of any one author with an implicit veneration, when he sees that, among those remains of the antients, which all the world admires, there is so great variety.'[118] Ware would like it to be understood that the architect's genius 'is not to be tied down by laws established by any one man, however great or judicious, but to expatiate through all those roads of freedom which the antient masters have travelled before him.'[119]

What he upholds is, of course, *classical* freedom; that is to say, he advocates 'liberty with moderation', not 'rash and wild liberty', but 'a fancy corrected by judgment'; he advises the architect to be as free as the ancients were, to 'select with discretion', and warns him that 'it is dangerous to give a loose to fancy without a perfect knowledge how far a variation may be justified'. It is a freedom 'limited within certain bounds of judgment', but it is a freedom just the same.[120] His insistence on this important aspect heightens our awareness that classical architectural thought had a wider range than a first glance might suggest. This in itself is valuable; but in our context more important is the contribution Ware thus made to our understanding of Perrault's theory. Because he borrowed so heavily from Perrault, his book highlights more strongly

116. ibid., p. 132.
117. ibid., p. 131.
118. ibid., p. 233.
119. ibid., p. 152.
120. The quotations come, in the sequence as they appear in the text, from the following pages: pp. 161, 681, 233, 135, 134.

than any other the fact that this notion of freedom, never mentioned in the *Ordonnance*, was rejected by Perrault.

In spite of this, Ware found in Perrault's Preface all the arguments which, in his opinion, sanctioned the wide choice offered to the architect. When setting out his case in general terms, therefore, he relied as much on the *Ordonnance* as he did when discussing detailed proportions, except that he adapts the text, though rarely copies it. In the preface to the whole treatise, he states that 'in speaking of the orders we shall shew what is fixed, and what is arbitrary; for the variations which are found in them among the works of antiquity shew that something is left to fancy even here.' In one of the introductory chapters to the part dealing with the Orders he comes still closer to Perrault's ideas. The measurements transmitted to us through the buildings of the ancients are prescribed by laws; but, he wonders, 'what do we suppose was the law or rule to them? it was no more than fancy... The proportions we have shewn varied greatly in their several works: we may now add they were arbitrary. They pleased when they were executed, and they became examples; because being in themselves good, and custom having approved them, it was proper to follow in the same road.' It is with the origin of architectural rules as with those of poetry: 'men have found beauties in antient works and upon those beauties they have founded rules; but they had none who made them.' If we try to find 'their reason for certain exact proportions, we cannot find it: for there appears nothing in nature that could be a reason: we have therefore great cause to suppose there was not any. Those who enthusiastically admire antiquity, declare these proportions to be incomprehensible and admire them, not only although they will not, but because they cannot understand them: this may be the way to reverence the antique: but it is not the path by which it can be imitated.' He then ends these observations by once more appropriating Perrault's text. He thinks it 'more rational to conclude that those things ... for which we can discover no reason, were not founded upon any, but were the result of fancy.'[121]

---

121. ibid., Preface; pp. 133 f. 'Fancy' is for Ware, throughout the treatise, synonymous with imagination.

Although a good many of these passages sound as if Perrault had written them, Ware made some distinct, possibly deliberate, and, in any case, significant deviations. When Ware had said, with Perrault, that 'certain exact proportions ... are the result of fancy,' he found that Perrault added that they are due to 'the Humour of the Workmen' who did not apply reason 'in the Determination of those things, the Preciseness of which was of no Importance'.[122] This was not acceptable to Ware. Instead, he speaks of the genius of the ancient architects who, like the poets, are entitled to take liberties and then adds: 'The preciseness of these measures was not of importance, and *therefore they boldly varied them.*' (my italics)[123] Thus, Perrault's low opinion of ancient variety was changed by Ware into undiluted praise. When on another occasion, Perrault demonstrates that the different projections of ancient entablatures cannot be due to adjustments made for optical reasons, Ware, on the whole, follows him, but, Perrault's conclusion 'that all this Diversity has no other Foundation than Accident', Ware leaves out, although up to this point he had been copying the text.[124] In its place, he inserts his own, very different conclusion. For him, these variations prove that the ancients aimed at 'more than has been conceived by any', that they always considered the effect of the whole building, in short, that what they did 'is above rule and must be the effect of genius'.[125]

Ware welcomes Perrault's insistence on the arbitrary nature of beauty, on custom and fancy, because he saw these notions as warrant for the artistic liberties he cherished so much. He parted company with Perrault, not because he thought him moving towards too much liberty, but because he saw him keeping out freedom altogether. No doubt, Ware was influenced by Perrault; but this influence made him map out a route which Perrault himself had never intended to take.

It is ironic that the first time an author preferred the *Ordonnance* to any other book on the Orders, and the first time its proportions were offered

122. *Ordonnance* (Engl. ed.), pp. XVf.
123. op. cit., p. 134.
124. *Ordonnance* (Engl. ed.), p. 35.
125. op. cit., p. 171.

as an alternative to those of Palladio, the most renowned master of the art, this author completely disregarded Perrault's main objective, namely that proportions should be fixed arbitrarily.[126] Perrault believed that, by clearing away the barrier of ancient authority only common sense and reason were needed to achieve this aim. Ware disagreed. His motto, derived from the study of ancient monuments, was that 'there is a great variety in them, and yet there is beauty throughout'.[127]

BRISEUX

It obviously never occured to Ware to see the *Ordonnance* as the embodiment of a theory likely to upset the evenly-poised balance of classical architecture, This, however, was precisely the charge levelled at Perrault by the French architect Charles-Etienne Briseux. When, a few years prior to Ware's treatise, Briseux published, in two volumes, a *Traité du Beau*, he had already made a name for himself, not so much by a small number of houses of a somewhat conventional character, as by another publication, written a decade earlier.[128] It had dealt competently with distribution and interior decoration, the field in which France had made her major contribution to contemporary architecture. Now in his seventies, Briseux was highly critical of the way in which the young generation thought fit to deal with architectural problems: not that he was opposed to the latest fashion for he had himself published in his earlier book designs for interiors in pure Rococo style, praised the works of Vassé and Pineau and, in his latest book, was still filled with admiration

126. Batty Langley, *A sure Guide to Builders*, London, 1729, shows on Pls XXII, XXIV, XXV, XXVI Perrault's Ionic, Corinthian and Composite Order next to those of Vitruvius, Palladio, Scamozzi, Vignola, Serlio, Bosse and Michelangelo.
   In France, the publisher Ch.-A. Jombert brought out, in 1766, as the fourth volume of his *Bibliothèque portative d'architecture* an edition of Fréart's *Parallèle* which included a comparison of Perrault's Orders with those by Charles Errard. Almost a hundred years later they formed part of another comparison, comprising those of the great masters of the Renaissance (F. A. Renard, *Architecture décimale, Parallèle des Ordres d'architecture*, Paris, 1854).
   127. op. cit., p. 134.
   128. *Traité du beau essentiel dans les arts*, Paris, 1752.
L'art de bâtir des maisons de campagne, Paris, 1743.

for Pineau's 'uncommon genius'.[129] What he objected to was a trend he thought he had detected among modern architects which made them surrender to taste and see it as the only principle that should guide them. What causes 'the innovators to broadcast so loudly the word taste', he asks himself, how can they have 'the audacity to assert that architecture has no other rule', why should it 'be deprived of solid principles, while the subsidiary arts all have fixed rules?'[130] Students, nowadays, were taught that 'there is no other rule than that of taste, that is to say, of caprice and chance', whereas in fact real success can only be achieved by the application of firm rules, 'rules of mathematical truth, rules based on nature'.[131] The teaching of the fundamental principles of architecture, of proportions, has ceased, 'the only source from which the great masters drew what is beautiful, elegant and noble in their works.' No wonder, that architecture has become decadent, that 'the truth has been hidden under the veil of falsity and arbitrariness'. The man responsible for this state of affairs, in Briseux's eyes, is no other than Perrault. He is for him the villain of the piece who through his pernicious notion that 'proportions have no share in the beauty of buildings' has brought about this decline in quality, this capitulation to taste.[132]

Seventy years had passed since Blondel had fought Perrault's paradoxical arguments. Now, once more, a repudiation of these, as it seemed to Briseux, subversive ideas had become indispensable if architecture was to assume again its former pre-eminent position. Briseux had studied with great care the *Ordonnance*, in particular its preface, and the relevant notes in Vitruvius. This enabled him to consider Perrault's theory as a whole, the first writer to do so after Blondel; like him, he takes up an uncompromising position.

In a preliminary chapter, Briseux selects from the preface of the *Ordonnance* Perrault's most provocative statements, each followed by his own reasoned response. It is, of course, easy for Briseux to refute

129. *Beau essentiel*, II, p. 6.
130. ibid., I, pp. 99 ff.
131. ibid., I, pp. 45, 65.
132. ibid., I, pp. 2 f.

Perrault's *système du hazard*, as he contemptuously calls it, and easy for him to show that proportions are, on the contrary, the mainstay of beauty, independent of custom, fashion or chance; he is at great pains to prove that, whatever Perrault had said to the contrary, acoustic harmonies and visual proportions are identical, both being founded on nature, a principle of fundamental importance to his own aesthetic theory.[133]

He is the first who was struck by the 'score of contradications to be met with' in the Preface, in particular by the strange fact that Perrault 'in spite of his obvious opposition to proportions, followed them'.[134] He could not understand 'what use the mean proportions could have if chance and caprice ought to be the artist's sole guide', if, as his followers claim, there are no other rules than those of taste.[135] Briseux was puzzled by Perrault's inconsistency and looked for an explanation, just as our intepretation has been aimed at resolving the apparent contradictions. Others, unaware of them, but shocked by the monstrosity of his *paradoxes*, had charged Perrault with insincerity. Briseux, equally discounting the possibility of a rational explanation, thought he had found it in the personal rivalry between Blondel and Perrault.

Briseux wants us to believe that Perrault, having been charged by Blondel with *singularité*, composed 'in revenge a preface of twenty-seven large pages to destroy, or at least obscure, through fallacious paradoxes the learned lectures which Blondel had given in his *Cours d'Architecture*.'[136] Perrault himself knew (of this Briseux is certain) that his system was wrong, but 'resisted the evidence and his own inner conviction' because 'his wounded pride' made him feel in honour bound to cling to his eccentric system.[137] This explanation runs counter to all the verifiable

133. ibid., I, pp. 4–11.
134. ibid., I, pp. 2, 91. The same point is made in *Examen d'un Essai sur l'architecture*, Paris, 1753, p. 179. The author of the book, La Font de Saint-Yenne, states on p. VIII that for his examination he had consulted 'habiles architectes'. The references to Perrault on pp. 178–83 of an appendix entitled 'Remarques sur ce qui est dit de l'Architecture dans *L'esprit des beaux arts*' are in phrasing as well as in tendency so close to those of the *Traité du béau* that there can be little doubt that they stem from the pen of Briseux.
135. *Examen*, p. 182, *Traité*, I, p. 65.
136. *Traité*, I, p. 2.
137. ibid., pp. 1 f., 11, 66. *Examen*, p. 183.

facts. Perrault had already expressed his 'eccentric' ideas in rudimentary
form in the first edition of *Vitruvius*: Blondel's refutation was, therefore,
a consequence, not the cause of Perrault's statements. Furthermore, when
they were finally formulated in the *Ordonnance*, the relevant volume of
the *Cours* had not yet been published. It is true that Blondel's book was
based on lectures which he gave twice weekly, from 1672 onwards, but
apart from the unlikelihood of Perrault's having attended these lectures,
it is even more improbable, to say the least, that Blondel delivered his
attack in public and at a time when, in prestige and influence, the two
brothers had reached the height of their careers. Briseux's explanation is
absurd; but its very absurdity shows how perplexed and incredulous
those were who examined the *Ordonnance* in detail.[138]

Briseux thought that, in consequence of Perrault's statement about
beauty, the architects who succeeded Blondel as professor at the Academy
'ceased teaching the fundamental principles of architecture'. This was an
effect which, Briseux imagined, not even Perrault 'had dared to expect,
although he had the boldness to risk it.'[139] In this way, Blondel's lectures,
which should for ever have been upheld to the honour of architecture,
were only too well undermined by Perrault.[140] In fact, it has come about,
Briseux complains, that nowadays 'the majority (of architects) march
confidently under the banner of Perrault and refuse to make beauty
dependent on proportions'.[141]

This is a strange statement for which our review of the architectural
literature has provided hardly any evidence. Only Frézier seems to have
been influenced to some extent by Perrault. Leclerc speaks of the 'rules
and proportions (of the Orders) as being only arbitrary', but simply in
order to establish the value of universally approved proportions, especially
those of Palladio; he never mentions Perrault.[142] Nobody subscribed to

138. On II, pp. 1 f., Briseux makes another, grotesque, statement, for which there is no evidence
at all, alleging that Blondel's publisher yielded to the pressure exerted by Perrault's followers
and suppressed Book V of Blondel's *Cours* which contained the charges against Perrault.

139. ibid., I, p. 2.

140. ibid., I, p. 11.

141. ibid., I, p. 4.

142. op. cit., p. 16.

Perrault's dubious views on proportion and beauty; many disregarded the Preface altogether, and often quite different conclusions were drawn from seemingly similar statements. As to Briseux's allegation that Perrault's writings influenced Blondel's successors, the absence of any reference to Perrault in the still extant lectures of La Hire, Desgodets and Courtonne is conspicuous; the last named going out of his way to praise Blondel's *Cours*.[143] But how is it, Briseux wonders, that though, in his opinion, Perrault's ideas were generally adopted, his Orders were rejected and never executed by a single architect; how could this inconsistency be explained?[144] In Briseux's opinion, Perrault's measurements were ignored (and it is true that only a few authors adopted them, Cordemoy and Ware being the notable exceptions) because 'the few changes which Perrault made to the Orders of the ancients ... altered the beauty visibly.'[145] Examining each Order and each part in detail, Briseux marked as a fault any occasion when the proportion adopted by Perrault fell short of the correct one; correct proportions being for him those that were based on arithmetical, geometrical or harmonic ratios.[146] (Pl. 38). Understood in this limited sense, proportions were, indeed, not taught any more, and it could be said with some justification that architects 'refused to make beauty dependent on proportions'. They treated the problem of proportions pragmatically, and in this respect their attitude was not different from Perrault's. It is also true that Blondel was the last author to discuss in detail the science of mathematical, and in particular harmonic, proportions, and that it was left to Briseux to re-state this theory. However, it was quite unreasonable to make Perrault responsible for a trend that had been gradually leading architects away from the observance of strict proportional systems – a trend which had set in long before Blondel had tried, without success, to revive the practice.

For the same reason, it was misleading to blame Perrault for having

143. Courtonne, op. cit., fol. 110 r. On his and the other academic lecture courses see my article in *The Art Bulletin*, XL, 1958, p. 36, note 77.

144. op. cit., I, p. 2.

145. ibid., I, p. 3. Also p. 96.

146. ibid., I, pp. 88 ff.

brought about a point of view which allowed taste to take up a controlling position. This, too, was the outcome of a trend the roots of which reached further back than Perrault's writings, and although it is possible that his emphasis on the arbitrary qualities of beauty were understood – or rather misunderstood – as a plea for taste to become the supreme authority, there is little evidence to prove his influence in this direction. The ascendancy of taste and the intricate problems arising out of this notion were phenomena that dominated aesthetics during the eighteenth century and were not confined solely to architectural theory. Taste took the centre of the stage, and it was absurd to suppose that a book of limited scope, such as the *Ordonnance*, could have given rise to this fundamental change. As always happens when new vistas are opened up, the word that signifies the new conception becomes a fashionable catchword. It may well be that Briseux, the septuagenarian, took the constant citation of taste for nothing more than a fashion, in which case one can understand why he thought of it as the unfortunate consequence of a single author's 'wounded pride'.

If the majority of architects had really been 'marching under the banner of Perrault', Briseux's treatise should have had the effect of rallying them to Perrault's defence. This certainly did not happen. On the few occasions when writers refer to the book, the attack on Perrault is hardly ever mentioned.[147] They all rejected the system of mathematical ratios as being too restricted and thus, implicitly, demolished the main argument on which Briseux's case against Perrault rested.[148] Pierre Estève

147. Frézier wrote a critical review of the book in the *Mercure de France*, July 1754, pp. 1 ff., without referring to Briseux's attack; J.-F. Blondel, *Arch. franç.*, IV, p. 5 note, believes that Briseux had been critical of Perrault 'dans le dessin sans doute de préconiser François Blondel'; in his *Cours*, IV, p. 188, he says that the book had little success and in his *L'homme du monde*, Amsterdam, 1774, II, p. 315, that it was 'peu estimé'; Laugier, *Essai*, 1755, refers to the book, but not to the attack, in several places (pp. XXVI, 108 f., 260). Much later, Viel de St. Maur in his *Lettres sur l'architecture*, Paris, 1787, lettre VI, p. 12, observes that 'Briseux déclamoit contre Perrault'.

148. Frézier, loc. cit.; Laugier, op. cit., pp. 260 f.

Gauthey, *Mémoire sur les règles d'architecture*, Bibl. de l'Ecole des Ponts et Chaussées, MS 1826, fols. 187 f., opposes, without explicitly naming Briseux, 'l'exactitude scrupuleuse de ces proportions qui, suivant ceux qui ont adopté ce sistème, est la seule cause de tout le plaisir que nous ressentons à la vue des beaux ouvrages de cet art.'

clearly perceived this: writing one year after publication of the *Traité du beau*, he observes: 'It would be a sign of bad faith, or rather of stupid ignorance, to allege that by rejecting arithmetical or geometrical proportions one sanctions ill-proportioned buildings and wants to make out that art is arbitrary.'[149] Those who refer to Perrault in the years following the publication of Briseux's book do not give the impression of wishing to defend him against unwarranted criticism. Comments, at times favourable, are never vindicative. Patte, discussing the preface of the *Ordonnance*, thinks little of Perrault's device of averaging, but agrees with him on many points, mainly because it opens up for him, too, the way for proposing a new system of the five Orders.[150] Another author, oblivious of Briseux's strictures on Perrault's corrupting influence, hailed him as 'the famous Perrault, the greatest architectural writer of the preceding century, the most profound theoretician' and advises those wishing to 'save architecture from eccentric opinions' to look to François Blondel and Claude Perrault who had dealt thoroughly with the principles of art.[151] Many, besides Briseux, were conscious of decadence and were as much concerned about the decline in quality as he had been, but in the opinion of most writers the artist guilty of introducing a licentious, lawless art was Borromini, not Perrault. 'The confused forms of Borromini,' wrote Patte looking back to a time when Rococo was at its height, 'threatened to make men forget the precepts of a Perrault.'[152]

Briseux's book made no difference to the general attitude towards Perrault. The response remained the same in the second half of the century as it had been during the first. His fame as an architect still eclipsed the eccentricity of his theoretical views; the treatise itself was still thought to be comparable to those of other writers, with details of his proportions occasionally being adopted, while it was still the generally held opinion that nobody had so far attained sufficient authority for

149. *L'esprit des beaux-arts*, Paris, 1753, II, p. 206.
150. *Mémoires*, 1769, pp. 76 ff.
151. Fréron, *L'Année littéraire*, 1755, II, pp. 254 f.
152. op. cit., Epître.

laying down the law.[153] Whether invariable proportions exist, whether taste is only a matter of fashion and caprice or based on nature and truth – these questions were often asked. They were topics for which a general interest then existed, an interest that cannot be directly linked to Perrault and seems to have been little influenced by Briseux's revival of the Blondel-Perrault dispute.

It is only towards the end of the century that we meet with writers who give to Perrault's statements the meaning Briseux had ascribed to them. In 1780, Le Camus de Mézières, architect of the functional Halle au Blé in Paris, criticized Perrault for his statement that 'there should be no fixed proportions, that taste alone must decide'.[154] It is significant that Camus is the only writer at that time who accepted the system of harmonic proportions, with which he had become acquainted through Ouvrard's work. Some twenty-five years later, Soane gave Perrault's text the same meaning. He, however, warned his students of the 'fanciful opinions' derived from Ouvrard's treatise on harmonic proportions, while, on the contrary, 'according to Claude Perrault, the learned translator of Vitruvius, and Architect of the celebrated façade of the Louvre, Architecture is not confined to any shackled mechanical system. It has no fixed Proportion: Taste, good sense, and sound Judgment, must direct the mind of the Architect to apply harmony and justice of relative Proportion.'[155]

Thus, the two architects, Camus and Soane, arrived at an identical

153. For favourable references to the *Ordonnance*, see *Encyclopédie*, sub *Ordre* by Jaucourt ('très-bel ouvrage') and sub *Architecture* by J.-F. Blondel ('avec des observations fort intéressantes') and *Recueil de quelques écrits*, p. 179, note 10, where the writer ranks it, along with Blondel's *Cours*, Perrault's own *Vitruvius*, Fréart's *Parallèle* and Desgodets's *Edifices*, as one of the best textbooks produced in the 17th century. Another of the above mentioned amateurs who favoured Perrault's Orders was Ribart de Chamoust, *L'ordre français trouvé dans la nature*, Paris, 1783.

154. Nicolas Le Camus de Mézières, *Le génie de l'architecture*, Paris, 1780, p. 13. K. Dézallier d'Argenville, *Vies des fameux architectes*, Paris, 1788. I, pp. 382 ff., accepts Briseux's case in his biographical article on Perrault; he repeats his explanation that 'wounded pride' made Perrault write what d'Argenville calls that 'galimatias', believing it to be 'inconcevable qu'un homme aussi habile se soit livré dans la Préface de sa traduction (*sic*) à l'esprit de paradoxe, qui depuis est devenu si commun.'

155. *Lectures on Architecture*, London, 1929, p. 100.

interpretation – one accepting, the other rejecting what in their opinion Perrault had meant to say. How this meaning could be reconciled with Perrault's clearly proclaimed intentions is as difficult to see as when, at about the same time, Boullée alleged that 'the author of the peristyle of the Louvre could in all known monuments only see fanciful products', or that, in his discussion with Blondel, Perrault had taken the extreme view that architecture is 'un art fantastique et de pure invention.'[156] Boullée's knowledge of the *Ordonnance* was, however, superficial, as is borne out by his belief that, when he stressed in his own *Essai* the basic difference between musical and visual proportions, he was presenting a point of view opposite to that of Perrault.[157] Owing to the same confusion about Perrault's text and about the stand taken by the two protagonists, Boullée was unaware that he was following Perrault when he established symmetry as the main architectural law, and that, when he finally arrived at the great principles of regularity, variety and order, he only re-stated the orthodox classical dogma which Blondel had elaborately set out more than a hundred years earlier.[158] Boulée's claim of 'having seen further than the short-sighted men who preceded me' had plainly been an idle boast.[159]

While there is, therefore, some evidence that, around the turn of the century, Perrault was believed to have acclaimed taste and imagination as the best guide available to the artist, it must be kept in mind that Soane's lectures and Boullée's treatise were only published in our time, so that any effect these opinions could have had were, particularly in Boullée's case, confined to a small circle.[160] At any rate, the apparent

156. op. cit., fols. 71v, 75v.
Reading this meaning into Perrault's writings, Boullée's reaction, when noticing the discrepancy between the Colonnade and the thoughts expressed in the Preface, is unusual: it made him slightly doubt his authorship. 'J'étais indigné de trouver dans les écrits de celui qui passe pour en être l'auteur qu'il cherchât à ravaler l'art qui l'honorait, et qu'il dénommât un art fantastique.' (f. 137r.).
157. ibid., fol. 137r, also fol. 80r.
158. ibid., fols. 81r, 139v f. This is also Pérouse de Montclos's conclusion (p. 68, note 24.).
159. ibid., fol. 137v.
160. An echo of Soane's remark, but joined to Briseux's criticism, may be detected in John Aiken, *General Biography*, London, 1813, VIII, sub Perrault: '. . . he maintains that there is no natural

discrepancy between preface and main body of the *Ordonnance* was so great that his intentions could be interpreted in diametrically opposite terms. While Boullée believed that Perrault saw in architecture only 'un art fantastique', a German writer, at almost the same time, blamed him for expecting to create a work of art 'through cold *raisonnement* and dry rules and calculations', and for being the kind of designer who 'lacking experience and the spirit of art . . . works out proportions with the treatise in his hand.'[161]

These words herald a change in taste, soon becoming more prominent and gradually causing people to scorn the architectural styles of the preceding two centuries. For this reason, the last champion of the classical style, Quatremère de Quincy, was also the last writer before the emergence of art-history to take note of the *Ordonnance*. When his *Encyclopédie* was first published, the neo-classical style reigned supreme. It did not seem necessary, then to do more than name the *Ordonnance* among the list of Perrault's literary works, but when, more than forty years later, he revised the *Encyclopédie*, the situation had changed. Classical taste was on the defensive, the romantic movement in the ascendancy. Now Quatremère thought it expedient to underline the merits of the *Ordonnance*, and described it as a book that 'comprises the best doctrine on the general principles of architecture and a complete analysis' of the classical system and praised the Preface for containing 'a general theory that includes excellent notions'.[162]

Quatremère was 75 years old when making these observations. It is unlikely that the younger generation was at all interested in a treatise dealing with the unimaginative classical dogma.[163] Nevertheless, Perrault's

foundation for the architectural proportions, but that they may be infinitely varied according to taste and fancy; an opinion which has given much offence, though justified by the practice of the ancients themselves.'

161. J. Fr. Freiherr zu Racknitz, *Darstellung und Geschichte des Geschmacks*, s.l.a. (after 1798), p. 31.

162. Quatremère de Quincy, *Encyclopédie méthodique. Architecture*, Paris, 1788; 2nd ed. 1832 (sub Perrault). The entry in the second edition was published already as a separate paper in his *Histoire de la vie et des ouvrages des plus célèbres architectes*, Paris, 1830, II, pp. 207 ff.

163. César Daly in *Revue générale d'architecture*, VII, 1847/48, p. 436: '. . . les travaux de M. Quatremère ont la plupart de leurs racines dans le XVIIIe. Autre temps, autres doctrines.'

name was not forgotten: the Louvre façade remained one of the masterpieces of French art, and Perrault was generally accepted as its author.
Viollet-le-Duc, anxious to rouse Frenchmen into trusting their own
architects, called him 'un homme de coeur et d'esprit' because he had
succeeded in ousting the 'clumsy workman, called Bernini,' while
Laborde, exceptional in his interest in the architecture of the immediate
past, spoke of Perrault as the 'celebrated author of the famous colonnade
of the Louvre' which, with all its faults, cannot 'detract from his reputation, established so well and firmly, more firmly perhaps than the
colonnade itself.'[164]

A few years earlier, on the eve of the revolution of 1848, César Daly,
the spirited editor of the influential *Revue générale de l'architecture*, had
called for 'liberty in art', demanding that 'every artist be free to listen
to the inspiration of his genius and the voice of his time'.[165] In the following
year, still moved by the revolutionary spirit, he described how at the time
of Louis XIV 'the finger of scorn was pointed at those who had been
pleading the cause of freedom for the modern artists.' It would be understandable if the modern reader were to pause at this point, expecting that
here at last will be given a new interpretation of Perrault's rôle among
architectural writers. Daly did not make clear whom he had in mind.
From the context, the persons most likely meant were those who still,
in the seventeenth century, saw beauty in Gothic works. Whoever
they were, Daly did not think of Perrault. In the sentence immediately
following the one just quoted, he does refer to the 'works of Blondel, of
Perrault', but only as witnesses for the different attitude towards antiquity
held during their time, compared with that held during the Renaissance.[166]
Perrault and liberty were not connected – yet!

Perrault, architect of the Louvre: it is in this capacity that he appeared

164. Viollet-le-Duc in *Annales archéologiques*, IV, 1846, p. 270. He cites in the article Charles
Perrault's *Mémoires*, published in Avignon 1759. In this way, Charles's version of the Louvre
'affair' was kept alive; it was not until Lance's critical article on Perrault appeared in his *Dictionnaire
des architectes français*, Paris, 1872, that the correctness of Charles's statements was seriously
challenged.
    A. de Laborde in the *Revue générale*, X, 1852, p. 199.
    165. *Revue générale*, VII, 1848, pp. 392 ff. (the quotation on p. 398).

in the comprehensive architectural histories written around the middle of the nineteenth century. In some of the books – provided, of course, that the author thought it worth his while to deal with post-medieval styles – Perrault's Colonnade was still admired. Readers were told that of all the buildings erected under Louis XIV this was 'the most notable', unsurpassed in modern times 'either for elegance or propriety', that its effect was 'truly grandiose and magnificent' and that it deserved 'the admiration expressed for it'.[167] These tributes are the more remarkable for coming from writers whose censure of the 'modern' style was harsh. Some scholars of the next generation took a serious interest in the art of the seventeenth and eighteenth centuries, but the competent treatment of Baroque architecture had to wait until a professional architect and historian choose this subject because he was genuinely attracted by the unique beauty of Baroque monuments.

CORNELIUS GURLITT

Gurlitt is the first modern historian who deals at length with the Blondel-Perrault dispute, and the first who tries to evaluate the issue afresh.[168] He begins with Blondel, showing that his conception of beauty was based on harmony and proportions, on simple ratios and a system of unified measures, and on figures which, in Gurlitt's opinion, Blondel found out 'through ingenious, but really untenable inquiries into the

---

166. ibid., VIII, 1849, p. 10.
On Daly and the various trends of architectural thought during this period see the informative book by Peter Collins, *Changing Ideals in Modern Architecture 1750–1950*, London, 1965.

167. The quotations have been selected from the following handbooks:
Franz Kugler, *Handbuch der Kunstgeschichte* (1st ed. 1842), Stuttgart, 1872, p. 314.
Léonce Reynaud, *Traité d'architecture*, Paris, 1863 (1st ed. 1850), II, p. 543.
Léon Chateau, *Histoire et caractères de l'architecture en France*, Paris, 1864, p. 525.
James Fergusson, *History of the Modern Styles of Architecture*, London, 1862, p. 215.
Joseph Gwilt in his edition of Chambers's treatise, London, 1825, p. 163, note 5 speaks of 'the admirable façade of the Louvre'.

168. *Geschichte des Barockstiles des Rococo und des Klassicismus in Belgien, Holland, Frankreich, England*, Stuttgart, 1888, pp. 154 ff.
I suspect that Gurlitt's name is hardly known today. Yet the three volumes of his *Geschichte des Barockstiles*, published from 1887 to 1889, were as much the cause of encouraging further research on Baroque architecture as Wölfflin's *Renaissance und Barock* which appeared at the same time (1888). For many decades Gurlitt's book remained an indispensable standard work.

nature of musical consonance'. Convinced that 'any deviation, any complicated fraction would produce dissonance', Blondel tried, in Gurlitt's vivid phrase, 'to catch beauty in the meshes of tables.'[169]

Having outlined Blondel's rigid system, Gurlitt next presents Perrault's views, as he sees them. Perrault he writes, was aware of the inaccuracies in the proportions of ancient monuments and was, for that reason, 'of the opinion that these do not need to be strictly adhered to, that one can change them at will, as long as one does it with taste, skill and understanding.' The proportions of the Orders were not based on nature, but had been the result of mutual consent among architects; eventually, through force of custom, a universally-valid taste had been achieved. That is the reason why Perrault 'wants to have preserved the right for the architect to change the Orders according to each architect's sense of beauty'. Next, Gurlitt mentions Perrault's notion of dual beauty and declares that he called arbitrary that kind of beauty 'which follows the changing taste of the period and the opinions of the Court, in short, which is modish'. Perrault, according to Gurlitt, was of the opinion that 'the Orders of the ancients were the result of an arbitrary, that is free act of brilliantly gifted artists and, therefore, it ought also to be possible for a great modern architect to create something that, although it deviates from the proportions as applied until now, is yet beautiful.' This is the most difficult part for the architect, whereas the creation of beauty according to rules demands only common sense. 'The task of the architect,' exclaims Perrault in Gurlitt's rendering, 'could not possibly consist only in the mechanical application of the rules; on the contrary, he must try to invent new and apparently right . . . proportions which do not deviate too much from the traditional and customary ones.' Gurlitt's final conclusion is that 'Perrault thus demands for his fellow-artists the right of making independent changes to traditional forms'.[170]

It is obvious that Gurlitt in this summary disregarded some of the most

169. op. cit., pp. 154 f. In a strange reversal, Gurlitt uses phrases in his interpretation of Blondel's theoretical views which rather fit those of Perrault.
170. ibid., pp. 155 f.

important points of Perrault's theory. No mention is made of his contention that beauty is independent of proportions, or that custom has the power of giving arbitrary beauty the semblance of positive beauty, nor is reference made to his statements about optical adjustment which so much contradicted the views which Gurlitt made out to be Perrault's. Clearly, Gurlitt selected only those passages which, taken together, form a consistent point of view. The paraphrasing itself is done so loosely that at times it is difficult to relate it to the relevant passage in Perrault's text. In addition, Gurlitt also introduced phrases of his own which give the whole selection an even stronger bias. Nowhere had Perrault said that one 'could change proportions at will', nor that architects could change the Orders, 'according to their sense of beauty', nowhere had he mentioned the 'free act of brilliantly gifted artists' and never had he denounced the 'mechanical application of rules'.

Where Gurlitt keeps nearer to the wording of Perrault's remarks, he alters in many cases the emphasis and, as it were, the direction which Perrault gave them. For Perrault, these were incidental remarks, not important links in a thoroughly argued case; they were meant only to support his main claim that proportions are not instrumental in the creation of beauty. Gurlitt turns them into precepts which Perrault advises architects to adopt. In this way, he conveys the impression of Perrault's really demanding 'the right for his fellow-artists to make independent changes' and of asking them to emulate the 'free act' of the brilliantly-gifted architects of Antiquity. Gurlitt deals in the same way with Perrault's notion of arbitrary beauty. He selects the simile of the fashion at Court, used by Perrault as an analogy illustrating his principle of transference of qualities, and, disregarding all other explanations given by Perrault, makes it into an all-embracing definition of this class of beauty. It is because of this 'extremely significant' remark that Gurlitt feels justified in calling Perrault 'the spiritual father of the Rococo.'[171]

---

171. ibid., p. 156. See Appendix VII for a comparison of Gurlitt's text with Perrault's relevant passages.

Others had already interpreted Perrault's text in a way similar to
Gurlitt's summary. They also believed him to have advocated arbitrary
changes, but they had invariably condemned his theory.[172] Gurlitt
was the first to transform the blame for preaching lawlessness into
praise for upholding the artist's right to freedom of action. It is in
line with this appreciation that he dismissed Blondel's 'counter-arguments . . . (as) very superficial.'[173] As a competent historian, Gurlitt
was, of course, aware of the complicated pattern of French Baroque
architecture with its cross-currents of classicism. He recognized that, in
spite of the fundamental difference between Blondel and Perrault, the
two had this in common: that they both preferred classical simplicity
to Baroque profusion.[174] At no time, however, are his readers left in any
doubt as to which of the two contestants was nearer to his heart. Thus,
two hundred years after the inception of the *Ordonnance*, the scales are
weighted heavily in Perrault's favour.

This positive attitude, which makes Gurlitt look for and appreciate
the progressive elements of a period, is the natural consequence of his
sensitivity to the beauty of these styles, but this does not sufficiently
explain why he arrived at this particular interpretation, nor why it was
put forward at this particular time. I believe that for an answer one must
look to those of his writings which are not strictly art-historical. This
will force us to make a digression which, it may be thought, leads too
far away from Perrault, but unless we know more about Gurlitt's taste
and aesthetic outlook, both of which must to some extent have influenced
his evaluation of Perrault's ideas, the explanation we are seeking will not
be forthcoming.

At the same time that he was engaged on his research into Baroque
and Rococo architecture, Gurlitt was active as an art-critic. His concern
for the art of his own time – painting, sculpture and architecture – was
as intense as was his interest in periods that were long past, and his

172. With the exception of Soane. See above p. 175.
173. ibid., p. 156.
174. ibid., p. 155.

comments in this field were equally knowledgeable and competent. He saw clearly that his individual response to art determined his standpoint as an art-historian. Once, when looking back over his life, he declared: 'Art is something I want to perceive with my senses, and if I learned at an early date to understand the Baroque style, it is just because of my aversion to aesthetic principles.'[175] This is borne out by his numerous articles on contemporary art and artists, his regular reviews on art exhibitions and his book on *Die Deutsche Kunst des 19ten Jahrhunderts*.[176] In these writings he reveals his whole attitude towards art and towards those problems of an aesthetic, and sometimes also of a more general, nature which were, at the time, the subject of lively discussion.

Again and again, he warns the reader about the pernicious influence of abstract rules, seeing real progress only in the liberation from their restrictive control. He compares the 'liberating force' of Menzel's art to a 'battering ram' used by the young generation in their attack against the 'senseless habit of making laws', and hails Wallot's Reichstag building as evidence that 'not rules, but only artistic vigour' can produce the right work.[177] He derides 'the rules of the measuring rod' when analysing Schinkel's architecture, and 'the rigid rule of the system' when dealing with the Viennese buildings of Theophil Hansen.[178] In a lecture given in 1883, he denounces 'the regularity and uniformity, the strict observance of proportions which at one time were considered to be beautiful' as the main evil which 'impedes and restrains us everywhere'.[179] Against the 'spirit of the law' he opposes the 'uncompromising activity of the individual and the free representation of one's own taste', commends the true artist, who, not concerned with rules, creates by following his own free choice, and – reiterating Daly's maxim of a generation earlier – also exclaims that 'Art is freedom'.[180]

175. In J. Jahn (ed.), *Die Kunstwissenschaft der Gegenwart in Selbstdarstellungen*, Leipzig, 1924, p. 11.
176. Vol. 2 of *Das 19te Jahrhundert in Deutschlands Entwicklung*, ed. P. Schlenther, Berlin, 1899.
177. ibid., pp. 510, 643.
178. ibid., pp. 261, 438 f.
179. ibid., p. 483.
180. ibid., pp. 73, 510; 'Ästhetische Streitfragen,' *Die Gegenwart*, XLIII, 1893, p. 186.

Gurlitt's belief in the freedom of the arts and the artist, unfettered by any extraneous rules, springs from his adherence to 'individualism', a particular brand of *Weltanschauung* which can be traced back to the rise of German liberalism around the middle of the nineteenth century. Individualism became a creed effective in all walks of life. In the political and economic field it meant a demand for the free activity of the individual unhampered by any intervention of the State, on the cultural level the conviction that great art is created through free expression of the artistic individuality without the constraint of an aesthetic system, and on the art-critical level faith in a radical subjectivism.[181] This attitude was adopted by a wide section of the educated public. It has, in fact, been said that 'for the men of the nineteenth century a mental climate other than individualistic seemed to be unthinkable'.[182] Gurlitt was introduced to this philosophy when, in 1885, he made the acquaintance of a man who five years later published *Rembrandt als Erzieher*, one of the most debated books of the century. Its author, Gurlitt acknowledged later, helped him 'to a clear understanding of the essence of individualism'.[183]

It was with these beliefs sincerely held that Gurlitt set out to write his history of Baroque architecture. Of course, this is not to say that he thought the standard he had adopted as a critic of contemporary art to be equally valid for his work as a scholar.[184] Whatever we may think today – he wrote in his appreciation of the Louvre – about the praise lavished on this building by the critics of the eighteenth century, 'we must respect (this judgment) as a fact and recognize that it places the exceptional art-historical importance of this work beyond question.'[185] Nevertheless, he

181. For examples of Gurlitt's outspoken subjectivism, see *Die Gegenwart*, XLIII, 1893, pp. 185 f., XLV, 1894, p. 315.

182. Georg Steinhausen, *Deutsche Geistes-und Kulturgeschichte von 1870 bis zur Gegenwart*, Halle, 1931, p. 303.

183. *Deutsche Kunst*, p. 494; *Westermann's Monatshefte*, LV, 1911, p. 677. For Langbehn, the anonymous author of the *Rembrandt*, and his position within the wider framework of German cultural development during the late 19th and early 20th centuries, see the interesting study of Fritz Stern, *The Politics of Cultural Despair*, Berkeley, 1961, chapter II, pp. 97 ff.

184. See *Deutsche Kunst*, p. 154 for his view on the need of the art-historian's unbiased attitude.

185. *Barockstil*, p. 148.

THE SEQUEL

185

is equally aware of the fact 'that it is quite impossible to grasp a period
correctly, as impossible for a historian as it is for a poet or an artist. . .
Whoever does not share Schiller's idealism or Mommsen's political
views, will consider both their accounts to be wrong.'[186] The introduction
to his book on Italian Baroque contains a good example of how an
author's involvement in the leading ideas and problems of his time gives
direction to his enquiry into the trends and structure of a particular
historical situation. In this passage Gurlitt points out that as a result of the
intensified study of ancient remains the masters of the High Renaissance
'did not judge any more solely according to a taste based on personal
sentiment, but rather according to ever more precisely conceived
aesthetic and, above all, formal laws.' In contrast, the artist of the Gothic
style did not suffer from this conflict between imagination and judgment.
Only from the High Renaissance onwards, did this conflict exist and
was bound to lead to 'disputes on the dividing line between the free
individualism of the artistic genius and the ever more stringently formulated laws . . . the question was bound to be asked whether superior
right should be accorded to the unhampered development of the individual
or to the law.'[187]

Although Gurlitt clearly preferred the Baroque to the classical trend
when tracing the two strands throughout the periods under discussion,
he was, nevertheless, sensitive to the high quality of French architecture
where the classical trend is predominant. Perrault's Colonnade, he
wrote, has 'a sublime beauty,' it is distinguished as the result of a happy
master-stroke and bears the stamp of effortless creation, of a 'greatness
free and unrestrained.' The Colonnade, he continued, 'grew naturally,
was not puzzled out at the sweat of the brow; it satisfies the strict demand
of French rule, but it does not show up, as was the case with Mansard,
that the rule was a hindrance to the creative impulse.'[188] Obviously, here

186. *Deutsche Kunst*, p. 280.
187. *Geschichte des Barockstiles in Italien*, Stuttgart, 1887, pp. 2 f.
188. *Deutsche Kunst*, p. 23; *Barockstil*, p. 148.

was an artist to Gurlitt's liking. In spite of the uniformity and standardization imposed by rules, Perrault had been able to retain his individuality
and spontaneity. It was quite unthinkable that a great artist of Perrault's
standing would in his writings simply reiterate a sterile dogma.

It is true that Gurlitt, a few pages before he discusses the Blondel-
Perrault dispute, refers to Perrault's remarks in the introduction to his
Vitruvius, which we have cited at the beginning of the second chapter.
Gurlitt paraphrases this passage correctly, even underlining Perrault's
demand for rules by adding to the text a warning (not, in fact, made by
Perrault) about the dangers inherent in the 'unrestrained freedom of the
imagination' which would subject beauty to 'the worst fluctuations'.[189]
It must have seemed impossible to Gurlitt that the creator of the Colonnade, an undoubtedly sensitive artist, could have meant these statements,
appropriate enough in an edition of Vitruvius, to represent his artistic
credo. When he, therefore, came to deal with what Perrault had to say
in the preface to the *Ordonnance*, he completely disregarded this passage,
to such an extraordinary extent that he did not notice, or in any case did
not comment upon, the obvious contradictions between the two texts
he had paraphrased. Instead, he looked at the *Ordonnance* through the
lenses of his own individualistic conceptions, and only those passages
came into clear focus that accorded well with the ideal of individualism,
while all the rest, remaining blurred, seemed to have no great significance.

Thus, once again, the high reputation which Perrault enjoyed as the
author of the Louvre façade prevented a just interpretation of his thoughts.
However, while on previous occasions his fame caused writers to disregard the Preface altogether, Gurlitt looked for and found in it statements
which seemed to him equal to Perrault's work and worthy of an artist
of his distinction. In the past, this misinterpretation had been of no
consequence; this time it was different: Gurlitt's notions of what he
thought Perrault had intended to convey were instrumental in mapping
out the place which modern art-history has assigned to Perrault and his
architectural theory.

189. ibid., p. 152.

Gurlitt's interpretation was given considerable support by a book on the *Querelle*, published at the beginning of this century.[190] Its author, Gillot, saw the *modernes* very much as a political party with a clearly defined programme, the main article of which was to fight authority in any shape or form and to assert 'with eloquence and determination the rights of liberty in the arts.'[191] The Moderns, according to Gillot, represented the link between the century of authority and that of liberty of thought.[192] 'By proclaiming loudly (these) rights,' Gillot concludes, using words reminiscent of Gurlitt, 'the Moderns prepared that decisive emancipation of the *individual*, that triumph of *individualism*, which the romantic revolution was finally to establish.' (Gillot's italics).[193] Gillot hardly mentions Perrault's architectural writings, and discusses only his treatise on ancient and modern music, but his conclusion is meant to apply to his whole personality: he was a Modern who subscribed to the 'programme' as imagined by Gillot.

The picture which Gurlitt had drawn of Perrault was new and exciting: the picture emerged of a man who was in advance of his time, who had a vision, however blurred, of things to come. Although our views about the age in which Perrault lived have changed considerably since Gurlitt wrote his book, it is, I think, fair to say that Perrault's image, as reflected in Gurlitt's summary, is still thought to be valid.[194] Exaggerated features have been erased, while others have been drawn even more sharply, and note has been taken of contradictions – but, on the whole, he remained the writer whose progressive thoughts benefited the generations which succeeded him.[195]

190. Hubert Gillot, *La querelle des anciens et des modernes*, Paris, 1914.
191. ibid., p. 178.
192. ibid., p. 561.
193. ibid., p. 561.
194. This is still the interpretation which L. Tatarkiewicz recently advanced in 'L'esthétique du Grand Siècle,' *XVIIe siècle*, 1968, pp. 21 ff.
195. Kurt Cassirer, *Die ästhetischen Hauptbegriffe der französischen Architektur-Theoretiker von 1650–1780*, Diss., Berlin, 1909, p. 25, rejected Gurlitt's remark about Perrault's being 'the spiritual father of the Rococo'.
More recently, Fiske Kimball, *The Creation of the Rococo*, Philadelphia, 1943, p. 14, criticized 'modern interpretations which would make of Perrault the spiritual destroyer of the academism he in fact so actively promoted', a remark that gives support to our own interpretation.

The examination of Perrault's views, as offered in these pages, has not lent support to this interpretation. It showed that his paramount intention was to bring proportions into a clearly defined and strictly followed system. In this way, he conformed to the analogous designs of those in authority, while it brought him into conflict with the artistic aspirations of the architects who cherished the restricted freedom which allowed them to vary the accepted norm. Far from realizing the contradictions existing within the spheres in which he was interested, and far from wishing to overcome them, he was proud of what had been achieved during his lifetime in the sciences and the arts – as conscious and proud, no doubt, as his brother of witnessing an age that came to an extraordinary degree close to the blissful state of perfection.[196] When setting forth his thoughts on architectural theory, Perrault hoped to make his own contribution to these achievements, not to question them, but, although in this sense he was conforming, his mind was by no means dull. Being intelligent, inquisitive and interested in every aspect of human activities, he preferred to go his own way, convinced that by looking at things from a point of view opposed to that commonly held, he would be in a position to make new discoveries, to succeed where others had failed. For this reason, he made ample use of *paradoxes*, even though he thus became open to the charge of aspiring after *singularité*. This strongly pronounced trait in his character caused him to express his ideas in provocative statements. However, reading the *Ordonnance* carefully, and seeing how he shrank from crossing swords with Blondel on one of the vital points of his theory, it becomes evident that these statements, though provocative, were not challenging; that, though disturbing to the profession – and probably meant to be – they did not reach any depth. Later generations were also shocked by them, but, as we have tried to show, were little influenced by them.

196. Charles Perrault, *Parallèle*, I, pp. 98 f.: 'Je me rejouis de voir nostre siècle parvenu en quelque sorte au sommet de la perfection. Et comme depuis quelques années le progrez marche d'un pas beaucoup plus lent, et paroist presque imperceptible, de mesme que les jours semblent ne croistre plus lors qu'ils approchent du solstice, j'ay encore la joye de penser que vrai-semblablement nous n'avons pas beaucoup de choses à envier à ceux qui viendront après nous.'

Our interpretation makes Perrault's views on architecture less radical and far-seeing than a first glance suggests. On the other hand, it may have helped to make them more comprehensible by explaining them as the necessary building material for a theory, consistent and free from contradictions. While he accepted the basic beliefs and conceptions of his age, he approached architectural problems from an unconventional point of view. In this way, he succeeded in producing a book that is a valuable contribution to the architectural literature of the seventeenth century, a book that widens the scope and thus enriches our understanding of this period.

APPENDIX I

The Machines for
the Pediment of the Louvre

It is generally assumed that the specially-devised wooden constructions for transporting and raising the stones were Perrault's invention (L. Vitet, *Le Louvre et le nouveau Louvre*, Paris, 1882 (first ed. 1833), p. 139; L. Hautecoeur, *Le Louvre et les Tuileries*, Paris, 1927, p. 174, note 7; R. Blomfield, *A History of French Architecture*, London, 1921, I, pp. 77 f.). However, there is no evidence for this. The main reason for crediting Perrault with the invention derives from the fact that an illustration, added to the second edition of *Vitruvius*, p. 341 (Pl. 7), shows the same machinery as depicted in an engraving by Sébastian Leclerc (Pl. 6) which was to commemorate the successful execution of this risky operation. All that can be deduced from it is that Perrault had asked Pierre Lepautre, when commissioning him with the illustration, to copy the machines as shown on Leclerc's engraving – the contraption for transporting the stones in every detail, and the one for raising the stones equally exactly, but in a manner that showed clearly what Perrault wished to demonstrate, namely that the precariousness of the operation made it necessary for the foreman to test continuously the tension of the various cables. In addition to these two machines, Lepautre's engraving shows a third one.

In his note 4 on pp. 339 ff. and in his explanation to the plate (p. 340), Perrault never claims to have invented the first two machines. He refers to the operation carried out at the Louvre only as 'un exemple de l'usage que peut avoir la connoissance de cette tension des cables', an expert knowledge which Vitruvius had mentioned when discussing the stringing and tuning of catapults (*Vitruvius*, X, xii), and speaks of fig. I of his illustration as representing 'la machine qui a servy à amener la pierre' and of fig. II as the one 'qui a servy à élever et poser la pierre'. After having explained in detail the hazards involved in raising stones as heavy and as long as those used for the pediment of the Louvre, he adds that 'dans cette veue et dans la crainte qu'on pouvoit avoir de ne pas connoistre assez exactement les différentes tensions des cables ... j'avois proposé une manière qui fut jugée tout-à-fait infaillible, et suivant laquelle il estoit impossible qu'un endroit de la pierre fust soulevé qu'elle ne le fust également par tous les autres.' This new machine, fig. III on his plate, is the only one which he claims to have invented. His own remarks thus prove that he had nothing to do with designing the constructions of the other two machines which were actually used in the operation. Furthermore, the problem of how to handle these huge stones had already arisen in 1672, when they were cut in the quarry at Meudon and brought down to the Seine (*Comptes*, I, pp. 595 f.). By that time, Colbert and the architect in charge at the Louvre must have been satisfied that efficient technical means for transporting and lifting these stones existed. Had Perrault been concerned with this problem, he would have taken the opportunity of referring to the proposed procedure in the first edition of *Vitruvius*.

What in fact happened was that the man in charge of carpentry work at the Louvre and other Royal buildings, Poncelet Cliquin (he is mentioned in the *Comptes* from 1664 onwards), was entrusted with the task of constructing devices for the operation. Cliquin was, according to Sauval, experienced in this kind of work, his 'fort ingénieuse' machine being 'dans le goût et semblable à une autre qu'il avoit dressée pour l'élever le cheval de bronze, amené de Nanci quelque tems auparavant.' (Henri Sauval, *Histoire et recherches des antiquités de la ville de Paris*, 1724, II, p. 61. Sauval, who died in 1678, had written the main text in the 1650's; subsequently he must have added this passage which refers to September 1674 as the date of the stone-laying and also mentions the engraving. The additional information that 'l'on trouve dans la dernière edition de Vitruve' is an interpolation). Clichin was paid for the machines in 1674 (*Comptes*, I, p. 741).

The question remains of when Perrault designed his improved version. He implies that he submitted his design in competition to the method finally used. However, it is then difficult to understand, not only why a machine considered to be 'infallible' was not adopted, but also why he failed to refer to it in the first edition. It is much more likely that, having witnessed the actual performance of raising the stones and placing them in position, he realized the difficulties and thought of an improved method. The opportunity for making use of it, however, did not arise. 'J'en fis faire un modèle qui est au Cabinet des machines de la Bibliothèque du Roi.' (p. 342).

Laprade, op. cit., p. 56, note 4, is also of the opinion that the machines had been invented by Cliquin, not by Perrault. On the other hand, he assumes that Perrault was responsible for the idea of constructing the pediment from two monoliths and supervised its execution; an assumption which comes somewhat unexpectedly from an author who is inclined to decry Perrault's architectural capability. The reason for this seemingly generous attitude towards Perrault is that, in Laprade's judgment, the whole idea was a 'tour de force' (App. C2), which he did not wish to attribute to d'Orbay.

Literary Appreciation
of Perrault's Scientific Work

The most explicit tribute to the value of Perrault's scientific work comes from no less a person than Leibniz. During Leibniz's stay in Paris, that is between 1672 and 1676, Perrault had sent him a paper on the causes of gravity, elasticity and other physical phenomena (later published in the *Essais*). In reply, he received a long letter (*Sämtliche Schriften und Briefe*, herausgegeben von der Preussischen Akademie der Wissenschaften, Zweite Reihe, Erster Band, Darmstadt, 1926, pp. 262 ff.). 'J'y ay pris,' wrote Leibniz, 'd'autant plus de plaisir, que je trouve beaucoup de conformité entre quelqu'uns de vos sentimens, et de ceux que j'avois eu sur le même sujet. . . . Ainsi je tiens que la cause que vous apportée du ressort et de la dureté . . . est tout à fait asseurée; et il n'en faut pas chercher de meilleure. Aussi les conséquences qui vous en tirez sont d'autant plus belles, que vous estes mieux informé que la plus part de ceux qui se meslent d'écrire en physique des phénomènes particuliers de la nature. C'est pourquoy je souhaitterois fort que vous vous puissiez appliquer à des recherches de la texture intérieure des corps. . . .' While disagreeing with Perrault's explanation of the cause of weight, Leibniz shows how much he valued Perrault's understanding of these matters by setting out – for the first time – his own theory of weight and gravity. At the end of the letter, he expresses the hope that by his own, analytical, method 'estant joint avec les méditations des personnes aussi versées dans les belles connoissances de la physique particulière que vous l'estes, j'oserois espérer qu'on pourroit au moins parvenir à quelque chose d'utile aux hommes . . .'

Both these men – Perrault as well as Leibniz – must have benefited by these exchanges. The similarity between Perrault's conception of 'pensées négligées et confuses' and Leibniz's 'petites perceptions' is unlikely to have been coincidental. A. Bertrand, *Mes vieux médecins*, Lyons, 1905, p. 188, even believes that Perrault's ideas on the subject 'font pressentir Leibniz'. (Similarly, F. Fearing, *Reflex Action*, Baltimore, 1930, p. 33). Leibniz himself testified on another occasion to the debt he owed to Perrault. Discussing with Huygens the geometrical problem of a certain curve, he wrote (October 1693, *Oeuvres Huygens*, X, p. 540): 'Vous estes tombé de vous même sur une idée, que j'avois déja, mais que j'ay apprise d'un autre. C'est de feu M. Perrault le Médecin qui me proposa de trouver (a curve having these properties).' (Leibniz acknowledged it again in a letter to Guido Grandi, published in *Allgemeine Monatsschrift für Wissenschaft und Literatur*, 1854, p. 223). For other instances when Leibniz referred to Perrault's scientific work see

Catalogue critique des manuscrits de Leibniz, Poitiers, 1914 ff., Fascicule II, Nos. 784, 785, 945C, 1204.

Huygens is less generous in this respect, but the fact that he carried out experiments with Perrault (*Oeuvres*, X, p. 323, XIX, p. 372) and showed him, as the first person, some of his own inventions (*Oeuvres*, VII, p. 410, VIII, p. 479) proves that he appreciated Perrault's judgment in scientific matters. (Various references to Perrault's work, attributed by Barchilon, op. cit., p. 29 to Huygens, are, however, not made by Huygens, but by the editor of the *Oeuvres*).

At about this time, the eminent German philosopher Johann Christoph Sturm (father of the architect and writer on architectural theory Leonhard Christoph Sturm) was much impressed by Perrault's sceptical statement that in Physics we cannot attain more than probability; he cites the relevant passages from Perrault's preface and acknowledges that owing to these remarks and the title of Perrault's book he added 'hypothetica' to the title of his own book (*Physica electiva sive hypothetica*, Nürnberg, 1697, preface and II, iii, 8).

Perrault's study on sound (Essais, II)

It was recognized as the best work so far on the subject by his colleagues J.-G. Duverney, *Traité de l'organe de l'ouie*, Paris, 1683, Avertissement, and by Denis Dodart, 'Mémoire sur les causes de la voix de l'homme,' *Histoire de l'Académie Royale des Sciences*, 1700, note p. 271. Dodart, when realizing that Perrault had stated a certain fact before him, admitted this, saying that 'ce seroit la moindre justice que je deusse à un Auteur d'un si rare mérite, dont je fais gloire d'avoir été disciple deux ans de suite . . .' J.-B. Duhamel, the secretary of the Academy, refers to Perrault's accurate and lucid anatomical descriptions of the ear and his research on sound (*Philosophia vetus et nova*, Paris, 1681, VI, p. 112), and J. de Hautefeuille speaks of the treatise and its author in the most exalted terms (*L'art de respirer sous l'eau . . .*, (Paris), 1681, pp. 21 f.). In the next century, the Chevalier de Jaucourt, author of the article 'oreille' in the *Encyclopédie*, believes that 'on ne lui a point rendu toute la justesse qu'il méritoit'. The next reference is that of Kurt Sprengel who in his important standard work, *Versuch einer pragmatischen Geschichte der Arzneikunde*, Halle, 1827 (1st ed. 1800), IV, p. 438, states that Perrault 'erläuterte zuerst aus mechanischen Prinzipien die Theorie der Stimme'. Many modern historians of medical science recognize the importance of Perrault's work in this field. J. Lebovits thinks that 'sa conception sur le bruit se rapproche beaucoup de la conception moderne du son' and that to his description of the outer and middle ear 'on n'a rien eu à ajouter depuis sauf les détails histologiques'. (*Claude Perrault physiologiste*, Paris, 1931, pp. 47, 76). Of the same opinion is j. Lévy-Valensin, 'Claude Perrault, physiologiste,' *Livre jubilaire offert au professeur G.-H. Roger*, Paris, 1932, p. 152. C. Mettler, *History of Medecine*, Philadelphia, 1947, p. 1073, calls his Essai on sound 'the first consequential physiologic study'.

The most recent comment on this part of Perrault's research is by E. Bastholm, *The History of Muscle Physiology*, Copenhagen, 1950, pp. 177 f., who speaks of Perrault as the 'eminent anatomist who contributed important discoveries, for instance the finer anatomy of the ear'.

Perrault's theory of Panspermatism

Here the situation is different. On the whole the theory was not accepted. The object of quoting below a number of authors who discussed panspermatism, often without naming Perrault, or who arrived independently at a similar conception, is to show that the theory, to us an abstruse notion, was then taken seriously. Perrault could well imagine that he had made a significant contribution to biology.

By having mentioned panspermatism already in his programme of 1667 (see above p. 9), Perrault was apparently the first to have proposed the theory in modern times. On Perrault's claim to that effect and on scientists, such as Redi and Swammerdam who mention it at about the same time, see J. Roger, op. cit., pp. 334 ff. Roger, however, is unaware of Perrault's having referred to the subject as early as 1667.

Later in the century, Pierre Dionis, *Dissertation sur la génération de l'homme*, Paris, 1698, pp. 80 f., considers the theory of panspermatism 'vraisemblable', while D. Tauvry, *Traité de la génération*, 1700, p. 2, and J. B. Verduc, *Traité de l'usage des parties*, Paris, 1696, I, p. 42, are critical; so is the Cartesian Pierre-Sylvain Regis in his *Système de philosophie*, Paris, 1690, II, p. 641 (cf. J. Roger, op. cit., pp. 348 ff.). J. Chr. Sturm admits that, having read the *Essais*, he finds that the theory he had explained in his lectures had already been stated by Perrault; he passes other theories in review, but finally returns to Perrault's (*De plantarum animaliumque generatione*, Altdorff, 1687, repr. in v. Haller, *Disputationum anatomicarum selectarum volumen*, Göttingen, 1746, V, pp. 61 ff.). Haller himself remarks that in his own time the theory had few followers. The most outstanding among these – 'one of the adherents to panspermatism' (A. W. Meyer, *The Rise of Embryology*, Stanford, 1936, p. 93) – was Buffon (*Histoire naturelle des animaux*, *Oeuvres*, ed. Sonnini, XVII, pp. 30, 67 ff.). Buffon refers occasionally to the *Essais*, but not to Perrault's particular contribution to the problem of *génération*. However, it was not entirely forgotten. With the rise of *Naturphilosophie* in Germany around the turn of the century, these ideas, though in a more sophisticated form, were taken up again. In the opinion of Lorenz Oken, *Die Zeugung*, Bamberg, 1805, p. 91, 'ist die Panspermie die älteste, ehrwürdigste Idee in der Geschichte der Naturphilosophie'; he speaks of the 'Zuflucht zur Panspermie, welche mehrere von Anaxagoras bis Perrault und Sturm . . . ergriffen.' (p. 17). In more recent times Perrault's claim that he was the first to have voiced these ideas was recognized in a paper by Wilhelm His, 'Die Theorien der geschlechtlichen

Zeugung', *Archiv für Anthropologie*, V, 1872, pp. 82 f.: 'Der Begründer dieser Theorie ist Claude Perrault, der berühmte Erbauer des Louvre. ...' His recapitulates Perrault's theory as set out in *Essais*, III, pp. 302 f. Lastly, T. Bilikiewicz, *Die Embryologie im Zeitalter des Barock und des Rokoko*, Leipzig, 1932, p. 89, acknowledges that 'Claude Perrault, Dionis und andere bereiteten den neuen Weg vor.'

Perrault's theory of sense perception

'L'opinion de Mons. Perrault est que l'âme est également par tout le corps, et que le sentiment se fait in ipso sensorio dans les yeux, dans les pieds,' wrote Leibniz in a note dating from the end of 1675 or the beginning of 1676. (E. Bodemann, *Die Leibniz-Handschriften der ... Bibl. Hannover*, Hannover, 1895, p. 118 and *Catalogue critique*, No. 1204). Leibniz then indicates the snags encountered in this theory and sets out his own version. Since Perrault did not publish his ideas on sense perception till 1680, he must have had discussions with Leibniz on the subject, which the latter apparently found interesting and which helped him to clarify his own views.

Some fifteen years later, Regis was the first who, in a book, considered Perrault's theory at length, though he finally rejected it (op. cit., II, pp. 97 ff.: 'Examen de l'opinion d'un Auteur Moderne touchant l'explication du Toucher,' identified in the margin as 'Monsieur Perrault'). More important than this critical review by a Cartesian is the fact that Perrault's ideas influenced Georg Ernst Stahl, the German physician who founded the animistic school of medicine. Stahl never referred to Perrault, but the similarity between Perrault's and Stahl's notions was so obvious that it was soon noted. The first to sense a connection was, it seems, La Mettrie who in his *L'homme machine* of 1747 refers to Stahl and Perrault in the same context (see the latest edition, Princeton, 1960, with excellent introduction and notes by A. Vartanian. The reference to Perrault on p. 188, the editorial notes on Stahl and Perrault on pp. 240, 243). Albert v. Haller is more definite. He saw in 'Claudius Perrault verus doctrinae Stahlianae auctor' (*Elementa physiologiae corporis humani*, Lausanne, 1757, IV, p. 295, also pp. 394, 555). Haller, who, incidentally, uses Perrault's *Essais* extensively throughout the many volumes of his monumental work, repeats this observation in his article on Perrault in his *Bibliotheca anatomica*, Zurich, 1774, I, pp. 549 ff. A few years later, it is taken up by N. F. J. Eloy, *Dictionnaire historique de la médecine*, Mons, 1778, III, p. 517. In the next century, the relation between Perrault's and Stahl's views was examined in detail by the eminent scholar Francisque Bouillier who recognized that 'ce que Claude Perrault avait fait en France, Stahl le fit en Allemagne avec plus de profondeur, de succès et de renommée.' (*Le principe vital et l'âme pensante*, Paris, 1862, p. 227). She devoted a whole chapter to a discussion of Perrault's theory. A. Bertrand, op. cit., pp. 177–198, arrives at the same conclusion in a chapter dealing with

'L'animisme de Claude Perrault,' while A. Lemoine, *Le vitalisme et l'animisme de Stahl*, Paris, 1864, p. 194, though not denying that Perrault was a forerunner of Stahl, is more critical of his work. Another aspect of Perrault's animistic theory was the importance he placed on custom. In this connection, it is interesting to note that his *Essais*, and, no doubt, his remarks about custom, were known to Maine de Biran, author of the important book on *Influence de l'habitude sur la faculté de penser* (1st ed. 1803), ed. Tisserand, Paris, 1954. Maine de Biran mentions, p. 68, Perrault's experiment demonstrating the retention of memory by a beheaded viper (Essai, II, p. 276). Perrault's radical views on the force of habit were still referred to, although critically, by F. Ravaisson, *De l'habitude*, Paris, (1st ed. 1838), 1927, p. 49, note 2.

Recently, Perrault's work on the anatomy of animals and on sense perception has been the subject of an interesting article by A. Tenenti ('Claude Perrault et la pensée scientifique française dans la seconde moitié du XVIIe siècle,' *Hommage à Lucien Febvre*, Paris, 1953, II, pp. 303 ff.). Tenenti emphasizes the fact that mechanical conceptions are preponderant in Perrault's work. While this, of course, is true, it must not be overlooked that mechanism was at that period the only possible basis for scientific thought and that modifications could only be visualized within the framework of this system. To say that 'le concept de machine et de "mécanique" occupe le centre de l'ouvrage' does not really help in the evaluation of Perrault's work. Its main merit must, on the contrary, be seen in the fact that Perrault was conscious, more perhaps than anybody else at this early period, of the limitations of the mechanical system. Throughout his *Essais*, he stressed the complex nature of the living organism, subjected as much to animistic influences as to mechanical laws.

Perrault's anatomical work

Since he was generally thought to be the author of the fundamental work on the *Histoire des animaux*, his fame rested mainly on this publication and on the third volume of his *Essais*, dealing with 'La méchanique des animaux.' Quotations from one or the other work occur frequently, (Haller has already been mentioned). Much later, the *Essais* were still being used in the study of comparative anatomy (J. F. Blumenbach, *Handbuch der vergleichenden Anatomie*, Göttingen, 1805, *passim*). In fact, Perrault's work in this field was so highly valued that P. Flourens, the biographer of Cuvier, went so far as to say that 'l'histoire de l'anatomie comparée compte trois époques nettement marquées: l'époque d'Aristote, celle de Claude Perrault, et celle de Cuvier,' and that 'c'est en effet des Mémoires de Claude Perrault sur l'anatomie des animaux que date la véritable renaissance de l'anatomie comparée'. ('Eloge historique de G. Cuvier', *Institut royal de France*, séance 29 December 1834, p. 16; *Histoire des travaux de Georges Cuvier*, Paris, 1858, p. 83.). Even F. J. Cole, the outstanding modern historian on medical science, is hardly less appreciative of Perrault's work as an anatomist: '*La Mécanique des animaux* of Claude Perrault ... is one of the few classics in which a speculative approach to the bare facts of comparative anatomy is even attempted.' (*A History of Comparative Anatomy from Aristotle to the Eighteenth Century*, London, 1944, p. 324, also pp. 394 ff.). E. Nordenskiöld, *The History of Biology*, London, 1929, pp. 154 f., comes, after an analysis of Perrault physiological work in general, to the conclusion that 'Perrault may thus be regarded, side by side with Borelli, as one of the pioneers of modern biology.'

APPENDIX III

Comments on
Perrault's Translation of Vitruvius

Only more explicit comments are included in this appendix, not short references which, usually with a laudatory attribute, are numerous.

François Blondel in a new edition of L. Savot, *L'architecture françoise*, Paris, 1673, p. 3, note: '... Monsieur Perrault Docteur en Médecine, qui nous a donné une excellente traduction de Vitruve, dont il a heureusement expliqué les endroits les plus difficiles, et par les conjectures judicieuses et des Notes sçavantes il a trouvé du sens aux passages ausquels les autres interprètes n'avoient osé toucher.'

Procès-verbaux, 11 June 1674 (I, p. 76): 'Ensuite l'on a commencé la lecture de Vitruve, traduit par Monsr Perault où, dans la préface qu'il y a fait on a remarqué plusieurs choses nécessaires et très utiles, à sçavoir à ceux qui voudront entreprendre la lecture de cet autheur, et que personne n'a encore rapportées, (tant) pour ce qui regarde l'intelligence du texte latin, que plusieurs choses très particulières concernant l'architecture ...'

A. Félibien, *Des principes de l'architecture*, Paris, 1676, p. 8: 'La Traduction que M. Perrault en vient de donner est si exacte et si sçavante; les Notes en sont si recherchées et si pleines d'érudition, qu'il y a lieu d'espérer que le public en tirera un très-grand secours; et qu'après un travail si considérable, l'on n'aura plus rien à désirer pour l'intelligence de cet Auteur que tant de sçavans hommes avoient tâché d'expliquer, mais que M. Perrault seul a rendu clair et facile dans tous les endroits où jusques à présent l'on ne voyoit que des difficultez et une obscurité impénétrable.'

R. Ouvard, *Architecture harmonique*, Paris, 1679, p. 15: '... Vitruve, qui est devenu le grand Maistre de l'Architecture depuis que M. Perrault l'a fait parler françois et rendu intelligible par ses doctes Remarques ...'

François Blondel in L. Savot, *L'architecture françoise*, ed. of 1685, pp. 340 f., note: 'Nous avons à présent une traduction de Vitruve infiniment plus exacte et plus juste (than the one by Martin), et qui peut même être appellée parfaite, laquelle est donnée au public par Monsieur Perrault, qui l'a remplie de mille observations curieuses. La seconde Edition du même Vitruve que l'on nous fait espérer dans peu est augmenté de plusieurs remarques très-utiles, et de quelques figures de bâtimens antiques qui ont été démolis de nôtre temps et dont Monsieur Perrault est bien aise de conserver la mémoire à la posterité. Nous avons encore un excellent petit livre qu'il appelle, Abrégé des dix livres d'Architecture de Vitruve dans lequel il a mis en ordre les matières que Vitruve a traitées confusément et a ramassé sous le même Chapitre ce qui se trouve dispersé en plusieurs endroits

... qui est une méthode qui peut beaucoup servir à apprendre la doctrine de cet Auteur et à la retenir avec plus de facilité.'

The high opinion which the profession had of the translation can be judged from the fact that members of the Academy used it for their periodical readings of the Vitruvian treatise, first in 1674–6, then again during 1690–1, again in 1707–8 and 1714–15. (*Procès-verbaux*, I–IV.).

L. Moreri, *Le Grand Dictionnaire historique*, Paris, 1707, p. 203: 'Sa *Traduction de Vitruve* ... enrichie par lui de Notes sçavantes ... lui fit tout l'honneur qu'il pouvoit espérer: et il y fit connoître qu'il entendoit parfaitement toutes les différentes choses dont parle Vitruve, telles que sont la Peinture, la Sculpture, la Musique, les Hydrauliques, les Machines et tout ce qui appartient aux Méchaniques.'

Giovanni Poleni, *Exercitationes Vitruvianae primae* ..., Patavii, 1739, pp. 122 ff.: After a critical review of the translation, he concludes: 'Sed ut eo revertar, unde discessi; licet quaedam sint, quae in hac quoque Perraultii Editione desiderari quidem posse videantur; concludam tamen, Editionem hanc inter utiliores adipiscendae Vitruvii Librorum intelligentiae, jure meritoque esse reputandam.'

C. F. Lambert, *Histoire littéraire du Règne de Louis XIV*, Paris, 1751, III, bk. X, p. 101: 'La belle traduction de Vitruve...est un ouvrage qui seul suffit pour l'instruction des plus grands Maîtres, et ce qui rend cet ouvrage plus parfait que tous ceux qui avoient paru jusqu'alors sur la même matière, c'est qu'ou ils avoient été composés par des Sçavans qui n'étoient point Architectes, ou par des Architectes qui n'étoient pas sçavans; et c'étoient là deux qualités qui se trouvoient heureusement réunies dans M. Perrault. Aucune des parties dont il est parlé dans l'ouvrage de Vitruve qu'il ne possedât parfaitement.'

Berardo Galiani, *L'Architettura di M. Vitruvio Pollione*, Naples, 1758, p. IV: 'Il Perrault senza dúbbio è il solo, che merita sopra tutti finora singolare stima e per l'utilità delle sue note ben ragionate, e per la nettezza della versione.'

Ch.-E. Briseux, *Traité du beau*, Paris, 1752, II, p. 38: '(Le Roi) fit faire une traduction de Vitruve par Claude Perrault qui en dévoila l'obscurité, et y ajouta des notes aussi sçavantes qu'utiles.'

S. Riou, *The Grecian Orders of Architecture*, London, 1768, preface: 'The French translation by Perrault, above all others, deserves singular esteem, his notes are judicious, and the version is clear.'

J.-F. Blondel, *Cours d'architecture*, Paris, 1771, I, p. 215, note n: 'Perrault, l'un de nos plus célèbres Architectes, l'a aussi commenté; ses notes importantes ont rendu l'étude de Vitruve indispensable aux Architectes.'

W. Newton, *The Architecture of M. Vitruvius Pollio*, London, 1791, I, p. V: 'After this comes the pompous French translation, executed by the learned Claude Perrault. ... This was published in 1673 and indeed much excelled all the preceding translations.'

de Bioul, *L'architecture de Vitruve*, Brussels, 1816, p. XI: 'Claude Perrault en donna une magnifique traduction qu'il enrichit d'excellentes notes.'

Joseph Gwilt, *The Architecture of Marcus Vitruvius Pollio*, London, 1826, p. XXVII: 'Though in many parts it is impossible to agree with him in his Interpretation of the Text, yet it is a most valuable work.'

M. Nisard reprints Perrault's text and notes in *Celse, Vitruve, Censorin*, Paris, 1852. In the *avertissement*, he declares: 'Pour l'architecture de Vitruve que pouvions-nous mieux faire que de reproduire la traduction de Perrault?'

F. A. Renard, *Architecture décimale*, Paris, 1854, p. 18: '. . . Perrault sut se mettre à la hauteur de sa mission et put livrer, après plusieurs années d'une application soutenue, un travail que l'on considère comme une des meilleures interprétations du texte de Vitruve qu'on ait faites jusqu'à ce jour.'

E. Tardieu et A. Coussin, *Les dix livres d'architecture de Vitruve avec les notes de Perrault*, Paris, 1859, p. IV: Perrault enriched his translation 'de notes nombreuses et excellentes au fond, mais qui deviennent souvent obscures à cause de leur longueur, étant entachées du défaut de l'époque dont Perrault n'a pas su se garantir.'

Bodo v. Ebhardt, *Die zehn Bücher der Architektur des Vitruv und ihre Herausgeber seit 1884*, Berlin, s.a., p. 52: 'Über den Wert der ziemlich freien Übersetzung kann kein Zweifel sein. In dieser kurzen Übersicht muss Perrault's Vitruv-ausgabe auch als die äusserlich bedeutendste des 17ten Jahrhunderts hervorgehoben werden.'

J. Prestel, *Zehn Bücher über Architektur des Marcus Vitruvius Pollio*, Strassburg, 1913, I, p. XIX: 'Von den Übersetzungen aus fremden Sprachen dienten mir vornehmlich die ausführlichen Werke von Perrault, W. Newton, Don José Ortiz sowie Marini als vergleichende wissenschaftliche Grundlagen . . .'

R. Blomfield, *A History of French Architecture*, London, 1921, I, p. 88: 'His edition of Vitruvius is not only a learned and scholarly work, and much the best interpretation of that obscure writer issued up to that date, it was also a valuable essay in criticism.'

M. Borissavliévitch, *Les théories de l'architecture*, Paris, 1951 (first publ. 1926), p. 52: 'Nous nous sommes proposé de chercher . . . une explication des concepts esthétiques de Vitruve. . . . Dans ce but, nous nous sommes servi du texte original, des traductions françaises de Choisy et de Perrault et de la traduction allemande du Dr Prestel.' p. 86: 'Claude Perrault fut un des meilleurs traducteurs et commentateurs de Vitruve de son temps, et même, à certains points de vue, du nôtre.'

Vitruve, *Les dix livres d'architecture. Traduction intégrale de Claude Perrault 1673, revue et corrigée sur les textes latins et présentée par André Dalmas*, Paris, 1965, p. 9: '. . . cette traduction est aussi une oeuvre véritable. Il faut ajouter que les éditeurs, traducteurs et commentateurs français (et étrangers) de Vitruve ont, quelquefois, négligé de rappeler que leurs travaux n'eussent pas été possibles sans le secours de l'album de Perrault. . . . Une traduction n'est pas lettre morte. Il la faut entretenir. Nous l'avons fait. Tous, cependant, et nous les premiers, devont rendre à Perrault ce que nous lui devons.'

APPENDIX IV

The Need for Expert Judgment

1. When Blondel asserted that professional skill and experience were needed for the successful adjustment of proportions, he condensed Vitruvius's, remarks VI, ii, 2–4, into the following citation (op. cit., p. 722.):

'... le plus grand soin d'un Architecte doit estre de proportionner les parties de son bâtiment, et de prévoir ce qu'il doit augmenter ou diminuer à leurs mesures; Que c'est en cela qu'il doit faire paroistre la force de son esprit; Qu'il faut beaucoup de jugement et de connoissance pour pouvoir se déterminer heureusement sur ce qu'il y a à faire dans les rencontres. Et qu'enfin cela dépend plus de la vivacité de l'esprit et du génie de l'Architecte que des règles que l'on puisse donner.'

(Other places where Vitruvius refers to skill and judgment needed when making adjustments: V, vii, 7; VI, iii, 11).

2. Vasari, *Le vite de' piu excellenti Pittori, Scultori ed Architettori*, Florence, 1550 (ed. Milanesi, Florence, 1878, Opere, I, p. 148): Having set out the measurements of the Orders, Vasari stresses the need for harmony 'che i fusi ... non sian lunghi o sottili, o grossi o corti, servando sempre il decoro degli ordini suoi; nè si debba a una colonna sottile metter capitel grosso nè base simili, ma secondo il corpo le membra, le quali abbiano leggiadria e bella maniera e disegno. E queste cose son più conosciute da un occhio buono; il quale, se ha guidicio, si può tenere il vero compasso, e l'istessa misura, perchè da quello saranno lodate le cose e biasimate.'

3. Serlio, *Tutte l'opere d'architettura*, Venice, 1619, fol. 161 v: Ionic Order: '... il tutto s'intende sempre per regola generale, lasciando sempre molte cose nell'arbitrio del prudente Architetto.'

4. ibid., fol. 169 r. (Corinthian base): 'ma secondo i luoghi, dóve le base saran poste, fa di bisogno che l'Architetto sia molto accorto.'

5. ibid., fol. 170 v. (Corinthian architrave): 'Onde il prudente Architetto può sempre far elettione di quelle parti, che piú al suo commodo tornano.'

6. ibid., fol. 184 r. (Composite Order): 'Perché gli antichi Romani han fatto diverse mescolanze, io ne sceglierò alcune dell piú note ... accioche l'Architetto possa col suo bel giudicio, secondo gli accidenti, fare elettion di quello, che piú al proposito gli tornerà.'

7. ibid., fol. 187 r. (Composite Order): 'Gran giudicio veramente convien haver l'Architetto, per le diversità delle compositioni ... percioche sono alcuni luoghi nell'Architettura, a i quali posson esser date quasi certe regole: perché non sono accidenti che intervengono fuori della nostra opinione, anzi tutto di si

veggono alcune colonne, che con le varie positioni loro dimostrano in se varie misure, secondo i luoghi dove sono.'

8. Pietro Cataneo, *L'architettura*, Venice, 1567, p. 126. (Corinthian base): 'Avertendo che secondo minore o maggiore distanza o altezza, fa di bisogno ancora accrescere o diminuire quei membri che sono occupati da gl'altri membri, e in ciò è molto necessario il guidicio del prudente architetto.'

9. Philibert de l'Orme, *Architecture*, Rouen, 1648, fol. 145 r: 'Mais 'telles mesures des chapiteaux Doriques, et encore de toutes leurs parties, se doivent faire selon le bon jugement de l'Architecte . . .'

10. ibid., fol. 172 r: '. . . il faut cognoistre et avoir jugement d'y sçavoir bailler une certaine proportion de modules et augmentation de mesures, afin que l'on puisse donner belle apparence et beauté aux édifices.'

11. Jean Vredeman de Vries, *Architectura*, Antwerp, 1577, text to Tuscan Order: having prescribed the exact measurements, he continues: 'Au surplus ce que le sage Architecte, expert en cecy, trouvera servir et expédient à l'ouvrage, . . . cela je recommande à sa discretion et bon jugement d'un chacun.'

12. Fréart, op. cit., p. 14: 'C'est pourquoy j'ay estimé nécessaire d'apporter icy divers exemples antiques sur chaque ordre, afin de donner moyen à ceux de la profession de s'en servir judicieusement, eu égard au lieu et à l'occasion.'

13. Félibien, *Principes* (ed. 1690), p. 6: '. . . Vitruve établit dans chaque Ordre une seule mesure, qui doit engendrer cette unique Beauté, que chacun recherche, mais qui se ne donne aux ouvrages que quand les Ouvriers sçavent par la force de leur esprit, et la lumière de leur jugement, conduire toutes les parties d'un édifice selon sa grandeur, sa situation et le lieu, ou la distance d'où on le peut voir.'

14. ibid., p. 27: '. . . car plus on regarde en haut et plus on a de peine à reconnoistre la largeur et la hauteur des parties d'un Edifice. C'est pourquoy il dépend du jugement de l'Architecte d'augmenter ou de diminuer ses mesures, pour donner plus de beauté et de grâce à ses Ouvrages.'

15. Félibien, *Entretiens*, p. 17: 'Or comme les choses que l'on considère de près, et qui sont élevées, paroissent à nos yeux tout d'une autre manière que celles qui sont éloignées de nous, et que l'on voit ou basses ou moins exhaussées; et que les objets qui sont dans un lieu renfermé font encore un autre effet à la veue que ceux qui sont à découvert: c'est dans ces différens aspects et dans ces diverses situations qu'un sçavant Architecte doit employer ses lumières et ses connoissances pour bien conduire ce qu'il veut exposer en public.' . . . 'Quand il a une fois déterminé ses mesures . . . il travaille à la proportion des parties . . . et ainsi par la force de son imagination, par la conduite de son jugement, et par les règles de son art, il donne à tout son ouvrage cette union et cet accord qui le rendent agréable.'

16. ibid., p. 20: 'C'estoit dans ces rencontres que les Anciens employoient toutes les connoissances et les lumières qu'ils avoient receues de la Géométrie et de l'Optique, afin de plaire à la vue, et empescher que l'oeil ne rencontrast

quelque chose qui pust l'offenser. Et c'est par cette science et par cette conduite qu'un Architecte se rend célèbre, et s'élève au dessus des autres.'

17. ibid., pp. 327 f.: 'Mais ce qu'un excellent Architecte est indispensablement obligé de sçavoir, est l'effet que chaque chose doit faire selon le lieu où elle est posée, par les règles de l'Optique, et par les raisons naturelles.'

18. Blondel, op. cit., I, p. 10: 'Ces mesures se sont même quelquefois trouvé assez alterées dans leurs bâtimens, qu'ils ont judicieusement ajustez à la différence des lieux et de la situation de leurs Colonnes.'

19. ibid., II, pp. 34 f.: 'Ce que je rapporte afin de faire voir que tout ce qui se trouve dans les livres des Auteurs, ou même dans quelques ouvrages de l'Antique, ne doit point passer pour des règles infaillibles, et qu'il faut beaucoup d'expérience pour se former un bon goust qui puisse discerner dans cette variété infinie d'exemples et d'enseignemens, ce qui n'a de beauté qu'en apparence.'

20. ibid., p. 729: According to Philander 'un Architecte a besoin de beaucoup de génie, de beaucoup de sçavoir et d'expérience; mais surtout de beaucoup de jugement et de prudence, qui puisse dans la construction de son bâtiment se départir quelquefois de la rigueur des préceptes de l'art pour luy donner plus de commodité ou de grâce. Car les mêmes proportions ne font pas par tout les mêmes effets.'

21. *Procès-verbaux*, II, p. 36 (9 August 1683): Criticizing Vignola for carrying standardization too far, they remark that 'lorsque l'on parle de règles générales des ordres d'architecture, on suppose qu'ils soient veus . . . à une distance médiocre . . . car autrement, suivant le sentiment de Vitruve, les sujettions obligent à changer les proportions: ce qui demande un jugement d'architecte consommé.'

APPENDIX V

Tolerance

1. Serlio, op. cit., fol. 141 v (Doric Order): 'Et perché io trovo gran differenza dalle cose di Roma . . . a gli scritti di Vitruvio, ho voluto dimostrarne alcune parti, delle quali si veggono ancora in opera con gran satisfattion de gli Architetti . . . le quai tutte cose ho voluto dimostrare, accioche lo Architetto possa fare elettion di quelche piú gli aggrada in questo ordine Dorico.'

2. ibid., fol. 161 r (Ionic entablature): the architrave can be either 1/16th or 1/12th of column according to their heights, and the frieze 'se si haverà da scolpire . . . si farà piú alto dell'architrave la quarta parte: ma se senza sculture e schietto si farà, deve esser la quarta parte minor dell'architrave.'

3. ibid., fol. 161 v (Ionic Order); 'Et perche le cose di Roma son molto diverse da gli scritti di Vitruvio, io formerò un altra colonna . . .'

4. ibid., fol. 170 r (Corinthian Order): having described in detail the usual proportions according to which the entablature should be the fourth part of the height of the column, he adds: 'e si potrà ancora far questo architrave, fregio e cornice la quinta parte dell'altezza della colonna.'

5. ibid., fol. 170 v (Corinthian entablature): 'L'architrave, fregio e cornice . . . l'altezza del tutto è manco della quinta parte dell'altezza della colonna.'

6. Palladio, op. cit., I, p. 19 (Base of Tuscan pedestal): Using the method of subdivisions, he allocates one unit to the fillet and then adds: 'il quale si può fare ancho un poco manco . . .'

7. ibid., p. 26 (Doric entablature): 'Onde l'Architrave, il Fregio, e la Cornice vengono ad esser alti la quarta parte dell'altezza della colonna. E queste sono le misure della Cornice secondo Vitruvio: dalla quale mi sono alquanto partito alterandola de'membri, e facendola un poco maggiore.'

8. ibid., p. 42 (Corinthian Order): 'La basa della colonne è l'Attica: ma in questo è diversa da quella, che si pone all'ordine Dorico, che lo sporto è la quinta parte del diametro della colonna. Si può ancho in qualche altra parte variare, come si vede nel disegno.'

9. Pietro Cataneo, op. cit., p. 113 (Attic base): '. . . e se la base serà superiore all'occhio . . . il quadretto del toro inferiore occupato da esso si doverà fare alquanto maggior dell'altro . . . e similimente la scotia in tal caso si farà alquanto maggiore.'

10. ibid., p. 127 (Corinthian capital): after describing Vitruvian measurements: 'Alcuni ad imitatione di più capitelli antichi per più sveltezza del capitello, lo fanno più alto di quel che s'e detto tutte l'Abaco: il che per mio aviso si puó molto bene approvare.'

11. Philibert de l'Orme, op. cit., fols 173 f. (Preface to Book VI): He warns the architect not to apply the measurements he has found on ancient monuments

indiscriminately, but to take account of the difference in scale and circumstances: 'pour autant que si vous aviez affaire de mille sortes de colomnes, et encores qu'elles fussent toutes d'un mesme ordre, fust-il Dorique, Ionique, Corinthien ou autre, pourveu qu'elles soient de différentes hauteurs il les convient aussi faire de différentes mesures: et non seulement les colomnes, mais aussi tous leurs membres. . . . Et encores quand les colomnes se trouveroient toutes d'une mesme hauteur, si les unes sont d'un ordre de quatre colomnes, elles ne conviennent point à celles de six, ny celle de six à celles de huict . . . parquoy elles doivent estre d'une autre sorte de mesures selon leur hauteur et nombre, autrement elles ne donneroient aucun contentement à l'oeil. . . . Et afin de la faire mieux cognoistre, j'ay proposé et proposeray cy-après plusieurs sortes d'ornemens et mesures de colonnes . . .'

12. ibid., fol. 137 r (Tuscan entablature): the ratio of architrave to frieze and cornice is given as 1:1:1; on fols. 140 r f.: as 5:7:8.

13. ibid., fol. 154 v (Ionic Order): 'Les colomnes Ioniques doivent avoir de hauteur selon leur grosseur, et aussi selon les lieux ausquels on les veut appliquer. . . . Il les faut donc faire de différentes mesures . . . pour les rendre plus agréables . . . les Ioniques doivent avoir huict fois leur diamètre . . . comme je l'ay trouvé et observé en plusieurs colomnes; mais à d'autres j'ay trouvé différentes hauteurs; de sorte que quelques unes avoient plus de huict fois leur diamètre, les autres huict et demy, et huict avec trois quarts ou environ, selon le jugement de l'architecte qui les avoit faictes, comme il luy avoit semblé pour le mieux.'

14. ibid., fol. 175 r (Corinthian Order): '. . . on leur donne pour leurs hauteurs plus de huict fois leur diamètre par le bas, voire neuf et plus quelquefois, selon le lieu auquel on les applique. Voilà qui les faict monstrer plus gresles et délicates que la Ionique, qui ne doit avoir de hauteur que huict fois et demie son diamètre pour le plus, et quelquefois moins.'

15. ibid., fol. 190 v: 'Pour encores d'abondant cognoistre la grande différence des colomnes Corinthiennes, nous en mettrons icy quelquesunes, afin qu'on puisse . . . choisir ausquelles on se voudroit arrester, selon l'oeuvre qu'on auroit à faire.'

16. ibid., fols. 191 r f. (Corinthian Order): 'Considérez . . . lesdites mesures . . . et par la cognoistrez s'il ne faut pas avoir bon jugement quand on veut mettre telles colomnes en oeuvre . . . et s'il n'y faut pas observer beaucoup de choses pour se garder d'y faire faute . . . Laquelle faute s'y commettra incontinent, si on n'entend la raison et pratique des proportions, non seulement aux colomnes, mais aussi à tous leur ornements tousjours différents, selon la grandeur des oeuvres qui se présentent.'

17. Lomazzo, op. cit., p. 100: The Composite Order should have 11 modules, the Corinthian 10, the Ionic 9, the Doric 8, the Tuscan 7 'o piú o meno secondo che piú converrà al guidicion di quelle che haverà da operare.'

18. J. Mauclerc, *Le Premier Livre d'Architecture*, Rochelle, 1600, fol. I: 'Je ne mets cy que d'une sorte de chapiteau dorique, par ce que ceux qui seront plus curieuxe d'en rechanger, auront recours si bon leur semble au quatrième livre de Serlio,

chapitre sixième, où ils en trouveront nombre, qu'il dit avoir trouvé entre les antiquitez d'Italie.' He then names several examples 'à celle fin qu'ils choississent ceux qui leur seront les plus agréables, et au contentement de leurs esprits, s'ils ne sont satisfaits des deux sortes icy descrites.'

19. ibid., fol. N: 'Il y a encor une autre manière de colomne Ionique . . .'
'. . . se fait une autre division de Cornice . . .'

20. ibid., fol. O: He will describe two kinds of Ionic Order 'selon leurs deues et parfaicte proportions.'

21. Scamozzi, op. cit., II, pp. 40 f. (Orders in general): '. . . quando i Fregi doveranno esser ornati . . . allhora essi si faranno alquanto piú alti.'

22. ibid., II, p. 56: 'Le Colonne Toscane . . . devono esser alte Moduli VII e mezo, e non ingrate riusciranno d'otto Moduli.'

23. ibid., II, p. 70 (Doric entablature): '. . . allhora tutto l'Ornamento eccederà poco piú del quinto dell'altezza delle Colonne.' (Doric pedestal): '. . . e tutto insiéme fanno a punto due Moduli, e poco piú d'un quarto di Modulo di tutto il Piedestilo.'

24. ibid., II, p. 99 (Ionic entablature): 'Ma nell'opere piú reali, dove il Fregio si doverà intagliare, l'Ornamento si faccia tra il IV e V dell'altezza delle Colonne.'

25. Fréart, op. cit., p. 5: '. . . dans ce recueil . . . j'ay rapporté ponctuellement leurs desseins l'un en parangon de l'autre . . . tellement que par le moyen de cette comparaison chacun a la liberté d'en faire choix à sa fantaisie et de suivre lequel il voudra des Autheurs que je propose, parce qu'ils sont tous dans l'approbation commune.'

26. ibid., p. 9: '. . . j'ay estimé nécessaire après les desseins qu'ils (les maîtres) nous ont donnez pour règle, de revenir tousjours aux Antiques . . . parmi lesquels il se trouve encore assez de variété pour contenter raisonnablement le goust de ceux qui veulent choisir.'

27. ibid., p. 12: The Doric column 'n'est point bornée ni à quatorze modules, ni à quinze même, pouvant quelquefois aller jusqu'à seize, et encore à davantage selon l'occasion.'

28. ibid., p. 35: 'C'est donc le modèle que je suivray et qui servira icy du règle pour cet ordre, l'ayant préféré avec conseil . . . à celuy qui est au théâtre de Marcellus, d'où j'ay tiré mon Dorique: lequel néanmoins je proposeray encore en suite, afin d'en laisser le choix aux autres qui ne seront pas de mon opinion.'

29. ibid., p. 64: Having explained why he has adopted the proportion of the Pantheon where the architrave is a fourth of the whole Order, he remarks: 'Mais je l'avertis auparavant, qu'il y a trois sortes de proportions différentes toutes belles et qui peuvent convenir à cet ordre Corinthien: à sçavoir le Quart . . . les deux Neuvièmes . . . et le Cinquième . . .'

30. ibid., p. 72: Palladio's and Scamozzi's Corinthian Orders do not follow the rules derived from ancient monuments: 'Néanmoins ayant égard à leur grande réputation . . . je ne sçaurois contredire à leur sentiment, ny blasmer ceux

qui les voudront suivre, quoy que ma maxime soit toujours de me conformer précisement au goust des antiques ...'

31. Abraham Bosse, *Traité des manières de dessiner les ordres de l'architecture antique en toutes leurs parties*, Paris, 1664, p. I: 'Palladio ... fait que les traverses de (Tuscan) et du Dorique sont du quart de leurs colonnes, et pour l'Ioniques, Corinthien et Composite du quint; et moy j'ay jugé devoir donner à toutes ces Traverses le Quint quoyque pour satisfaire à tout si je puis, je les donne encore du Quart ...'

32. Blondel, op. cit., I, pp. 19 f. (Tuscan pedestal): 'Le Tronc est mis entre deux plattes bandes dont la hauteur en chacune est de module $\frac{3}{4}$ ou module $\frac{3}{5}$, c'est à dire égale au quart ou mesme au cinquième de la hauteur du tronc.'

33. ibid., I, p. 23 (Vitruvian Tuscan Order): 'Mais comme elle ne plaist pas à tout le monde ... j'ay cru que l'on verroit icy volontiers les sentimens ... (de Vignole, Palladio et Scamozzi) ... afin d'en laisser le choix au jugement de ceux qui auront à s'en servir.'

34. ibid., I, pp. 71 f. (Ionic entablature): '... la hauteur de l'architrave estant de mod. 1, celle de la Frize est de mod. $\frac{3}{4}$, quand elle n'est point ornée, et celle de la corniche de peu plus de mod. $1\frac{1}{4}$. Qui fait pour l'entablement peu plus de mod. $2\frac{3}{4}$. Mais si la Frize est chargée, sa hauteur est de mod. $1\frac{1}{4}$ et celle de la corniche mod. $1\frac{1}{7}$, qui font pour l'entablement un peu plus de mod. $3\frac{1}{2}$.'

35. ibid., II, p. 9: 'Quant aux mesures des Colonnes que nous avons attribuées aux Interprète de Vitruve dans la première partie de ce Cours, et que nous avons triées dans cette confusion; Elles sont beaucoup mieux proportionnées qu'aucune des autres, et l'on peut seurement les mettre en pratique, aussi bien que celles de Vignole qui a fait à peu près le même raisonnement.'

36. ibid., II, p. 13: 'Il ne faut pourtant point croire que ces hauteurs (des colonnes) puissent estre alterées au point que cette règle le veut permettre. Il faut qu'un Architecte ait le jugement de sçavoir se contenir dans certaines bornes pour ne rien produire d'extravagant: C'est à dire que l'on peut dans le besoin augmenter la hauteur d'une Colonne d'un ou de deux mod. ou même de mod. $2\frac{1}{2}$ dans les bastimens d'une grandeur extraordinaire et aux ordres fort élevez au dessus de l'oeil, mais je doute que l'on puisse passer ces termes sans donner dans le goust Gothique.'

37. *Procès-verbaux*, I, pp. 272 f. (28 January 1680): '... la compagnie s'est appliquée sur les proportions des colonnes ioniques ... et, après avoir aprofondi cette matière, elle est tombé dans ce sentiment qu'aux colonnes isolées, qui ne sont pas extraordinairement eslevées audessus de l'oeil ... la haulteur peut estre depuis huict à huict et demi et mesmes jusques à neuf diamètres ...'

38. ibid., II, pp. 181 f. (5 August 1689): 'On a réglé qu'on pouvoit se servir des trois manières de bases pour l'ordre corinthien, sçavoir: de ceux de la *Rotonde*, du *Frontispice de Néron* et des *Thermes de Dioclétien*, dont l'application (se fera) selon la grandeur des édifices et de la situation des lieux.'

APPENDIX VI

Perrault's Mistakes
in Calculating the Mean

The table on p. 10 deals with entablatures. Its purpose is to show by how many minutes various entablatures are either above or below Perrault's own norm, which consists of 120 minutes. There are a number of careless mistakes: Serlio's Tuscan should be minus 30, not minus 3, Scamozzi's Doric is 127 minutes high, therefore exceeding Perrault's norm by 7, not 27 minutes, Vignola's Doric equals his own, so the correct entry is 0, not minus 10, nor is Vignola's Corinthian minus 12, but is a full module higher than his own. The greatest mistake happened in the last column, dealing with the Composite Order. The dividing line between 'plus' and 'minus' should have been drawn after Palladio – in other words, all examples of Composite entablatures exceeded his norm, with the exception of Palladio's, who made it the same size, and Scamozzi's, which was slightly lower. This was, no doubt, due to carelessness which, however, was aggravated by the fact that Perrault took these mistakes over into the text (p. 10, the paragraph above the table). Even a cursory glance at Vignola's Composite Order, with an entablature two whole modules higher than he assumed it to be in his table, should have warned him that something had gone wrong. However since he did not use the table for calculating the mean, it was of no consequence. To conclude from these careless mistakes that Perrault was incompetent or acted in bad faith, as Sigwalt, op. cit., pp. 52 ff., does, is unjustified.

With the table on p. 23 he was going to show that 'les Anciens n'ont point fait les diminutions différentes selon les différens Ordres, ny suivant les différentes grandeurs des Colonnes' (p. 21), and cited the columns of the Temple de la Fortune Virile and the Portique de Septimius, which both have the same diminution, but of which 'l'une est d'Ordre Ionique, et ayant seulement vingt et deux piés, et l'autre est d'Ordre Corinthien, qui a jusqu'à trente-sept piés.' (ibid.) The last figure, he copied wrongly from Desgodets; it should have been 27 feet. Although a difference in height existed between these two columns, it was not as spectacular as Perrault made it out to be. Similarly, the projection of the cornice of the Temple de la Fortune Virile on table p. 28 was probably entered by him in his manuscript as 23 (Desgodets: 22 1/3rd), but appeared in print as 13. This makes his own 'mean' figure of 17 to be of a magnitude exceeding everything else. However, this may have been a printer's error. More disturbing is the fact that the height of the pedestals, set out in the last column of this table, are different from those he had already given in another table on p. 17.

In this table, on page 17, wrong figures are of greater consequence, since he arrives – or pretends to arrive – at his measurements for the height of the pedestals by calculating the mean between the highest and the lowest figure recorded in the table. 'La plus grande hauteur dans le Toscan,' he explains on p. 16, 'laquelle est de cinq modules dans Vignole jointe à la plus petite qui est de trois dans Palladio, fait le nombre de huit modules, dont la moitié fait les quatre de la grandeur moyenne que je prens.' He thus arrives at the desired figure, but Palladio's measurement is clearly shown in the *Quattro libri*, I, p. 20, as two normal modules, while Vignola's is less than five. 'Dans l'Ordre Dorique la plus grande hauteur qui est de six modules dans Serlio jointe à la plus petite, qui est de quatre modules cinq minutes dans Palladio, fait le nombre de six (printer's error for 'dix') modules cinq minutes, dont la moitié est les quatre modules vingt minutes . . .' In the first place, Palladio's measurement is 4 m 20 min. (as Perrault himself enters it in table p. 28), and in the second place his arithmetic is wrong: the correct mean would, of course, be half of 10 m 5 min., i.e. 5 m 2½ min!

The arithmetic for the Ionic in table p. 17 is correct; but the required mean is only arrived at by taking – probably intentionally – an actual for a modular measurement: the 3′ 8″ given by Desgodets as the size of the pedestal at the Theatre of Marcellus is changed by Perrault into 3 m 8 min. He thus found that the 'sept modules douze minutes au Temples de la Fortune Virile, jointe à la plus petite qui est de trois modules huit minutes dans le Théâtre de Marcellus, fait le nombre de dix modules vingt minutes, dont la moitié est les cinq modules dix minutes, qui répondent à huit petits modules.' (p. 16). He may have done something similar when trying to work out, from the same table, the mean for the Composite, where the correct figure for the Arc des Orfèvres would have ranked it as the lowest, not as the highest, measure. Again, if on table p. 25 (projection of bases) he had entered, instead of 40, the correct figure of 39 for Scamozzi's Tuscan base (Fréart, op. cit., p. 93), he could not have deduced that 'si l'on joint le nombre de la plus petite Saillie, qui est quarante dans le Corinthien du Colisée, au nombre de la plus grande, qui est quarante quatre dans l'Arc de Titus, on trouvera les quatre-vingt quatre dont la moitié fait les quarante deux dont il s'agit.' (p. 25).

All this may, however, have been due to negligence; but this cannot be the case when the text reveals that he himself was aware of the correct measurements. On page 18, when dealing with the parts of pedestals, Perrault states, correctly, that Palladio and Scamozzi 'font toujours la Base du double de la Corniche,' but drawing up the relevant table (p. 19), he is obviously intent on showing that his own proportions are an improvement on those commonly applied. Since Palladio's Corinthian and Scamozzi's Composite bases have proportions identical to his own, namely 30:75:15, he changes their figures slightly, thus giving the impression that Palladio and Scamozzi prescribed awkward, incommensurable ratios, while his own are the only regular ones. Forgetting that his text on page 18 patently contradicts the figures in the table on page 19, he remarks that 'on peut voir dans la Table suivante, de combien de peu de chose il s'en faut, que les ouvrages Antiques et les Modernes ne s'accordent avec les proportions que je propose.' (p. 18).

There is another discrepancy here between text (p. 18) and table (p. 19), one which indicates that Perrault revised his manuscript after having seen Desgodets's book. Having stated that the table shows how close ancient and modern measurements come to the proportions proposed by him, he sets out his own, uniform ratios: he divides the pedestal of each Order into 120 units of which he allots 30 to the base, 75 to the dado and 15 to the cornice. Then, however, having had the opportunity of measuring Desgodet's drawings, he finds that there are ancient buildings with extreme measurements which are far removed from those prescribed by him. Overlooking that he had just pointed out 'de combien de peu de chose il s'en faut' for making the ratios of ancient monuments agree with his own, he now shows that, for each part, the size he has prescribed is the exact mean between widely separated extremes.

Here again, he must have worked with so much haste that, when writing the sentence: 'Je trouve par la même méthode les dix particules, qui font la hauteur des Moulures de la Base, en joignant la plus grande hauteur qu'elle ait, qui est dix-neuf au Temple de la Fortune Virile, avec la plus petite, qui est onze au Colisée, qui font trente, dont la moitié est les quinze que je luy donne,' he was too careless to notice that the first part of the sentence refers to the *ten* units of the 'Moulures de la Base', whereas the second part relates to the mean of *fifteen* units of the 'Corniche'.

Another instance, indicating that Desgodets's book caused Perrault to make interpolations, occurs on pp. 11 f. Dealing in this place with the rate of increase in the length of columns, he explains that modern architects made the rate of the overall increase from the Tuscan to the Composite greater than Vitruvius 'car elle est dans Scamozzi de cinq modules et demy, dans Palladio et dans Serlio de six, ainsi qu'il se voit dans la Table qui suit . . .' (p. 12). But the table on p. 13 does not show this at all, since Scamozzi's fifth Order (the Corinthian) is not entered, Palladio's Orders stop short at the Ionic and Serlio's at the Corinthian. On the other hand, the table contains a number of examples some of which at least had been taken over from Desgodets. Obviously, some of Palladio's, Scamozzi's and Serlio's measurements had to make room for those of ancient columns. The table in its original version must have given only Vitruvius's, Scamozzi's, Palladio's and Serlio's measurements. On page 14 he evidently refers to this original table when he explains how it enabled him to arrive at his modular sizes for each Order. 'Après avoir établi la somme entière des quatre progressions qui sont depuis le Toscan jusqu'au Composite, laquelle je faits de cinq modules moyens et dix minutes, afin qu'elle soit moyenne entre les cinq modules de l'Antique et les cinq et demy des Modernes; je partage cette somme qui fait cent soixante minutes en quatre parties égales, donnant quarante minutes à la progression de chaque Ordre.' In this way, he arrives at the orderly progression from 22 *petits modules* for the Tuscan to 30 *petits modules* for the Composite. Having altered the table by inserting the measurements of ancient columns derived from Desgodets, Perrault decides to work out the mean separately for each Order from the high and low of each of the five sections. He interpolates this new calculation (which, of course, results in the same measurements for each Order as the first one) on page 12. It thus precedes, and in fact supersedes, the first calculation which follows on page 14.

There are many more mistakes, but since they are of no consequence, it would be pointless, and tedious, to record them all.

APPENDIX VII

Gurlitt's and Perrault's text

After each sentence of Gurlitt's text (op. cit., pp. 155 f.), which is given in full, follow those passages from the *Ordonnance* or *Vitruvius* that come nearest to Gurlitt's paraphrasing.

Gurlitt: 'Perrault ist aber in Erkenntnis der zahlreichen Ungenauigkeiten in den Verhältnissen der klassischen und italienischen Architektur der Meinung, dass diese nicht unbedingt eingehalten werden müssten, sondern dass man sie beliebig ändern dürfe, wenn man es nur mit Geschmack, Geschick und Einsicht mache.'

Perrault (*Ordonnance*, p. II, end of second paragraph): '... il ne se trouve point, ny dans les restes des Edifices des Anciens, ny parmy le grand nombre des Architectes qui ont traité des proportions des Ordres, que deux Edifices ny deux Auteurs se soient accordez et ayent suivy les mesmes règles.'

(ibid., end of first paragraph): 'on voit aussi dans l'Architecture des ouvrages avec des proportions différentes avoir des grâces pour se faire également approuver par ceux qui sont intelligens et pourveus du bon goust de l'Architecture.'

Gurlitt: 'Es komme wie beim menschlichen Körperbau nicht auf die Richtigkeit gewisser Verhältnisse, sondern auf die anmuthige Form an.'

Perrault (ibid., p. I): 'Ce qui fait voir que la beauté d'un Edifice a encore cela de commun avec celle du corps humain, qu'elle ne consiste pas tant dans l'exactitude d'une certaine proportion ... que dans la grâce de la forme ...'

Gurlitt: 'Die vollendete Schönheit sei gerade auf einem gewissen Wechsel der Erscheinung begründet.'

Perrault (ibid., p. I): '... grâce de la forme, qui n'est rien autre chose que son agréable modification, sur laquelle une beauté parfaite et excellente peut estre fondée, sans que cette sorte de proportion s'y rencontre exactement observée.'

Gurlitt: 'Die Verhältnisse der Ordnungen seien keineswegs aus der Natur der Bauten nothwendig sich ergebende, sondern entstanden durch die geistige Übereinstimmung der Architekten, von denen einer beim andern lernte, so dass sich ein gemeinsamer, nunmehr alle Welt beherrschender Geschmack durch die Macht der Gewohnheit ausgebildet habe.'

Perrault (*Vitruvius*, p. 105, note 7): '... la plus grande partie des Architectes ... croyent que les proportions des membres de l'Architecture sont quelque chose de naturel. . . . Pour moy j'ay traduit suivant la pensée que j'ay que ces proportions ont esté établies par un consentement des Architectes qui . . . ont imité les ouvrages les uns des autres, et qui ont suivy les proportions que les premiers avoient choisies, non point comme ayant une beauté positive . . . mais seulement parce que ces proportions se trouvoient en des ouvrages qui ayant d'ailleurs d'autres beautez positives . . . ont fait approuver . . . ces proportions. . . . Cette raison d'aimer les choses par compagnie et par accoustumance se rencontre presque dans toutes les choses qui plaisent . . .'

Gurlitt: 'Daher will er dem Architekten das Recht gewahrt haben, die Ordnungen seinem Schönheitsgefühl nach abzuändern, wie ja auch die Alten es gethan.'
Perrault (*Ordonnance*, p. II): 'Mais ces proportions ont une estendue assez ample pour laisser aux Architectes la liberté d'augmenter ou de diminuer les dimensions des parties, suivant les besoins que plusieurs occurences peuvent faire naistre. C'est en vertu de ce privilège que les Anciens ont fait des ouvrages dont les proportions sont si extraordinaires . . .'

Gurlitt: 'Mit den Verhältnissen verhalte es sich keineswegs wie mit den Tönen des Akkordes; denn hier bemerke jedes Ohr alsbald den Missklang, während der Architekt nur durch Nachmessen der Fehler den verwickelten Zusammenhang der regelrechten Verhältnisse mühsam erkennen könne.'
Perrault: Gurlitt's sentence is obviously based on Perrault's remarks about musical analogy (pp. III f.), but he fails to bring out Perrault's main point that, while musicians know naturally the correct consonance and are shocked by dissonance, architects, on the contrary, are not at all unananimous in condemning 'les ouvrages d'Architecture, qui n'ont pas ces véritables et ces naturelles proportions qu'on prétend qu'ils sont capables d'avoir . . .'

Gurlitt: 'Nach Perrault gibt es zwei Arten von Schönheiten in der Architektur: Erstens eine gesetzmässige, auf die klare Erkenntnis des Verdienstes and Werthes, wie auf den Reichthum des Materials, die Pracht und Durchbildung, oder auf die Symmetrie, auf die Masseinheit der Verhältnisse, Grösse, Lage und Anordnung begründete.'
Perrault (ibid. p. VI: '. . . il faut supposer qu'il y a de deux sortes de beautez dans l'Architecture . . j'appelle des beautez fondées sur des raisons convaincantes, celles par lesquelles les ouvrages doivent plaire à tout le monde, parce qu'il est aisé d'en connoistre le mérite et la valeur, telles que sont la richesse de la matière, la grandeur et la magnificence de l'Edifice, la justesse et la propreté de l'exécution et la symmetrie . . .' So far Gurlitt remained fairly close to Perrault's text. But 'die Masseinheit der Verhältnisse, Grösse, Lage und Anordnung' Perrault, of course, never included in the class of positive qualities. What happened was that when

Perrault, continuing the sentence just quoted, explained the different meaning of French *symétrie* and Latin *symmetria*, Gurlitt wrongly assumed that, when naming the characteristics of the latter, Perrault was still referring to his class of positive qualities.

Gurlitt: 'und zweitens eine willkürliche, die dem wechselnden Geschmack der Zeit, dem Urtheil des Hofes folgend, kurz modisch ist. Dieser Gedanke ist ungemein bezeichnend und macht Perrault geistig zum Begründer des Rococo.'

Perrault (ibid., pp. VII f.): ('car par cette liaison il arrive que l'estime dont l'esprit est prévenu pour les unes dont il connoist la valeur, insinue une estime pour les autres dont la valeur luy est inconnue. . . .) C'est aussi la prévention qui nous fait aimer les choses de la mode et les manières de parler que l'usage a establies à la Cour: car l'estime que l'on a pour le mérite et la bonne grâce des personnes de la Cour, fait aimer leurs habits et leur manière de parler . . .'

Gurlitt: 'Nach seiner Meinung entstanden die Ordnungen der Alten durch eine willkürliche, weil freie That glänzend begabter Künstler und daher müsse es auch für einen grossen modernen Baumeister möglich sein, etwas von den früher geschaffenen Verhältnissen Abweichendes und doch Schönes zu schaffen.'

Perrault (ibid., p. X): 'De manière que ceux qui les premiers ont inventé ces proportions, n'ayant guères eu d'autre règle que leur fantaisie, à mesure que cette fantaisie a changé, on a introduit de nouvelles proportions qui ont aussi plu à leur tour.'

Gurlitt: 'Und gerade dies bildet für ihn die schwerste Aufgabe des wahren Architekten. Die gesetzmässige Schönheit verlangt nur gesunden Verstand; die Aufgabe des Architekten könne unmöglich darin bestehen, blos die gewonnenen Regeln mechanisch zu verwerthen, sondern er muss versuchen neue richtig erscheinende (probables et vraisemblables), auf die richtige Erkenntnis begründete Verhältnisse zu erfinden, die sich von den überlieferten und gebräuchlichen nicht zu weit entfernten.'

Perrault (ibid., p. XII: '. . . c'est (la connoissance des beautez arbitraires) seule qui distingue les vrais Architectes de ceux qui ne le sont pas; parce que pour connoistre la plupart des beautez positives, c'est assez que d'avoir du sens commun; n'y ayant pas grande difficulté à juger qu'un grand Edifice de marbre taillé avec justesse et propreté est plus beau qu'un petit fait de pierres mal taillées, où il n'y a rien qui soit exactement à niveau, ny à plomb, ny à l'équerre.'

(ibid., p. XIV): 'il reste à examiner si l'on peut établir de probables (proportions) et de vray-semblables fondées sur des raisons positives, sans s'éloigner beaucoup des proportions recues et usitées.'

Gurlitt: 'Er warnt *sogar* (my italics) vor zu blinder Verehrung der Antike, vor den aus dem Ausspruche des Spaniers *Villalpanda* zu ziehenden Folgerungen, welcher meint, Gott selbst habe den Architekten beim Bau des Salomonischen Tempels die richtigen Verhältnisse gelehrt und die Griechen sie von diesem entlehnt.'

Perrault (ibid., pp. XVII, XVIII, *Vitruvius*, p. 104, note 2).

Gurlitt: 'So beansprucht Perrault für seine Kunstgenossen das Recht der selbstständigen Fortbildung der überkommenen Formen.'

PLATES

Il n'est point de secret dans la Nature entiere
Ny dans les Arts qu'Il n'ayt connu
Et modeste Il n'vsa de toute sa lumiere
Que pour voir non pour estre vû

Vercelin Pinxit   G. Edelinck Sculp. C.P.R. 1690.

1. Claude Perrault. Engraving by G. Edelinck after a painting by Vercelin

2. *Le voyage de Viry*. Titlepage. Drawing by Perrault. London, Brit. Mus.

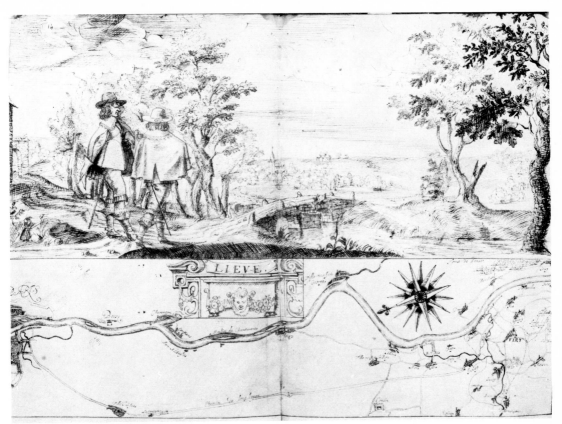

3. Illustration to *Le voyage de Viry*. Drawing by Perrault. London, Brit. Mus.

4. Dissection of a fox in the Bibliothèque du Roi. Vignette from *Mémoires pour servir à l'histoire des animaux*, 1671. Engraving by Sébastien Leclerc

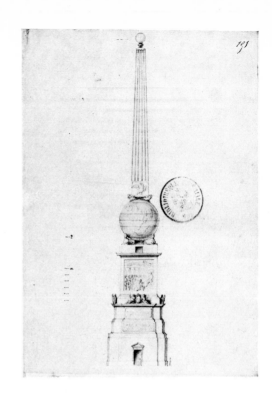

5. Perrault. Design for an Obelisk, 1667. Paris,
Bibl. Nat.

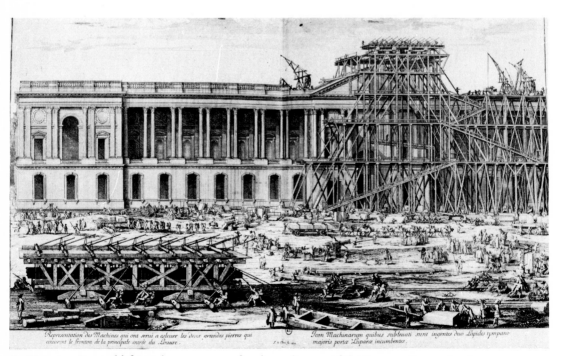

Representation des Machines qui ont servi a esleuer les deux grandes pierres qui
couurent le fronton de la principale entrée du Louure.

Icon Machinarum quibus sublevati sunt ingentes duo Lapides tympano
majoris portæ Luparæ incumbentes.

6. Transporting and lifting the two stones for the pediment of the Louvre. Engraving by
Sébastien Leclerc, 1677

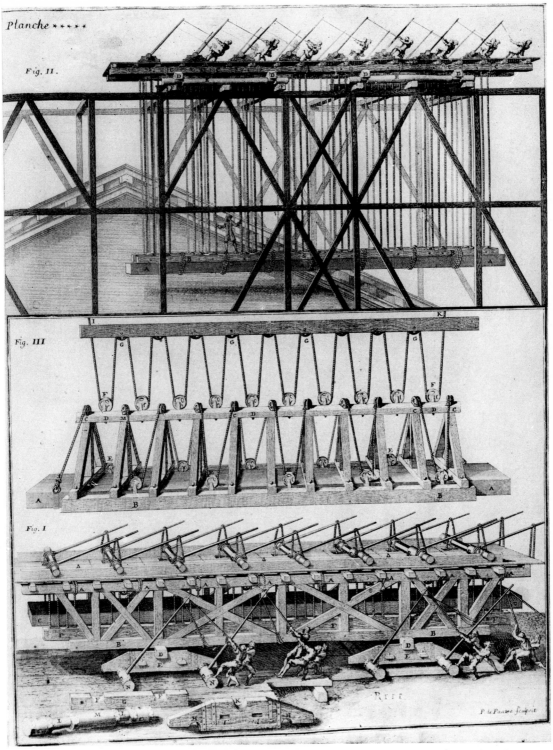

7. Perrault. Improved Machine for lifting large stones. Engraving by P. Lepautre from *Vitruvius*, ed. 1684

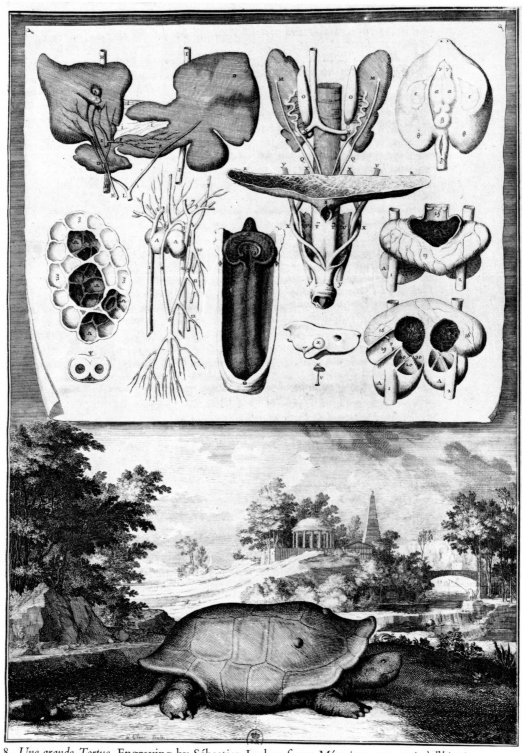

8. *Une grande Tortue*. Engraving by Sébastien Leclerc from *Mémoires pour servir à l'histoire naturelle des animaux*, 1676

9. *Deux Sapagons.* Engraving by Sébastien Leclerc from *Mémoires pour servir à l'histoire naturelle des animaux,* 1676

LES DIX LIVRES

D'ARCHITECTURE

DE

VITRUVE

CORRIGEZ ET TRADVITS

nouvellement en François, avec des Notes
& des Figures.

Seconde Edition reveue, corrigée, & augmentée.

Par M. PERRAULT *de l'Academie Royalle des Sciences , Docteur en Medecine*
de la Faculté de Paris.

A PARIS,
Chez JEAN BAPTISTE COIGNARD,
Imprimeur ordinaire du Roy , ruë S. Jacques , à la Bible d'or.

M. DC. LXXXIV.
AVEC PRIVILEGE DE SA MAJESTE.

10. Titlepage of *Vitruvius*, 2nd edition, 1684

11. *Bains des Anciens.* Engraving from *Vitruvius*, pl. XLVIII

EXPLICATION DE LA PLANCHE LIV.

Cette Planche represente la salle Egyptienne, qui reſſemble fort à ce que nous appellons une Chambre à l'Italienne. L'eſſentiel de ce genre d'Edifice conſiſte à ne prendre du jour que par en haut, & à
avoir l'exhauſſement de deux étages ; ce qui apporte trois commoditez conſiderables. La premiere eſt
que cette ſorte d'appartement peut eſtre dégagé des quatre coſtez, & répondre à quatre appartemens ;
La ſeconde qu'il eſt frais en Eſté ; La troiſiéme que le jour qui vient des quatre coſtez & par en haut
n'éblouït point, & laiſſe tout à l'entour aux Tableaux & aux autres ornemens, dont on le veut pa-
rer, la place qui eſt ordinairement employée à des croiſées.

Architraves

12. *La Salle Egyptienne.* Engraving from *Vitruvius,* pl. LIV

13. *Periptère*. Engraving from *Vitruvius*, pl. XXXVI

14. Perrault. Design for a Monopteros. Stockholm,
Nationalmuseum

15. Perrault. Design for the Temple of Jerusalem. Elevation from the East. Woodcut from
Maimonides, *De Cultu Divino*, 1678

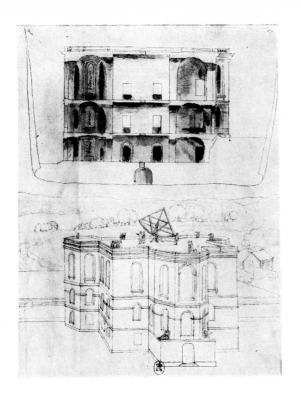

16. Perrault. Design for
    Observatoire. Preliminary
    drawing for *Vitruvius*,
    pl. III. Paris, Bibl. Nat.
    Cabinet des Estampes

17. Perrault. Design for the Arc de Triomphe at the Porte St Antoine. Drawing by
    Sébastien Leclerc. Paris, Louvre, Cabinet des Dessins

18. Frontispiece to *Vitruvius*, 1673, showing Arc de Triomphe, Louvre and, in background, Observatoire. Design by Sébastien Leclerc

19. Louis XIV visiting the Académie des Sciences. Frontispiece to *Mémoires pour servir à l'histoire des animaux*, 1671. Design by Sébastien Leclerc

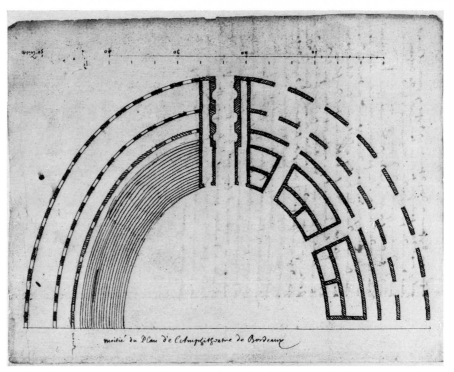

20. Bordeaux. Roman Amphitheatre. Plan. Sketch by Perrault from *Voyage à Bordeaux*, Paris, Bibl. Nat.

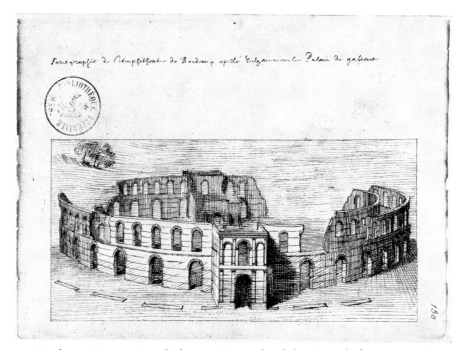

21. Bordeaux. Roman Amphitheatre. View. Sketch by Perrault from *Voyage à Bordeaux*, Paris, Bibl. Nat.

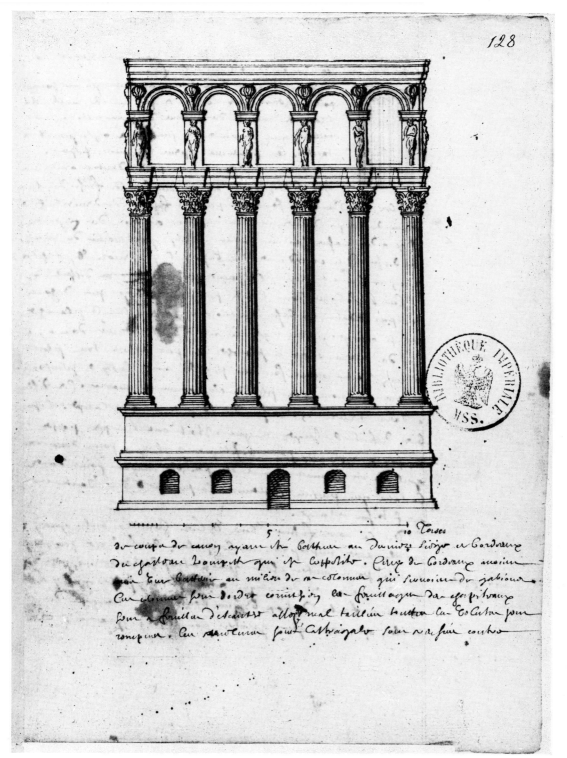

22. Bordeaux. *Les Piliers de Tutelle*. Sketch by Perrault from *Voyage à Bordeaux*. Paris, Bibl. Nat.

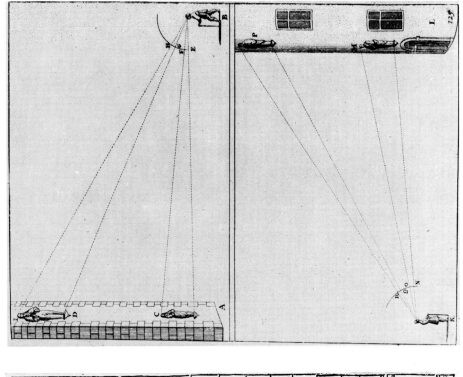

24. Jean Dubreuil. Device for counteracting foreshortening
(from *La perspective pratique*, 1642)

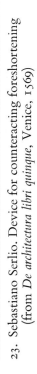

23. Sebastiano Serlio. Device for counteracting foreshortening
(from *De architectura libri quinque*, Venice, 1569)

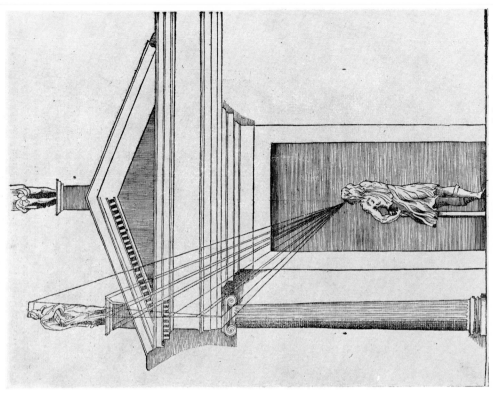

26. Jean Martin. Illustration to demonstrate need for inclining highly placed objects forward (from *Architecture . . . de Vitruve*, 1547)

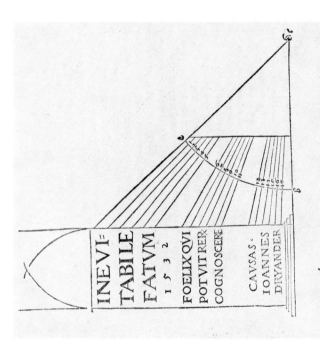

Vum itaque architecti, siue pictores, & alii aliquando scripturam ad altiores parietes effingere soleant, opere precium erit, vt rite deforment literas. Quaobrem hic aliquantulū de hac re volo offēdere: primūm alphabetum latinum præscribam, deinde textuale, quibus duobus generibus literarum maximè in talibus rebus vti confueuimus.
In primis ad literas romanas singulas fac quadratum æquum in quo contineatur vnaquæq; litera. At quando in eo ductis literæ tractuum maiorem, hunc fac latum parte decima lateris quadrati: & minorem tertiā parte latioris, idq; obseru un per omnes literas alphabeti.
Primo fac A, hoc pacto, Designa eius quadrati angulos literis a b c d, idē fac in omnibus reliquis literis, & diuide quadratum per duas lineas ad angulos rectos fefe fecantes: erectam e f, transuersam g h, deinde pone duo puncta i k inferne iuxta c d, decima parte distantia inrortium ab c & d, & ducito tractum tenuiorem furfum ab i, ad quadratum: inde deducito latiorem tractū deorfum, ita vt amborū

25. Albrecht Dürer. Device for making lettering on different levels appear to be of equal size (from *Elementa Geometrica*, 1532)

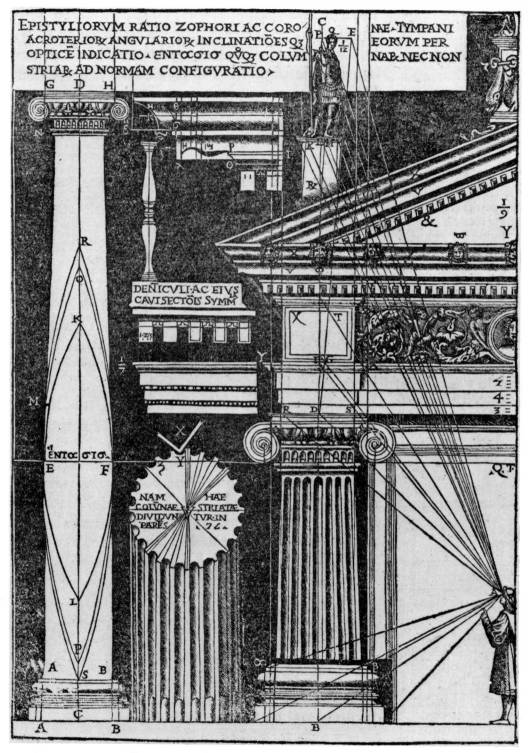

27. Cesare Cesariano. Illustration to demonstrate need for inclining highly placed objects forward (from *Di . . . Vitruvio*, 1521)

28. Paris, St Gervais

29. Rome, Column of Trajan. Engraving of 1589

30. Perrault. The five Orders. From *Ordonnance*, pl. I

31. Paris, Louvre. Intercolumniation of Colonnade (from Pierre Patte,
Mémoires sur les objets les plus importans de l'architecture, 1769)

32. Louvre, Colonnade. View from inside towards south (from Baltard,
    Paris et ses monuments, 1803)

33. Perrault. Corinthian Capital. From *Ordonnance*, pl. V

Soffite du larmier

Profil par le milieu du chapiteau des colonnes

34. Rome, Pantheon, Corinthian Capital (from Desgodets, *Les édifices antiques de Rome*, 1682)

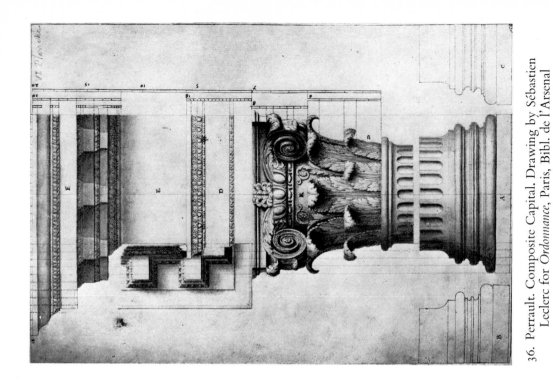

36. Perrault. Composite Capital. Drawing by Sébastien
Leclerc for *Ordonnance*, Paris, Bibl. de l'Arsenal

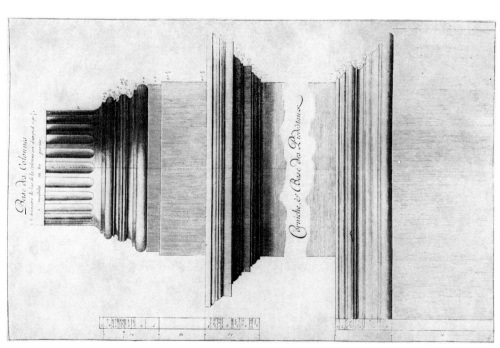

35. Rome. Arch of Titus. Base and Pedestal of Composite
Column (from Desgodets, *Les édifices antiques
de Rome*, 1682)

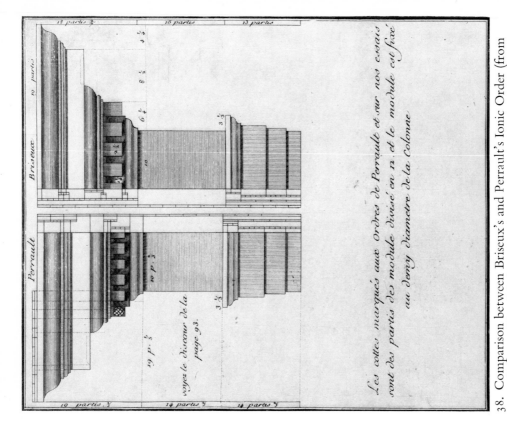

The following text appears within/around the upper illustration:

13 parts ¾   *16 parts*   *13 parts*

10 parts

Briseux

Perrault

*Les cottes marqués aux Ordres de Perrault et sur nos essais
sont des partis des module divisé en n. et le module est fixé
au demy diametre de la Colonne*

*voyez le discour de la
page 93.*

10 parts ¾   *14 parts ⅜*   *14 parts ⅜*

38. Comparison between Briseux's and Perrault's Ionic Order (from
    Briseux, *Traité du beau*, 1752)

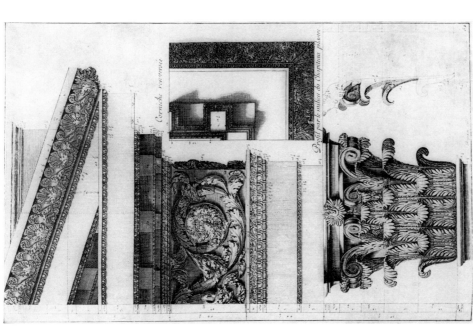

Cornicha reversée

Profil par le milieu du Chapiteau pilastre

37. Rome. *Frontispiece de Néron* (from Desgodets,
    Les édifices antiques de Rome, 1682)

Lud. de Chastillon fecit.

A MONSEIGNEUR
COLBERT
MARQUIS DE SEIGNELAY,
BARON DE SEAUX, &c.

MINISTRE ET SECRETAIRE D'ESTAT
& des Commandemens du Roy, Commandeur, & Grand
Threforier des Ordres de Sa Majefté, Contrôleur General
des Finances, Surintendant & Ordonnateur General des
Baftimens & Jardins de Sa Majefté, Arts & Manufactures
de France.

 ONSEIGNEVR,

Après avoir travaillé par vos Ordres à la tra-
duction & à l'explication de Vitruve, avec un fuccez

39. *Ordonnance*, Dedication

BIBLIOGRAPHY

WORKS BY PERRAULT

As the member responsible for publishing the results of anatomical work carried out by him and others at the Académie des Sciences:

Extrait d'une lettre écrite à Monsieur de la Chambre qui contient les observations qui onst esté faites sur un grand Poisson dissequé dans la Bibliothèque du Roy le vingt-quatrième Juin 1667 – Observations qui ont esté faites sur un Lion dissequé dans la Bibliothèque du Roy le vingt-huitième Juin 1667 tirées d'une lettre écrite à Monsieur de la Chambre, Paris, 1667.

Description anatomique d'un caméléon, d'un castor, d'un dromedaire, d'un ours et d'une gazelle, Paris, 1669.

Mémoires pour servir à l'histoire naturelle des animaux, Paris, 1671.

Mémoires pour servir à l'histoire naturelle des animaux. Dressez par M. Perrault . . . (2nd enlarged edition), Paris, 1676. In 1733, the *Mémoires*, reduced in size, were published again in the third volume of the *Mémoires de l'Académie Royale des Sciences depuis 1666 jusqu'à 1699*. Included were some of the drawings and descriptions prepared by Perrault for a third edition.

Translations:

Memoirs for a Natural History of Animals . . . Englished by Alexander Pitfeild, London, 1688.

Another edition under the title: *The Natural History of Animals . . . Done into English by a Fellow of the Royal Society*, London, 1702.

Perrault's own publications:

'Extrait d'une lettre de M.P. à M*** sur le sujet des Vers qui se trouvent dans le foye de quelques animaux', *Journal des Sçavans*, 1668, pp. 49 ff.

Les dix livres d'architecture de Vitruve corrigez et traduits nouvellement en François, avec des Notes et des Figures, Paris, 1673.

Les dix livres d'architecture de Vitruve . . . Seconde Edition reveue, corrigée et augmentée, Paris, 1684.

Abregé des dix livres d'architecture de Vitruve, Paris, 1674. (Perrault's name does not appear on the title, but only in the privilege).

Architecture générale de Vitruve reduite en abregé par M. Perrault . . . Dernière édition enrichie de figures en cuivre, Amsterdam, 1681.

Translations:

An Abridgment of the Architecture of Vitruvius . . . First done in French by Monsr Perrault . . . and now Englished with Additions, London, 1692.

The Theory and Practice of Architecture: or Vitruvius and Vignola abridg'd. The First by the famous Mr Perrault . . . (and carefully done into English) . . ., London, 1703. (Other editions, the last of 1729).

L'architettura generale di Vitruvio ridotta in compendio dal Sig. Perrault . . ., Venice, 1747.

Des grossen . . . Vitruvii Architettura, in das Kurze verfasst, durch Herrn Perrault . . . in das Teutsche übersetzt von H. Müller, Würzburg and Prag, 1757.

Compendio de los diez libros de arquitectura de Vitruvio escrito en francès por Claudio Perrault . . . Traducido al castellano por don Joseph Castañeda, Madrid, 1761.

Extrait des Registres de l'Académie Royale des Sciences contenant les Observations que M. Perrault a faites sur des fruits dont la forme et la production avoient quelque chose de fort extraordinaire', *Journal des Sçavans*, 1675, pp. 94 ff.

'Extrait . . . contenant quelques Observations que M. Perrault a faites touchant deux choses remarquables qui ont esté trouvées dans les oeufs', *Journal des Sçavans*, 1676, pp. 27 ff.

'Explicatio tabularum, quae figuram Templi exhibent' (followed by three plates showing the reconstruction of the Temple of Jerusalem) in Maimonides, *De Cultu Divino . . . ex Hebraeo Latinum fecit . . . Ludovicus de Compiègne de Veil*, Paris, 1678.

'Découverte d'un nouveau conduit de la Bile, sa description et sa figure par M. Perrault', *Journal des Sçavans*, 1680, pp. 183 ff.

Essais de Physique, ou recueil de plusieurs traitez touchant les choses naturelles, Paris, I, II, III, 1680, IV, 1688.

Reprinted in Claude et Pierre Perrault, *Oeuvres diverses de physique et de méchanique*, Leyden, 1721. (another edition 1727).

Lettres écrites sur le sujet d'une nouvelle découverte touchant la veue faite par M. Mariotte, Paris, 1682.

Ordonnance des cinq especes de colonnes selon la méthode des anciens, Paris, 1683.

Translation:

A Treatise of the Five Orders in Architecture . . . Written in French by Claude Perrault . . . Made English by John James of Greenwich, London, 1708. (*The Second Edition*, London, 1722).

Recueil de plusieurs machines de nouvelle invention. Ouvrage posthume, Paris, 1700.

These and additional four machines were again published by Gallon, *Machines et inventions approuvées par l'Académie Royale des Sciences depuis son établissement jusqu'à présent*, Paris, 1735, I, pp. 4–65: 'Machines inventées par M. Perrault.'

MANUSCRIPTS BY PERRAULT

Les Murs de Troye (second chant). Paris, Bibl. de l'Arsenal, MS 2956 (about 1653). Publ. by P. Bonnefon in *Revue d'Histoire littéraire de la France*, VII, 1900.

Dossier Perrault. Scientific notes and drawings from 1667 and following years. Paris, Archive of Académie des Sciences.

Mémoire on properties of chalk (17 December 1667). Paris, Académie des Sciences, Register, I, fols. 308–327.

Mémoire attached to the design for an obelisk (30 August 1667). Paris, Bibl. Nat. Manuscr. anc. franç. 24,713, fols 145–151.

Mémoire on coagulation (10 August 1669). Paris, Académie des Sciences, Register, VI, fols. 141–149a.

Relation du voyage fait en 1669 par MM. Du Laurent, Gomont, Abraham et Perrault. Paris, Bibl. Nat. Manuscr. anc. franç. 24,713. Publ. by P. Bonnefon, *Mémoires de ma vie Voyage à Bordeaux*, Paris, 1909.

Two *mémoires* relating to the supply of water for Versailles (1671 and 1676). Paris, Arch. Nat. o¹ 1854.

Letter dated 27 January 1674. Paris, Bibl. Nat., Mélange Colbert 167, fols. 245 a and b.

Preface to the *Traité de la musique*. Paris, Bibl. Nat. Manuscr. anc. franç. 25,350. Publ. by H. Gillot, *La querelle des Anciens et des Modernes*, Paris, 1914, pp. 576–91.

Tomb Mazarin. 'Avis de M. Perrault le médecin pour mettre le tombeau sous l'arcade qui fait la croisée à droitte (en) entrant par la grande porte de l'Eglise' (1676). Paris, Bibl. de l'Institut Manuscr. 368, fols. 169 v–171 v.

BIOGRAPHICAL NOTICES ON PERRAULT

H. Basnage, *Histoire des ouvrages des Sçavans*, Rotterdam, November 1688, pp. 310 ff.

Fontenelle, *Eloge de Monsieur Perrault* (written 1688), *Oeuvres*, ed. Paris 1759, IX, pp. 390–5.

Journal des Sçavans, 28 February 1689, pp. 80 ff.

Charles Perrault, *Les Hommes illustres qui ont paru en France pendant ce siècle*, Paris, 1696, pp. 67 f.

L. Moreri, *Le Grand Dictionnaire historique*, Paris, 1707.

Johann Heinrich Zedler, *Grosses vollständiges Universal Lexicon*, Leipzig, 1741, XXVII, pp. 550 f.

C. F. Lambert, *Histoire littéraire du Règne de Louis XIV*, Paris, 1751, III, bk. X, pp. 100–104.

Francesco Milizia, *Le vite di piu celebri architetti*, Rome, 1768, pp. 374 f.

A. Portal, *Histoire de l'anatomie et de la chirurgie*, Paris, 1770, III, pp. 383–92.

Condorcet, 'Eloge de Perrault' in *Eloges des Académiciens de l'Académie Royale des Sciences*, Paris, 1773, pp. 83 ff.

N. F. J. Eloy, *Dictionnaire historique de la Médecine*, Mons, 1778, III, pp. 515 ff.

J.-A. Hazon, *Notice des hommes les plus célèbres de la Faculté de Médecine en l'Université de Paris*, Paris, 1778, pp. 122 ff.

K. Dezallier d'Argenville, *Vies des fameux architectes*, Paris, 1788, pp. 382–96.

Quatremère de Quincy, *Encyclopédie méthodique. Architecture*, Paris, 1788, pp. 93 ff.

John Aikin, *General Biography*, London, 1813, VIII sub Perrault.

Quatremère de Quincy, *Histoire de la vie et des ouvrages des plus célèbres architectes*, Paris, 1830, II, pp. 207 ff.

L. G. Michaud, *Biographie universelle*, Paris, 1843 ff., XXXII, pp. 526 ff.

Nouvelle biographie générale, Paris, 1862, XXXIX, pp. 626 ff.

Adolphe Lance, *Dictionnaire des architectes français*, Paris, 1872, II, pp. 195 ff.

A. Jal, *Dictionnaire critique de biographie et d'histoire*, Paris, (2nd ed.), 1872, *supplément*, sub Perrault.

Ch. Bauchal, *Nouveau Dictionnaire biographique et critique des architectes français*, Paris, 1887, pp. 462 f.

E. von Cranach-Sichart, in *Thieme-Becker*, 1932, XXVI, pp. 430 ff.

Bates Lowry, in *Encyclopedia of World Art*, New York, 1966, XI, p. 181.

LITERATURE ON PERRAULT

Only those works are included in the following list in which either his theoretical views on architecture or his scientific work in general are being discussed. Studies dealing with buildings which he designed or for which his authorship has been claimed are not listed. Some of these studies have been quoted at the appropriate places in the text.

Cornelius Gurlitt, *Geschichte des Barockstiles des Rococo und des Klassizismus in Belgien, Holland, Frankreich, England*, Stuttgart, 1888.

Paul Bonnefon, 'Claude Perrault, architecte et voyageur', *Gazette des Beaux-Arts*, 3e période, XXVI, 1901, pp. 209 ff.

Paul Bonnefon, 'Charles Perrault Essai sur sa vie et ses ouvrages,' *Revue d'histoire littéraire de la France*, XI, 1904, pp. 365 ff.

Alexis Bertrand, *Mes vieux médecins*, Lyons, 1905, Chapter VI.

Paul Bonnefon, Introduction and notes to *Mémoires de ma vie par Charles Perrault Voyage à Bordeaux (1669) par Claude Perrault*, Paris, 1909.

Kurt Cassirer, *Die ästhetischen Hauptbegriffe der französischen Architektur-Theoretiker von 1650–1780*, Diss., Berlin, 1909.

Henry Lemonnier, 'Quelques idées de Claude Perrault sur l'architecture,' *Bulletin de la société de l'histoire de l'art français*, 1910, pp. 322 ff.

Henry Lemonnier, Introductions and notes to vols I and II of *Procès-verbaux de l'Académie Royale d'Architecture*, Paris, 1911 f.

Henry Lemonnier, *L'art français au temps de Louis XIV*, Paris, 1911, pp. 188 ff.

A. E. Brinckmann, *Baukunst des 17. und 18. Jahrhunderts in den romanischen Ländern*, Berlin-Neubablesberg, 1919, pp. 229 f.

R. Blomfield, *A History of French Architecture*, London, 1921, I, pp. 84 ff.

E. Kaufmann, 'Die Architekturtheorie der französischen Klassik und des Klassizismus,' *Repertorium für Kunstwissenschaft*, XLIV, 1924, p. 209.

K. Borinski, *Die Antike in Poetik und Kunsttheorie*, Leipzig, 1924, II, pp. 90 ff.

André Hallays, *Les Perrault*, Paris, 1926.

M. Borissaviliévitch, *Les théories de l'architecture*, Paris, 1926.

J. Lebovits, *Claude Perrault physiologiste*, Paris, 1931.

J. Lévy-Valensin, 'Claude Perrault, Physiologiste,' *Livre jubilaire offert au professeur G.-H. Roger*, Paris, 1932, pp. 147 ff.

J. Lévy-Valensin, *La médecine et les médecins français au XVIIe siècle*, Paris, 1933.

L. Hautecoeur, *Histoire de l'architecture classique en France*, Paris, 1943 ff., II (1948), pp. 462 ff. (especially pp. 487 ff.)

A. Sigwalt, *Une mystification de Charles Perrault*, Paris, 1948, (specially pp. 50 ff.).

P. Vallery-Radot, 'Un architecte de génie: le docteur Claude Perrault,' *Histoire de la médecine. Revue technique et historique*, IV, 1952, pp. 12 ff.

Herbert Koch, *Vom Nachleben des Vitruv*, Baden-Baden, 1951.

Alberto Tenenti, 'Claude Perrault et la pensée scientifique française dans la seconde moitié du XVIIe siècle,' *Hommage à Lucien Febvre*, Paris, 1953, II, pp. 303 ff.

E. R. de Zurko, *Origins of Functionalist Theory*, New York, 1957.

P. H. Scholfield, *The Theory of Proportion in Architecture*, Cambridge, 1958.

P. Vallery-Radot, 'Un médecin architecte: Claude Perrault (1613–1688),' *Fureteur*, XVIII, 1959, pp. 67 ff.

L. Tatarkiewicz, 'L'esthétique associationiste au XVIIe siècle,' *Revue d'esthétique*, XIII, 1960, pp. 287 ff.

Albert Laprade, *François d'Orbay*, Paris, 1960.

J. Barchilon, 'Les frères Perrault à travers la correspondance et les oeuvres de Christian Huygens,' *XVIIe siècle*, 1962, pp. 19 ff.

L. Tatarkiewicz, 'Objectivity and Subjectivity in the History of Aesthetics,' *Philosophy and Phenomenological Research*, XXIV, 1963, pp. 157 ff.

Max Imdahl, 'Kunstgeschichtliche Exkurse zu Perraults *Parallèle des Anciens et des Modernes*' in Facsimile edition of the *Parallèle*, Munich, 1964, pp. 65 ff.

L. Tatarkiewicz, 'L'esthétique du Grand Siècle,' *XVIIe siècle*, 1968, pp. 21 ff.

INDEX